Routledge Revivals

The Taming of the Shrew

William Shakespeare's *The Taming of the Shrew* has succeeded in surviving in contemporary culture, and has even managed to penetrate to the most modern media of mass communications. This book, first published in 1991, examines some of the different literary and oral versions of *The Taming of the Shrew*. This book is ideal for students of literature, drama, and theatre studies.

The Taming of the Shrew
A Comparative Study of Oral and Literary Traditions

Jan Harold Brunvand

First published in 1991
by Garland Publishing

This edition first published in 2015 by Routledge
2 Park Square, Milton Park, Abingdon, Oxon, OX14 4RN
and by Routledge
711 Third Avenue, New York, NY 10017

Routledge is an imprint of the Taylor & Francis Group, an informa business

© 1991 Jan Harold Brunvand

The right of Jan Harold Brunvand to be identified as author of this work has been asserted by him in accordance with sections 77 and 78 of the Copyright, Designs and Patents Act 1988.

All rights reserved. No part of this book may be reprinted or reproduced or utilised in any form or by any electronic, mechanical, or other means, now known or hereafter invented, including photocopying and recording, or in any information storage or retrieval system, without permission in writing from the publishers.

Publisher's Note
The publisher has gone to great lengths to ensure the quality of this reprint but points out that some imperfections in the original copies may be apparent.

Disclaimer
The publisher has made every effort to trace copyright holders and welcomes correspondence from those they have been unable to contact.

A Library of Congress record exists under LC control number: 90039612

ISBN 13: 978-1-138-84274-8 (hbk)
ISBN 13: 978-1-315-72355-6 (ebk)

THE TAMING OF THE SHREW
A Comparative Study of Oral and Literary Versions

Jan Harold Brunvand

GARLAND PUBLISHING, INC. • NEW YORK & LONDON
1991

© 1991 Jan Harold Brunvand
All rights reserved

Library of Congress Cataloging-in-Publication Data

Brunvand, Jan Harold.
    The Taming of the shrew : a comparative study of oral and literary versions / Jan Harold Brunvand.
       p. cm. — (Garland folklore library ; vol. 5) (Garland reference library of the humanities ; vol. 1289)
    Originally presented as the author's thesis (doctoral—Indiana University) in 1961.
    Includes bibliographical references.
    ISBN 0-8240-7149-2 (alk. paper)
    1. Taming of the Shrew (Tale) 2. Shakespeare, William, 1564–1616. Taming of the shrew. I. Title. II. Series. III. Series: Garland folklore library ; 5.
GR75.T35B78   1991
822.3'3—dc20   90-39612
                                                                 CIP

Printed on acid-free, 250-year-life paper
Manufactured in the United States of America

Contents

Introduction to This Edition	xv
Preface	xxiii
Chapter I Introduction	3
Abbreviations	21
Table I. The Versions of the Tale	25
Table II. The Elements of the Tale	77
Chapter II Summary of the Combinations of Narrative Elements in the Versions	113
Chapter III Type 901: Historic-Geographic Study	119
Chapter IV Type 901: The Northern-European Elaborated Subtype and Shakespeare's *The Taming of the Shrew*	171
Chapter V Type 901: "That's Once," the American Subtype	213
Chapter VI Type 1370 and the Combination 1370 and 901	229
Chapter VII Other Tales in the Complex	249
Chapter VIII Summary of Conclusions	257
Appendix	269

References Cited

Azzolina, David S.
  1987 *Tale-Type and Motif Indexes: An Annotated Bibliography.* New York: Garland.

Brunvand, Jan Harold
  1966 "The Folktale Origin of *The Taming of the Shrew.*" *Shakespeare Quarterly* 17:345–359.

  1968 "The Taming of the Shrew Tale in the United States." In Jan Harold Brunvand, *The Study of American Folklore.* New York: Norton. Pp. 304–316.

Di Niscia, G.
  1903 "Per una fonte probabile della" *Bisbetica Domata.* In *Nózze Percopo-Luciani 30 luglio 1902.* Napoli: Luigi Pierro e figlio. Pp. 5–56.

Dragomanov, M.
  1898 "Taming of the Shrew, in the Folk-Lore of the Ukraine." In Helen Wheeler Bassett and Frederick Starr, eds., *The International Folk-lore Congress of the World's Columbia Exposition, Chicago, July, 1893.* Chicago: Charles H. Sergel Company. Pp. 368–373.

Goldberg, Christine
  1984 "The Historic-Geographic Method: Past and Future." *Journal of Folklore Research* 21:1–18.

Köhler, Reinhold
  1868 "Zu Shakespeares *The Taming of the Shrew.*" *Jahrbuch der deutschen Shakespeare-Gesellschaft* 3:397–401.

Morris, Brian, ed.,
  1981 *The Taming of the Shrew.* The Arden Edition of the Works of William Shakespeare. London: Methuen.

Oliver, H.J., ed.
  1982 *The Taming of the Shrew.* The Oxford Shakespeare. Oxford: Clarendon Press.

Roberts, Warren E.
  1958 *The Tale of the Kind and the Unkind Girls.* Berlin: Walter de Gruyter.

Thompson, Ann, ed.
  1984 *The Taming of the Shrew*. Cambridge: Cambridge University Press.

Thorne, William B.
  1968 "Folk Elements in *The Taming of the Shrew*." *Queen's Quarterly* 75:482–496.

Tillyard, E.M.W.
  1964 "The Fairy-Tale Element in *The Taming of the Shrew*." In Edward A. Bloom, ed., *Shakespeare 1564–1964: A Collection of Modern Essays by Various Hands*. Providence: Brown University Press. Pp. 110–114.

Introduction to This Edition
Jan Harold Brunvand

Thirty years ago I decided to begin a study of Aarne-Thompson Type 901, "The Taming of the Shrew," and related folktales because of two factors mentioned in the Preface of my Indiana University doctoral dissertation—first, the unknown relationship of Shakespeare's play to the folktales, and second, the story's apparent survival as a modern joke with the punchline "That's Once!" Three years later I finished the historic-geographic study published for the first time in the present edition. Although some further variants of the shrew tales have been collected and the method the study used is no longer followed, I believe my findings are still valid and could not easily have been reached by any other means.

If the historic-geographic or "Finnish method" of folktale analysis had not existed in the late 1950s when I began, I would have had to invent it. This is not as unlikely—or as egotistical—as it may sound, since the method, as Archer Taylor pointed out in 1927 (quoted on p. 15), may be regarded as ". . . only common sense codified into a rigid procedure and not applied at random" (1927–28: 486). The extent to which the method became refined into a set of strict procedural axioms is suggested by the following passage from Taylor's own study of "The Black Ox." Here, in magisterial periodic sentences, Taylor indicates just how convinced some scholars of his day were that the approach of the Finnish school would yield completely reliable results in deriving the archetypes of international folktales:

> The most determinedly hostile critic must, however, concede that a trait which is widely distributed, which appears frequently in the variants, particularly in the fuller and better ones, which is attested at an early period in the tale's recorded history, which is *per se* old (involving some ancient religious or superstitious idea), which is useful in the tale's economy, which permits competing forms to be derived from it by some natural and readily explicable alteration or substitution, which yields evidence in agreement with that deducible from other traits, and which shows a development in accord with a known or a probable cultural trend, *must* belong to the earliest ascertainable form of the tale. I insist upon the word *must*. Granted that the trait meets these requirements, one is *compelled* to accept it as original; no option is conceivable. [1927: 7]

I soon realized that the historic-geographic method could not be applied to folktales as inflexibly as this, nor were the traits of an archetype to be determined with the certainty that Taylor's comment had suggested. (Taylor, in fact, followed this statement with the admission that ". . . such a fortunate conjuncture is relatively infrequent.") I incorporated in my study numerous refinements upon the method proposed by earlier folktale comparatists, plus inventing a few changes of my own as the data required. But I never saw these contributions to the procedural or theoretical sophistication of the method taken up by later historic-geographicists, for by the mid-1960s the method had fallen by the wayside as structural, semiotic, and contextual approaches to folktales gained adherents.

During my pre-computer graduate schooling, I earned my Ph.D. the old-fashioned way—by handwriting the documentation and analysis, then having it typewritten for submission in multiple carbon copies. Both the author and typist would have viewed the computer upon which I am composing this update as a sort of fairytale wonder, had we foreseen its emergence some twenty years or so down the road as a common tool for number-crunching data and word-processing text. In 1974 two folklorists did develop a computer program for speeding up future historic-geographic studies, but by then the method seemed to have no future, and to my knowledge a computerized Finnish method folktale study has never been attempted (Rosenberg and Smith, 1974).

In 1985, introducing papers from an Indiana University sponsored symposium "The Comparative Method in Folklore," Linda Dégh wrote, "Students in folklore programs may obtain a degree without learning how to use the type and motif indexes" (1986: 80). Robert A. Georges in his symposium paper declared, "From the viewpoint of many contemporary folklorists, the historic-geographic method is passé (1986: 87). While it is true that the conclusion of Georges' paper was that the *concepts* associated with the method had prevailed in folkloristics, despite the demise of the *method* itself, from the 1960s on most scholars interested in folk narratives had shunned the application of the Finnish method, which was even parodied in another Indiana University publication in these words:

> They [i.e., historic-geographic scholars] collected tons and tons of folktales and arranged them on a map in circles. This was known as the Finish Method, because it went around in circles and would never be finished. The Finish Method went on for a long time and is still not finished yet. [Magliocco, 1987: 132–133]

The unkindest cut of all—for me—was that Christine Goldberg's survey of the findings of historic-geographic studies, previously published in the *Journal of Folklore Research*, did not even mention my dissertation, nor did it list Type 901 as a folktale that had been studied comparatively. Goldberg, however, stated that the method "had been misunderstood and unjustly maligned," and she suggested that it still had a value and a future in folklore studies, even though she believed that "the last major historic-geographic study" had been published in 1958 (1984: 6, 9).

A possible joining of folktale comparatism and structuralism proposed by Alan Dundes in 1962 had failed to win followers or to bridge the gap between the two approaches (1962). "Unsuccessful repetition" was the binary structural trait that Dundes discovered in a number of tale types that seemed to be particularly common in the corpus of Lithuanian folktales. He speculated whether this meant that Lithuanian folklore reflected the actual historic past of that country marked by "a pattern of success followed by failure" (1962: 173). Dundes postulated that other patterns of repetition in folktales exist, and these may coordinate with other social, cultural, and historical factors. His approach might well be followed with "Taming of the Shrew" material, since the variants exhibit successful/unsuccessful, successful/successful, and even unsuccessful/successful repetitions in numerous widely distributed texts. Twenty-seven years ago I intended to write an essay extending and partly challenging Dundes' views expressed in this article; perhaps now I should get back to the project.

My findings with regard to Shakespeare's sources for "The Taming of the Shrew" were presented in my 1966 article in *Shakespeare Quarterly*. It is gratifying that the editor of this play for "The Oxford Shakespeare" felt that I argued "most convincingly that Shakespeare did not *need* a literary source for his taming story and that he is much more likely to have drawn on oral tradition." This literary historian projected my findings further to suggest that if the folktale about shrew taming was known to members of Shakespeare's audience, then Elizabethans may have arrived to see the play "'pre-conditioned,' as we might say, to enjoy the spectacle of the taming of one on whom they would not expect to waste a moment's sympathy" (Oliver, 1984: 49–50).

The anti-feminist "spectacle" of a shrewish woman being tamed by trickery and cruelty, however, has became as passé as the historic-geographic method since I finished my dissertation. One result of this raising of consciousness was that my essay "The Taming of the Shrew Tale in the United States," which was included in the first two editions of my textbook *The Study of American Folklore*, was replaced with another essay as of the third edition (Brunvand, 1968, 1978, 1986). The theme of the folktale—mastery in a marriage—was no longer tolerable to teachers and students in introductory folklore courses. Those who wish to read my update of the dissertation's American material will have to avail themselves of an earlier edition of the textbook.

Introduction to This Edition

But the tradition of telling jokes derived from "The Taming of the Shrew" tale was still alive a decade ago, at least in Utah. In 1978 a student in my American Folklore class reported the following encounter she had with the story. Her class in Latter-day Saints scriptures was studying the Mormon work called *The Doctrine and Covenants*. Section 98, verses 23–32, is a passage about how to behave "if men will smite you, or your families." The text advises Saints to follow God's teachings and "bear it patiently" for the duration of three such attacks before warning the enemy "in my name" to desist. Beginning a discussion of this passage , the LDS Institute instructor asked the class what they should do if someone should come against them, and one student called out, "That's Once!"

My student reported the response to this witticism: "Many knew the joke, and they laughed; then the teacher told the joke so the rest of the class would understand what everyone else was laughing about." I'm pleased to report, also, that my student told her class, "That's Aarne-Thompson Type 901!"

Salt Lake City, Utah
July 1989

References Cited

Brunvand, Jan Harold.
   1966 "The Folktale Origin of *The Taming of the Shrew.*" *Shakespeare Quarterly* 17: 345–359.

———.
   1968, 1978, 1986 *The Study of American Folklore*. 1st, 2nd, and 3rd editions. New York: Norton.

Dégh, Linda.
   1986 Introduction to Special Issue: "The Comparative Method in Folklore." *Journal of Folklore Research* 23: 77–83.

Dundes, Alan.
   1962 The Binary Structure of 'Unsuccessful Repetition' in Lithuanian Folk Tales." *Western Folklore* 21: 165–174.

Georges, Robert A.
   1986 "The Pervasiveness in Contemporary Folklore Studies of Assumptions, Concepts and Constructs Usually Associated with the Historic-Geographic Method. *Journal of Folklore Research* 23: 87–103.

Goldberg, Christine.
   1984 "The Historic-Geographic Method: Past and Future." *Journal of Folklore Research* 21: 1–18.

Magliocco, Sabina.
   1987 "Comment: 1846 and All That—A New History of Folkloristics, Including Good Things, Bad Things, and One or Two Really Weird Things." *Folklore Forum* 20: 128–137.

Oliver, H.J., ed.
   1982 *The Taming of the Shrew*. Oxford and New York: Oxford University Press.

Rosenberg, Bruce A., and John B. Smith.
   1974 "The Computer and the Finnish Historical-Geographical Method." *Journal of American Folklore* 87: 149–154.

Taylor, Archer.
   1927 "The Black Ox: A Study in the History of a Folk-Tale." *Folklore Fellows Communications*, No. 70. Helsinki: Academia Scientiarum Fennica.

———.
1927–28 "Precursors of the Finnish Method of Folklore Study." *Modern Philology* 25: 481–491.

Preface

Aarne-Thompson Type 901, *The Taming of the Shrew*, is a particularly interesting subject for a comparative folktale study because the relationship of the oral tradition to Shakespeare's comedy of the same title and to other literary versions has never been satisfactorily explained. *The Shrew* has long been an intriguing item for source studies in the Shakespearean canon. No text of the play earlier than the First Folio is known, though *The Taming of the Shrew*, an anonymous earlier quarto, is somehow related to it. Numerous studies of these and other literary versions have failed to take into consideration the widespread oral tradition of the tale. I was originally attracted by this situation to begin a study of the history of the plot.

In December 1958 I first realized that this folktale is still current in the United States. At that time my brother-in-law, then twelve years old, told me a version he had read in *Boys' Life* magazine (GEAm 1 in the study). Investigation soon revealed the tale to be well known to Americans at various age and cultural levels. For a seminar in Comparative Literature under Dr. Horst Frenz at Indiana University in 1959, I prepared a preliminary survey of the available texts of the tale. I found Type 901 to be an excellent example of that relatively rare folktale which has had a well-documented history in Indo-European oral tradition, continuing to the present day, and which inspired important literary works. The tale has managed to survive in contemporary culture and even to penetrate to the most modern media of mass communications.

When I began to gather all available versions of Type 901, I soon discovered that Type 1370*, *The Lazy Cat*, and certain other miscellaneous folktales and literary tales were logically and historically related to my central subject; I subsequently resolved to study this whole development, which I have called the Taming of the Shrew Complex. Eventually it became apparent that a really thorough study of all aspects of the complex would require texts, time, and funds well beyond the scope of the project. However, it has been possible to outline the general relationships of each of the related narratives to the major Tale Types which are discussed, and it is hoped that these notes will provide a satisfactory basis for close studies in the future of the other tales.

A large-scale comparative folktale investigation would be extremely difficult to carry out lacking our well-organized modern works of research or without help from many folklore scholars the world over. Having such aids, I found it possible to finish my study in a little less than three years of mostly part-time research. Even to list all those who facilitated my work indirectly would be impractical; many compilers of type and motif indexes, collectors, archivists, and editors of folktales are only mentioned in tables and footnotes, if indeed they are known to me at all. There are, however, many other scholars with whom I had direct contact, either by mail or in person, and I wish to thank them by name here.

For providing me with copies of folktale texts from other countries, I am grateful to Bo Almqvist of Reykjavík, Iceland; Walter Anderson of Kiel, Germany; Carl-Martin Bergstrand of the Västsvenska Folkminnesarkivet, Göteborg, Sweden: Olav Bø and Svale Solheim of the Norske Folkeminnesamling, Oslo, Norway; Laurits Bødker and Bengt Holbek of the Nordisk Institut for Folkedigtning, Copenhagen, Denmark; Maja Boškovic-Stulli and Zoran Palčok of the Institut za Narodnu Umjetnost, Zagreb, Yugoslavia; John Lorne Campbell of Isle of Canna, Scotland; James H. Delargy and Sean O'Sullivan of the Irish Folklore Commission, Dublin, Ireland; Brita Egardt of the Folklivsarkivet, Lund, Sweden; Ed Ertis and Erna Normann of the Kirjandusmuuseum, Tartu, Estonia; Béla Gunda of the Ethnological Institute of the University, Debrecen, Hungary; Jouko Hautala of the Folklore Archives of the Finnish Literary

Preface

Society, Helsinki, Finland; Luc Lacourcière of the Archives de Folklore, Quebec, Canada; Isidoe Levin of Leningrad, USSR; George Megas and Andrew Michaelides-Nouaros of Athens, Greece; G.R.S. Megaw of the School of Scottish Studies, Edinburgh, Scotland; Joachim Schwebe of the Institut für Volkskunde, Marburg, Germany; and J.J. Voskuil of the Centrale Commissie voor Onderzoek van het Nederlandse Volkseigen, Amsterdam, Holland.

For sending me miscellaneous information from other countries, I am indebted especially to Pertev N. Boratov of Paris, France; Reidar Th. Christiansen of Blommenholm, Norway; Gianfranco D'Aronco of Padova, Italy; Maurits de Meyer of Wilrijk Anvers, Belgium, Berze Nagy Janos of Pécs, Hungary; Julian Krzyzanowski of Warsaw, Poland; Åsa Nyman of Uppsala, Sweden; Roger Pinon of Liege, Belgium; Mihai Pop of Bucharest, Romania; Kurt Ranke of Kiel, Germany; Georges Henri Rivière of Paris, France; Einar ól. Sveinsson of Reykjavík, Iceland; and Paolo Toschi of Rome, Italy.

For aid in translations, I am grateful to Sean Cronin of Dublin, Ireland; Ealasaid Sinclair of Edinburgh, Scotland; Warren Kliewer of Lindsborg, Kansas; and Constantine Kazazis, Elli Köngäs, Meri Lehtinen, Nicholas Ochsner, and Mr. and Mrs. Merle Simmons, all of Bloomington, Indiana.

Numerous Americans helped me in various ways. I was provided with texts by Marion Moore Coleman and Anne H. Sidwa of *Polish Folklore*, Jesse Harris of Southern Illinois University, Américo Paredes of the University of Texas, Leonard Roberts of Morehead State College, Marie Walter of Brooklyn College, and Marie Berry, Head of the General Reference Department of San Antonio Public Library, San Antonio, Texas. Other American folklorists who sent information or advice were E.W. Baughman, Elizabeth Brandon, Thomas R. Brendle, Marie Campbell, Kenneth W. Clarke, Austin E. Fife, Herbert Halpert, Wayland Hand, Louis Jones, Hector Lee, and Archer Taylor. The editors of several folklore journals who printed my query for texts deserve my thanks, though these appeals were generally unsuccessful. Allan M. Trout, columnist for the Louisville, Kentucky, *Courier-Journal*, printed the only one of these notices which bore any fruit.

Professors Richard M. Dorson and Warren E. Roberts, both on my advisory committee, did me a great service by reading and criticizing the manuscript for this study. Professor Emeritus Stith Thompson was kind enough to allow me to consult his notes for the forthcoming revised edition of the *Type-Index*.

The Research Committee of Indiana University generously provided me with funds through a doctoral grant-in-aid for copying, translating, and providing the necessary postage for the completion of my project.

Finally, I am most deeply grateful to my very efficient typist, Mrs. Barbara Winkelman, and to my patient wife, Judith (who is *not* a shrew).

The Taming of the Shrew

CHAPTER I

Introduction

The Taming of the Shrew Complex

The title "Taming of the Shrew," apart from Shakespeare's comedy, is often loosely applied to various folktales, literary works, and subliterary works in which a bad wife is improved. However, by folklorists the designation has been chiefly reserved for Tale Type 901 in the Aarne-Thompson *Types of the Folk-tale*,[1] summarized there as follows: "The youngest of three sisters is a shrew. For their disobedience the husband shoots his dog and his horse. Brings his wife to submission. Wager: whose wife is the most obedient." This plot, or part of it, is recognizable in several early European literary sources, such as the Middle High German poem *Der vrouwen zuht*, an Old French fabliau *De la Dame Escolliée*, a chapter in the fourteenth-century Spanish *El Conde Lucanor* of Don Juan Manuel, one of Straparola's stories from the sixteenth century, and others. There is also an anonymous English play from 1594, *The Taming of a Shrew*, the relationship of which to Shakespeare has long been a subject of disputes. In addition, there are many folktale analogues of the tale, mostly unpublished, from Europe and the East.

A few scholars have pointed out, though none has studied, the similarity in a wife-taming method described in another folktale, Type 1370*, *The Lazy Cat*, which is reduced in the *Type-*

Index to two statements: "The cat beaten for not working. The wife must hold the cat and is scratched." (This tale is henceforth referred to without the star, as in Thompson's forthcoming revised edition of the *Type Index*.) The plots of Types 901 and 1370 both center on a husband who cures his bad wife by pretending to administer irrational punishment to a recalcitrant animal. The types differ, basically, not only in the species of animals usually involved, but also in that, while the wife is not really harmed in most versions of Type 901, she suffers rather severe physical punishment in version of Type 1370. These distinctions, however, tend to merge in many folktales; also combinations of both types in single narratives are not unknown. The scattered and brief discussions by scholars of the similarities in these tale types has had no effect on folktale classification. The *Type-Index* itself, with Type 901 classified as a *novella* about shrewishness reformed and Type 1370 in a category for miscellaneous stories about married couples, creates an artificial breach between the tales. Some annotators and archivists have not apparently found the description of Type 1370 under the starred numbers in the *Type-Index*, and so they have simply listed versions of *The Lazy Cat* with Type 901. (Both types were sent to me by archivists when I originally wrote asking only for Type 901.) The time is long overdue to reassert the relationships between these two folktales and to study them, along with other related tales and their literary parallels, as a tale complex.

In both Types 901 and 1370 there is considerable variation in exact details of the pretended punishment which is used to tame the wife. In Type 901 the species of animal that is killed may vary, and often several animals appear. Similarly, in about one-half of the versions of Type 1370, not a cat but some inanimate thing is beaten on the wife's back, ostensibly for being lazy and not doing the housework as the husband commanded. Sometimes the husband, who may not punish his wife directly because of her higher social status, pretends to punish something by beating it while his wife holds it. The object beaten may be an animal hide, a bag, or some other object. It seems legitimate to designate versions containing hides or other objects merely as subtypes of Type 1370.

Introduction

Various other devices to tame a wife, some ingenious and some merely cruel, are sometimes combined with Type 901 or Type 1370. Occurrences of these miscellaneous devices as separate tales have also been gathered for this study, though they are treated rather briefly. Epilogues that may be attached to the tales, such as an unsuccessful attempt to tame another wife, or the subsequent taming of the Shrew's mother (i.e., Type 901B), have been included as part of the complex. Similarly, special introductions or elaborations in the tales, when not obviously borrowed from other folktale types, have been taken into account.

In this study, therefore, "Taming of the Shrew" refers to a complex of tales and narrative elements from oral and literary tradition which cluster about Type 901 and its psychological and historical partner, Type 1370. Versions were admitted to the study if they involved taming a bad wife by pretending to punish an animal or object, or if they contained other taming methods which have repeatedly been combined with either of the two types based on this motif.

Previous Studies

The absence of a full-scale study of any part of the Taming of the Shrew Complex, and the lack (prior to the revised *Type-Index*) of even a fairly complete list of references to this popular theme of oral and printed tradition, would be difficult to understand were it not for two crucial gaps in the printed history of the tale. First, the Taming of the Shrew story was not in the Grimm brothers' collection, and second, the majority of recently collected versions lie unpublished in folklore archives. The result of the first condition is that not only are we without Bolte and Polívka's *Anmerkungen* for the Taming of the Shrew, but also the tale has not benefited from wide circulation in the Grimm canon and has thus not been called to the attention of folktale collectors as an item to be sought and preserved. (As a matter of fact, the Taming of the Shrew did not appear in any early collection which could be described as a "popular classic," except perhaps for Svend Grundtvig's books.) As a result of infrequent publication of oral versions, the scholars who are most interested in the tale,

Shakespeareans, have not realized that a large number of folktale analogues are extant. Studies dealing with Shakespeare's relationship to the oral tradition of the tale are discussed in Chapter IV; here we will only consider briefly writings concerned mainly with folktales.

The history of scholarly attention to the Taming of the Shrew Complex is no more than the history of annotations by the editors of some literary versions and by the collectors and publishers of some oral versions. The annotators of literary versions began earlier than the folklorists, but disappeared from the scene at about the period when folktale research was emerging as a recognized discipline. The folklorists who have dealt with the tale have been collectors and indexers who, in general, were interested in providing materials for research, rather than in producing studies of individual tales.

There is no value in summarizing in detail the annotations of literary analogues of the Taming of the Shrew, most of which date from the nineteenth century. Not only did succeeding editors often simply repeat notes from previously published lists, but theoretical opinions, when ventured, depended for folktale references upon guesswork concerning an oral stream, or on a few scant early reports from the field. One of the earliest of these editions,[2] it is true, does provide us with two eighteenth-century French versions of Type 901[3] and one version of a related tale,[4] but the editor disappoints us on the same pages by censoring his own fabliau text. Karl Simrock, who was interested in parallels for Shakespeare's plots in popular and oral tradition, provided the best early list of parallels for *The Taming of the Shrew*, along with summaries or translations of several versions, in 1831.[5] Simrock kept his notes up to date in later editions of his work; however, he confused Type 901 with Types 900 (*King Thrushbeard*) and 670 (*The Animal Languages*), and he made no theoretical conclusions beyond postulating an Italian variant standing between Straparola's and Shakespeare's versions of the tale.[6] The editors of *Der vrouwen zuht* (see GG Lit 1, Table I below)[7] and *El Conde Lucanor* (RS Lit 1)[8] limited their commentaries to repeating the list of well-known literary analogues and remarking on the curious appearance of the theme in folklore. An especially puzzling version for the early commentators was that reported from Persia in 1827 (Per 1) by

Introduction

an English traveler; it was apparently published in German as early as 1829. Simrock, it seems, first called attention to the Persian tale as an analogue to Shakespeare's comedy.[9] Joseph Bédier[10] and Albert Wesselski,[11] who would be expected to have been aware of folktales, were interested in the Taming of the Shrew at a time before a large number of oral texts had been collected; both of these scholars had strong feelings against comparative folktale studies, so it is doubtful whether they would have written their notes any differently even if they had been able to consult Aarne's or Thompson's indexes or the type catalogues for individual countries. Both Bédier and Wesselski gave only the standard list of old literary parallels. All of these nineteenth-century and early twentieth-century scholars may fairly be excused on the grounds of lack of information from approaching the Taming of the Shrew Complex *in toto*; this does not, of course, lessen the value of their spadework in locating early printed analogues of the tales.

As the collecting of folktales increased, scholars took more notice of the oral tradition of the Taming of the Shrew. It is interesting to note that Heinrich Pröhle, who in 1853 published one of the earliest texts of Type 1370 from oral tradition, pointed out in his note a basic relationship of *The Lazy Cat* to Shakespeare's plot. He wrote, "[this tale] is in its contents a counterpart to Shakespeare's comedy The Taming of the Shrew. As in the play, the man here *apparently* punishes another being (here an animal and there the servant) in order to improve his stubborn wife."[12] Pröhle's observation, however, produced no great response. Johannes Bolte, who commented on oral versions when he published two texts of Type 1370 from fifteenth-century manuscripts in 1908,[13] took no notice of Pröhle's observation except to cite a few examples of both of the tales in early literary sources. Bolte's only personal comment was that the folktales about the lazy cat were not merely recent garbled retellings of other Taming of the Shrew tales (i.e., of Type 901), but seemed to have a tradition of their own.

A contribution by Reinhold Köhler to the *Jahrbuch der deutschen Shakespeare-Gesellschaft* for 1868 [14] presented for the first time in a publication that would come to the attention of many literary scholars, a folk version of Type 901. Köhler had noticed the tale in Svend Grundtvig's 1854 collection (version GD 7 in Table I); he furnished a German translation of it, noted resemblances to Shakespeare's play, and listed the older literary versions and the Persian story once again. He dismissed the possibility that Shakespeare invented the plot and that the Danish tale could have been borrowed from his comedy; he thought that the evidence suggested older forms of the story from which both the Danish tale and the English play were derived. Köhler's article has attracted the interest of some Shakespeareans, who have taken the Danish text to be a unique oral survival; by comparing it with Shakespeare's plot and other literary analogues, they have sought to explain the relationships of all. Their conclusions will be examined in Chapter IV; here it is sufficient to say that Köhler's thesis of common early popular sources for both the play and the Danish tale—which seems almost axiomatic to a student of the folktale—has received short shrift so far from the literati. Probably none of these scholars has examined the reprinting of Köhler's paper in his *Kleinere Schriften*, or more interest might have generated in the oral parallels to Shakespeare's play. Bolte, the editor of Köhler's writings, added references to two further Danish folktales (GD 3 and GD 6 below) and one tale collected in India (Ind 1).[15] The first volume of the *Kleinere Schriften*, moreover, contained Köhler's previously unpublished notes to a French version of Type 901 first printed in 1886 (RF 1).[16] In Köhler's notes, then, we find the earliest list of references to several folktales belonging to the Taming of the Shrew Complex.

One further brief study of both literary and oral versions of the Taming of the Shrew was available before the turn of the century, at least to a pioneer group of American folklorists, and through their publication, potentially to others; it was a paper read *in absentia* in English for the Ukrainian scholar Mykhaylo Dragomanov at the International Folk-Lore Congress of the World's Columbia Exposition in Chicago, 1893.[17] Professor Dragomanov's essay, "Taming of the Shrew, in the Folk-Lore of the Ukraine," included one full translation and one summary of unpublished texts, and summaries of three versions from printed collections. Dragomanov assumed that Shakespeare had borrowed his basic taming-plot from Straparola's *novella*, but he thought that details of the play might have been derived from English oral versions similar to stories known elsewhere in Europe. Dragomanov apparently had rather full notes on analogues for the tales, for he mentioned, without always giving explicit references, folktales from Spain, Denmark, France, Germany, Russia, Bulgaria (!), and Persia. His theory concerning the genesis of the tales was that an Oriental original had only involved a cat being killed (i.e., Type 901) and that European imitations of this story, "impelled by a coarse vivacity on the subject," produced the versions with another animal killed or a cat beaten on the wife's back (Type 1370). Both forms, Dragomanov suggested, penetrated into the Ukraine, where, since such treatment of a wife does not accord with her position here, a new form was invented. In this form the husband is selected on the basis of his ability to handle animals and he tames his wife by denying food to her until she does some work (i.e., Motif W111.3.6., "Who will not work shall not eat.")

When the Aarne-Thompson *Type-Index* was published in 1928, there were further versions of Type 901 to report from Estonia, Finland, Swedish-Finland, and Russia.[18] Type 1370 was not included as a major entry in the *Index*, being only reported then from Estonia and Finland. Nearly two decades later in *The Folktale*, Thompson could add Spain, Scotland and Ireland to the list of countries from which Type 901 had been collected, but still there was no study of the tale to report; he commented, however,

> The tale goes back to the Exemplum literature of the Middle ages, where it appears in Juan Manuel's *El Conde Lucanor*. It was also retold by Straparola in the sixteenth century. Whether from these literary forms or otherwise, it is popular in the folklore of the Baltic states and Scandinavia. It has also been reported from Scotland, Ireland, Spain, and Russia. . . . It would seem most reasonable to suppose that we have here a literary tale which has become a real part of the folklore of northern Europe.

Further on in *The Folktale*, however, in discussing possible literary origins of folktales, Thompson by mistake credits Straparola with originating the tale. Here he writes,

> . . . an ultimate origin in European literature seems unmistakable for a dozen or more of the stories current today. . . . Many stories have undoubtedly originated among the people of Italy, and it is sometimes difficult to know whether a tale recounted by those great writers of *novelle* beginning with Boccaccio was learned from the people or was invented by the author. For at least three of our folktales such literary invention by the *novella* writer seems the most reasonable hypothesis. The wager on the Wife's Chastity (Type 882) is in Boccaccio's) *Decameron*; The Luck-Bringing Shirt (Type 844) is in the *Pecorone* of Ser Giovanni; and The Taming of the Shrew (Type 901) is in the *Nights* of Straparola.[19]

(Type 1370 was described in *The Folktale* only as being popular in Eastern Europe.)[20]

The most voluminous set of notes published with a version of the Taming of the Shrew, and the most ambitious attempt so far to analyze the whole complex, accompanied Espinosa's two Spanish texts published in 1946 to 1947.[21] Espinosa knew most of the literary sources used in the present study, but only the folktales which had been published from Spain, Spanish-America, Portugal, France, Denmark, and Hungary; on the basis of these versions he attempted to construct an outline of the fundamental elements of the tale and to describe major types which occur. Espinosa's typological discussion is not of much value now, since he lacked enough examples of different forms of the tale to make a really comprehensive outline; furthermore, he included in his outline only elements of the taming itself and not special introductions, elaborations, the wager, and other details studied here. Espinosa's references, despite some inaccuracies, are especially helpful for locating Spanish and Portuguese texts.

Lists of versions from Sweden and Denmark with brief annotations have been published in recent folktale collections; these may be taken as representative of the present state of knowledge, or lack of knowledge among folklorists, concerning the Taming of the Shrew. Waldemar Liungman, who himself collected several Swedish versions, summarized the examples he had of Type 901 by remarking that the Persian and Indic fragments may show the original form of the story and that the tale was told all over Europe, though it is uncommon. The form of the story known in Sweden, Liungman wrote, is more common than that collected in Spain.[22] Laurits Bødker's interest in Type 901 was local when he recently annotated one of Grundtvig's unprinted versions in the *Danmarks Folkeminder* series;[23] he only listed and briefly characterized other Danish texts. Finally, a version collected by the present writer was published in *Kentucky Folklore Record* with a headnote reporting on progress in gathering versions for this study.[24]

Materials for this Study

Thirty-five literary versions and three hundred and eighty-three oral versions of various forms of the Taming of the Shrew have been used in the present study; thirty countries or national groups are represented. Certainly it would be presumptuous to suggest that all known versions have been gathered, but, judging from the published indexes of folktales, remarkably few of the catalogued texts have not at least been available to me in summary form. The only sizeable group of versions listed in a published index but not accessible were the Lithuanian ones; here, fortunately, a number of printed texts was available to help fill the gap. Lack of collections and indexes and/or poor communications with certain countries probably has caused some artificial gaps in the distribution of the versions; one thinks at once of England, for instance, where there is no national archive and field collections of folktales have not been made; this is in contrast to neighboring Ireland, where folktale collecting has reached almost legendary proportions. Also, folklorists who wrote me from Italy, France, Switzerland, Poland, and other countries could not report any collected texts of shrew-taming tales, but they hesitated to state categorically that such tales might not exist in tradition. I was not successful in establishing communications with folklore scholars in Czechoslovakia, Bulgaria, and some other parts of Eastern Europe, or with South America, where versions might be expected; on the other hand, I had the good fortune to reach sympathetic and helpful scholars (whose names are given in the Preface) in Russia, Estonia, Yugoslavia, Romania, Greece, and many other countries, some of which have not always yielded their folktale riches to the inquiring student.

A large number of versions have come to me in summaries or in translations, often into French or German, which I in turn had to put into English. Greek, Russian, Hungarian, Spanish, Finnish, Irish and Scottish Gaelic, and Icelandic were translated for me by others. As a result I was able to use texts which would not otherwise have been accessible to me; at the same time a certain danger of misrepresentation of the originals existed. In no instance was a summary used when it was reasonably possible to acquire the full text of a version. All of my translators and summarizers have been professional folklorists or were working under the guidance of a folklorist.

Method of Study

The overall pattern followed in this study is the historic-geographic or "Finnish" method of comparative folktale research. The Finnish method has been conceived of here, to use Archer Taylor's words, as "only common sense codified into a rigid procedure and not applied at random";[25] my purpose, like Taylor's, in developing *Urforms* has been "by the procedure of reconstruction to look deeply into the structure and life of the tale."[26] The basic steps of this method, as outlined by Aarne, Krohn, Anderson, and Thompson,[27] have been used—gathering all possible versions, dividing them into individual traits or elements, and attempting to reconstruct hypothetical original forms of the traits and the tales. In its essential framework this study resembles Warren E. Roberts's recent historic-geographic study of Type 480,[28] upon which, indeed, it was originally patterned. As in Roberts's and other tale-type monographs, however, the exact methods followed have been partly determined by the goals of the researcher and partly by the specific nature of the material being examined.

Four important aspects of the Taming of the Shrew Complex have significantly affected the methods worked out for the study and the presentation of the findings. These are as follows: (1) Several narrative elements—types, motifs, and otherwise—have combined variously to make up individual versions; (2) There was found to be a large number of relatively nondistinctive versions of Type 901, in which, however, traces of more specific subtypes of the tale sometimes might appear; (3) There are a number of older literary versions relating to different forms of the complex, the best known example of which is Shakespeare's play; and (4) Type 901 persists, though in modernized dress, as a current American joke. My chief goals in studying this material have been to discover the major forms in which the tales have existed and to work out their relationships to each other, to attempt reconstructing life histories of the various tales and of the complex itself, to relate the oral and literary versions and to attempt to explain Shakespeare's connection to the whole tradition, and to discuss briefly the modern versions and their place in twentieth-century culture.

In examining a whole group of related narrative elements which may combine in different sequences or exist separately, I faced some of the same problems as did the student of "The Cinderella Cycle."[29] In some respects solutions to problems found by Rooth were applied to the Taming of the Shrew Complex, although there are important basic differences between the two studies. For example, in her monograph Rooth dispenses with the complete list of variable elements and summaries of the elements contained in each version; she has also developed some personal terminology. In my study the conventional lists of elements and the tale-summaries have been prepared; also, established terms, so far as possible, are employed.

Early in her monograph Rooth rightly comments, "It is impossible . . . in a research concerned with several different types, first to construct the original forms of the motifs and thereafter the earliest form of the type. The establishment of the former necessitates simultaneous consideration both of the motifs and the types."[30] This statement applies well to the Taming of the Shrew Complex. Obviously, it would be absurd to reconstruct the archetypal form of an element such as the device for taming the wife and do the same for the element of the wager on the wives' obedience, and then to combine these two "original" elements in an archetype for the whole tale. For while the basic taming tale is found in folktales literally from Ireland to India and in literature from at least the fourteenth century, the wager is attached to a number of tales but is limited in its distribution to northern Europe and is not found in the taming tale before Shakespeare's time. Several other important elements of the complex, as will be seen, are considerably more restricted in number and distribution than is the basic plot of Type 901. Each of these units must be established in its proper segment of the tradition before the reconstruction of the whole is attempted. Rooth, thus, examined the "motif-complexes"—small organic units within the larger unit of the tale[31]—before studying the types themselves. I have borrowed the technique, though not the term, in studying two "free-floating narrative elements"—the wager and the taming of the mother-in-law—before taking up the Taming of the Shrew proper. Also, in arguing the connections of certain versions within subtypes, I have often called attention to distinctive narrative elements or to "sequences of elements" which are paralleled in these versions but not elsewhere.

Rooth continues, "In order to present the subject more clearly, the section on the relationship and development of the types is inserted before the investigations of the motifs and geographical area. The types have been arranged in the order in which they seem to have been evolved."[32] In this study, likewise, the typological divisions, though actually plotted after consideration of the narrative elements and their distributions, are presented first in the hope of clarifying the following close analyses. In Chapter II the versions have been grouped according to the combinations of narrative elements contained in each; a chart has been prepared to show clearly the relationships of the parts of the complex to each other. In Chapter III, after the discussion of the free-floating elements, subtypes of Type 901 are defined and then subjected to individual historic-geographic analysis; these subtypes have been arranged in what is thought to be roughly chronological order. Because special problems and intentions are involved, the subtype to which Shakespeare's comedy belongs and the current American subtype are treated separately in Chapters IV and V. Types 1370 and miscellaneous tales in the complex are discussed in Chapter VI and VII, and conclusions follow in

Introduction

Chapter VIII. Archer Taylor has criticized this sort of arrangement of the material in an early monograph by Gaston Paris, but he also commended its value; he wrote:

> He arranges his material in groups of related stories. The arrangement implies a previous knowledge of the relations. In other words, he works out the whole study before writing it and this doubles his labor. In a systematic comparison based on historical and geographical considerations such groups present themselves of their own accord; more than that, the reader would not be tempted to raise the question whether other groups could have been found. Yet the merits of Gaston Paris' presentation, its perspicuity and strict organization, are not to be underestimated.[33]

For the clearness and orderliness it affords, the initial arrangement of versions into related groups has been followed. Readers may examine the data in Tables I and II to evaluate the groupings for themselves.

Possibly some forcing has been done on the material by working all versions, whatever their special forms, into a single outline of elements. After some initial experimentation with other systems, however, it was felt that a single outline did not seriously distort the data and was certainly preferable to a multiplicity of abbreviations, letter-and-number codes, and cross-references from one table to another. Every version has the same general course of action—the marriage, taming, and reform of a shrewish girl—and a suitable place in the outline could be designated for all of the variations.

The most crucial point in evaluating any historic-geographic study of a folktale is not the form of the tables of data or the order of presentation of subtypes, but the criteria by which traits are admitted or excluded in reconstructing the archetype. In this respect Aarne's considerations for traits that belong in the original form of the tale have been tempered with reference to Roberts's criticisms of them;[34] that is, the most frequently occurring and most widely distributed traits are preferred. Also, as Roberts pointed out, distribution of a trait only on the periphery of an area indicates that the trait must have been known earlier *within* the area, but it has died out there or been replaced by newer forms. Still, others of Aarne's criteria are sometimes applied here, especially the seventh, a trait's essential place in the story, without which the plot would suffer; the eighth, its presence in one tale only; and the ninth, the possibility of other forms having been developed from it.

The kinds of changes that Aarne pointed out to which oral narratives are subject as they diffuse have also been taken into account in constructing original forms of the tales.[35] The loss and addition of details and the stringing together of several tales are everywhere apparent. Both the specialization of general traits and generalizing of specific traits have occurred. Some changes have required others to be made in the tale; for instance, when the wager is present there must be more characters, usually husbands of the Shrew's sisters, to do the wagering. The setting of the tale in a scene where animals such as a horse or dog may logically appear has affected such an element as the roles of the human characters. Instances of modernization of older traits and even of updating the whole story with the addition of a gag "punch line" have been pointed out. Miscellaneous other internal evidence (such as references in texts to definite places) or external evidence (such as examples or certain borrowings form one nation to another in other tale types) has occasionally been made use of. Also taken into account have been the different amounts of collecting in various countries, the degree of representativeness of subtypes within countries, and the nature of colonial versions. Since particular criteria are emphasized more in one section than in others, methodology is briefly taken up from time to time within the sections of analysis themselves.

The literary versions have generally been easy to identify with definite oral subtypes; thus, they serve as markers showing that particular forms of the tales were known at least in certain areas by definite dates in history. The absence of old literary versions, of course, in many areas can in no way be taken to show that the oral tale could not have existed there. Elements which appeared to be strictly, or even largely, literary rather than oral have not been examined in any detail. Shakespeare's plot requires special attention since here elements which must ultimately go back to oral tradition have sometimes been altered to fit the conditions of the stage. The consideration of

Introduction 17

many other dramatic and musical adaptations of the Taming of the Shrew—most of which are based on Shakespeare—would extend too far beyond the scope of this study. A separate modern play (see RS Lit 3) which is based on a Spanish literary version, however, has been included.

In the study of the American subtype of Type 901 the major interest has been on the place of the old folktale in our mass-communications-dominated culture, rather than solely on the original forms of elements. This section is meant merely to be suggestive, certainly not definitive. The evidence concerning Type 1370 and the miscellaneous taming tales had been less full than that about Type 901; therefore, conclusions in these sections are more than usually open to amendment.

Although individual archetypes for the special subtypes and forms of the tales have usually been constructed following the main analysis of each, the final archetypes have been deferred to the section of conclusions about the life history of the whole complex.

Terminology, Abbreviations, and the Tables of Data

The term "complex" was preferred to Rooth's use of "cycle" because the latter is used ordinarily to signify a series of adventures of a definite character; we speak, for example, of "the Trickster Cycle," "the cycle of Hodscha Nasreddin tales," or "the cycle of stories about Old Marster and John." The use of "Complex" is intended rather to suggest an intricately related number of narrative elements clustering about a basic plot pattern and all dealing with a similar theme, here the improvement of a bad wife. "Trait" and "element" are used for the small units into which each version is divided. ("Version" and sometimes "tale" or "story" are used to mean one recorded text of a tale.) The terms "motif" and "type" are used, to avoid confusion, *only* in the sense of items which are catalogued in the *Motif-Index* and *Type-Index*. "Narrative element" has been used where Rooth might have employed her term "motif-complex." But my use of "narrative element" also includes parts of tale types, groups of motifs, and tale-sections not found in the indexes—in short, any units of narration larger than traits but smaller than whole tales, that have freely combined to make up the versions. The term "subtype" is used for a closely related number of versions which share distinctive elements—usually *sequences* of elements—not regularly found in other versions. "Group" and "form" have been used variously for other related numbers of versions which are to be discussed as a unit other than a subtype. Usually catchword titles are given to groups of versions when they are taken up.

The Taming of the Shrew, when underlined, indicates, of course, the title of Shakespeare's comedy. Following the custom in Shakespearean studies, however, the plays are often referred to simply as *The Shrew* and *A Shrew*.

In Table II, "The versions of the Tale," titles of published works and names of folklore archives are abbreviated after the first references. A list of the abbreviations for archives precedes the table; a second list shows the abbreviations used for countries in both tables. The contents of each version is summarized in Table I with numbers and letters referring to the sections of Table II, "The Elements of the Tale." (A figure in parentheses in a summary indicates an element which is slightly different from the standard form or only generally described in the version.) The literary versions have been grouped here by types—first Type 901, then Type 1370, and finally other tales. In Table II these three groups are given in the same order with diagonal lines setting off references to Type 1370, a plan that was found impractical to apply to the folktale versions.

The folktales so far as possible have been arranged in Table I from north to south except for two groups. The Finnish versions are arranged according to the areas used by Finnish folklorists. These areas progress northward from the southwestern corner of the country and are identified with letters of the alphabet. The letter designations are given with each Finnish version here. The Danish versions are arranged by the plan used in that country, first Copenhagen and the eastern islands, then the Jutland peninsula from north to south. Whenever known, the date and place of collection are stated at the end of each summary of an oral version. The summaries do not necessarily represent the exact order in which elements appear in the texts; unusual order is only indicated in the summary of a version if this seems to be significant to the study of the life history of the tale. A general element of tale has never been cited in a summary if a more specific form of the element of a tale can be given; for example, the element "husband kills a horse" was not listed in a summary if the reasons for his killing the horse were given and could be represented in the table of elements. The absence of an element has not been indicated in the summaries except for section III, the description of the wedding, and section VI, the wager on the wives' obedience. Numbers from the *Motif-Index*, where appropriate, are given with elements in Table II.

NOTES

1. FCC 74 (1928)
2. Pierre Jean Baptiste Le Grand d'Aussy, *Fabliaux ou contes du xiie et du xiiie siecle*, 2 vols. (Paris, 1779); contained version RF Lit 1.
3. pp. 353–354; RF Lit 2 and RF Lit 3 in this study.
4. pp. 356–357; RF Lit 4 in this study.
5. *Die Quellen des Shakespeare in Novellen, Märchen und Sagen*, 2 vols. (Bonn, 1831); *The Shrew* discussed, I, 327–254. Translation for the Shakespeare Society, *The Remarks of M. Karls Simrock on the Plots of Shakespeare's Plays* (London, 1850; *The Shrew* discussed here, pp. 80–93.
6. I compared the English translation of the edition of 1831 with the revised German edition of 1870.
7. Friedrich Heinrich von der Hagen, *Gesammtabenteuer*, 3 vols. (Stuttgart and Tübingen, 1850).
8. Hermann Knust, ed., Juan Manual, *El Libro de los enxiemplos del Conde Lucanor et de Petronio* (Leipzig, 1900).
9. See the English translation by the Shakespeare Society (1850), pp. 88f.
10. See *Les Fabliaux*, 5th ed. (Paris, 1925), pp. 464–465.
11. See *Märchen des Mittelalters* (Berlin, 1925), pp. 66–69, 216.
12. *Kinder-und Volksmärchen* (Leipzig, 1853), p. xli. My translation of the quotation.
13. "Der Schwank von der faulen Frau und der Katze," *Zeitschrift für Volkskunde*, XVIII (1908), 53–60.
14. "Zu Shakespeare's *The Taming of the Shrew*," *Jahrbuch*, III (1868), 137–401.

15. Reinhold Köhler, *Kleinere Schriften zur Märchenforschung*, ed., J. Bolte, III (Berlin, 1900), 40–44.
16. "Anmerkungen zu Bladé, *Contes populaires de la Gascogne*," *Kleinere Schriften*, I (Weimar, 1898), 114–137.
17. Published with this title (Chicago, 1898), pp. 368–373. For reprintings of this essay, see the note to version SRUk 1.
18. The *Type-Index* also lists a tale of Spanish provenance from the Zuni, but this text does not appear to be a version of Type 901; see note 25 to Table I.
19. *The Folktale* (New York, 1946), pp. 105 and 177–178.
20. Ibid., p. 211.
21. Aurelio Macedonio Espinosa, *Cuentos populares españoles*, 3 vols. (Madrid, 1946–47), texts no. 91 and 92.
22. *Sveriges Samtliga Folksagor i Ord och Bild*, II (Stockholm, 1949), 452.
23. *DFM*, No. 68, Niels Levinsen, *Folkeeventyr fra Vendsyssel*, Udgivet af Laurits Bødker, (Copenhagen, 1958), pp. 2213–240.
24. "Folktales by Mail from Bond, Kentucky," *KFR*, VI (1960), 69–76; Type 901, pp. 70–71.
25. Archer Taylor, "Precursors of the Finnish Method of Folklore Study," *MP*, XXV (1927–28), 486.
26. Archer Taylor, "The Predestined Wife (Mt. 930°)," *Fabula*, II, Heft 1/2 (1958), 78.
27. See Antti Aarne, *Leitfaden der vergleichenden Märchenforschung*, FFC 13 (1913); Kaarle Krohn, *Die Folkloristische Arbeitsmethode* (Oslo, 1926); Walter Anderson, "Geographische-historische Methode," *Handwörterbuch des deutschen Märchens*, II, Johannes Bolte and Lutz Mackensen, eds. (Berlin, 1934–1940), 508–522; and Stith Thompson, *The Folktale* (New York, 1946), "The Life History of a Folktale," pp. 428–448.
28. *The Tale of the Kind and the Unkind Girls*, Fabula Supplement, Serie B: Untersuchungen, Nr. 1 (Berlin, 1958).
29. Anna Birgitta Rooth, *The Cinderella Cycle* (Lund, 1951).
31. Ibid., p. 26.
31. Ibid., p. 31.
32. Ibid., p. 29.
33. Taylor, "Precursors," p. 488; he is referring to Gaston Paris's article "Die undankbare Gattin," *Zeitschrift für Volkskunde*, XIII (1903), 1–24, 129–150.
34. Roberts, op. cit., pp. 7–8.
35. See Aarne, *Leitfaden*, "Die Veränderungen in den Märchen," pp. 23–213; Thompson, *The Folktale*, p. 436.

Abbreviations for Folklore Archives

AF	=	Archives de Folklore de l'Université Laval (Québec)
AVM	=	Archiv für Volkskunde, Marburg
DFS	=	Danske Folkemindesamling (Now Nordisk Institut for Folkedigtning)
FLS	=	Folklore Archives of the Finnish Literary Society
IFC	=	Irish Folklore Commission Archives
INU	=	Institut za Narodnu Umjetnost Archives, Zagreb
KMT	=	Folklore Archives of the Kirjandusmuuseum, Tartu
LUF	=	Lund University Folkminnesarkiv
SSS	=	School of Scottish Studies
VF	=	Västsvenska Folkminnesarkivet

Abbreviations for Countries

GI	Iceland
GN	Norway
GS	Sweden
GSF	Swedes in Finland
GD	Denmark
GG	Germany
GNe	The Netherlands
GE	England
GEAm	The United States
CS	Scotland
CI	Ireland
FF	Finland
FE	Estonia
FH	Hungary
BLi	Lithuania
SP	Poland
SRW	White Russia
SRUk	The Ukraine
SR	Russia
SY	Yugoslavia
RF	France
RFAm	French in America

Abbreviations for Countries

RI	Italy
RP	Portugal
RS	Spain
RSAm	Spanish in America
RR	Romania
Gre	Greece
Per	Persia
Ind	India

TABLE I

The Versions of the Tale

Literary forms of Type 901

GG Lit 1—Friedrich Heinrich von der Hagen, *Gesammtabenteuer* (Stuttgart and Tübingen, 1850), I, 37–57, "Der Vrouwen zuht" [MHG poem]. IIalg, B3, C1f, 2a, IIIA2, E1ci, e, gi, 3b IVA4, Bla, dii, 2ai, 4bi, VI0, VIIA4e.

GG Lit 2—Johannes Bolte, "Eine Parallele zu Shakespeare's *The Taming of the Shrew*," *Jahrbuch der Deutschen Shakespeare-Gesellschaft*, XXVII (1892), 130–134, "Eine gantz böse Jungfrau wird eine gar fromme Frau," from *Gepflückte Fincken, Oder Studenten-Confect* [1667]. IIAlg, B3, Cla, IIIEO, IVA8, Blvi, di, 2ai, 4biii, D3, VI0.

GE Lit 1—*The Taming of a Shrew*, ed. by F. S. Boas (The Shakespeare Library: New York and London, 1908) [First edition 1594]. IB4, IIAlei, B17, Cla, IIIA8, B1, C1, Ela, b, 2b, 3a, IVA5, D3, 8a, c, d, VA3b, c, e, C2aii, b, VIA1, 3, B1, D1, 4ci, 5e, 7, VIIB2.

GE Lit 2—William Shakespeare, *The Taming of the Shrew*[1] [Written ca. 1596; first printed in First Folio, 1623]. IB4, IIAlfi, B17, Cla, IIIA2, 4, 8, B1, C1, Ela, b, ci, 2a, b, 3a, (b),

25

VIA4, 5, Blvii, iv, cv, D3, 8a, b, c, d, VA3b, c, e, C2aii, b, VIa1, 3, B1, D1, 4c, (5e), 7, 10, VIIB2.

GE Lit 3—Isaac Bickerstaff, Esq. [Richard Steele], *The Tatler*, Number 231 (from Thursday September 28 to Saturday September 30, 1710)[2] [Contains a tale dated "From my own apartment, September 29," which describes a shrew-taming in "a family wherein I was several years an intimate acquaintance . . . in Lincolnshire"]. IIA1dii, B17, (IIIElci, e, f, 3b), IVA4, B1bi, 1di, 2avii, VIa1, Blb, C1, D1.

RF Lit 1—Anatole de Montaiglon and Gaston Raynaud, *Recueil Général et Complet des Fabliaux des XIIIe et XIVe Siecles* (Paris, 1872-1890), I, 95–116, "De la Dame Escolliée." (Id1), IIA1g, B3, Clf, C2a, b, IIIB1, C4a, E2b, 3b, IVA4, Blaxi, 2axi, D8c, VIC, VIIA4c.

RF Lit 2—*Journal de Paris* (31 Juillet 1777) [Summarized in Pierre Jean Baptiste le Grand d'Aussy, *Fabliaus ou contes du xiie et du xiiie siecle* (Paris, 1779), II, 353–354]. ID4, IIIE0, IVB2a, VIO.

RF Lit 3—*Bibliotheque de Cour*, V, 186 [Summarized in Le Grand d'Aussy, II, 353–354]. IIA1h, B2, IIIE0, IVB1, 2, VIO.

RS Lit 1—Don Juan Manuel, *El Conde Lucanor*, ed. by Hermann Knust (Leipzig, 1900), no. XXXV, pp. 154–161[3] [Written ca. 1335, first edition 1575, first English translation in *The Athenaeum*, vol. I, no. 2071 (June 29, 1867), 846–847. The translation in James York, *Count Lucanor: or the Fifty Pleasent Stories of Patronio* (London, 1888), 200–207 is numbered 44 in the collection; the story has frequently been reprinted, retranslated, and renumbered]. IB4, IIA1g, B17, C1a, IIIA2, 3, 11, B4, E0, IVA5, Blaxvi, 2axiii, 3h, VC1d, VIO, VIIA2a.

RS Lit 2—*El Conde Lucanor*, Knust ed., no.XXVII, pp. 116–131 [York, no. 5, pp. 29–41]. IB4, IIA1eii, B17, Clf, IIIEO, VA2e, f, 3d, VIO.

Table I: The Versions of The Tale 27

RS Lit 3—Alejandro Casona Alejandro Rodriguez Alvarez, *Retablo Jovial* (Buenos Aires, 1949), 57–58, "Entremes del Mancebo que Caso con Mujer Brava"[4] [A dramatization of RS Lit 1]. IB4, IIA1g, B17, CIa, IIIA2, 3, 11, B4, EO, IVA5, B1axvi, 2axiii, 3h, VC1d, VIO, VIIA2a.

RI Lit 1—G.F. Straparola, *le piacevoli notti*, tr. by W.G. Waters (London, 1894), II, 86–92, second story of eighth night [first edition 1550]. IB4, IIA1f, B2, IIIEO, IVA5, B1bi, (D5), VIO, VIIA2b.

Literary Forms of Type 1370

GG Lit 3—Johannes Bolte, "Der Schwank von der faulen Frau und der Katze," *Zeitschrift des Vereins für Volkskunde*, XVIII (1908), 59–60, "Wie ein Bauer eines armen Edelmannes faule Tochter und träges Pferd meistert" [15th Century]. IIA1g, A2a, B1, C1b, F, IIIa11, Ci, EO, IVA5, C1b, VIO, VIIB3.

GG Lit 4—Bolte, *ZfV*, XVIII (1908), 55–58, "Jörg Zobels Gedicht von dem klugen Rossatäuscher und seiner faulen Frau" [1455–56]. IIA1g, B5, C1f, IIIA2, 11, C1, EO, IVA5, CIa, VIO.

GG Lit 5—W. Seelmann, ed. *Mittelniederdeutsche Fastnachtspiele* (Norden and Leipzig, 1885), pp. 1–20, "Wie man böse Frauen fromm machen kann"[5] [1540–50]. IIC2a, IIIEO, IVA5, C2ai, g, VIO.

GG Lit 6—Martin Schmidder, *Das new Morgens Fell* (Dören, 1582) [Summarized in Johannes Bolte and W. Seelman, eds., *Niederdeutsche Schauspiele älterer Zeit* (Norden and Leipzig, 1895), pp. *9–*15]. IIC2a, IIIEO, IVA5, C2ai, f, VIO.

GG Lit 7—"Eine approbirte Kunst, wie man die bösen Weiber kan fromm machen" [A tale from German jest books 1666f., summarized in Bolte-Seelmann, p. *19]. IIA2diii, B4, IIIA11, EO, IVA5, C2ci, f, (VIC4, D3).

GG Lit 8—Joseph Clemens, Archbishop of Köln, *La Peau-de-boeuf, ou remède universel pour faire une bonne femme d'une mauvaise* (Valenciennes, 1710) [A play written by a German in exile, summarized in Bolte-Seelmann, pp. *19–*20]. IIB3, IIEO, IVA5, C2d, f, D4, VIO.

GG Lit 9—Samuel Grosser, *Die versteckte aber auch mit sonderbahrem Ruhm entdeckte Höflichkeit* (Görlitz, 1716) [Summarized in Seelmann, p. xxi]. IIB4, IIIA11, EO, IVA5, C2c, VIO.

GNe Lit 1—Georg Macropedius, *Andrisca* (Utrecht, 1538) [A *Schulkomedie* in Latin, summarized in Bolte-Seelmann, pp. *7–*8]. IIB14, IIIEO, IVA5, C2ai, f, D5, VIO.

GNe Lit 2—*Moorkensvel* [First edition ca. 1550, printed in Bolte-Seelmann, pp. 1–14 and summarized in German pp. *5–*6]. IIC2a, IIIEO, IVA5, C2ai, f, VIO.

GE Lit 4—W. C. Hazlitt, *Remains of the Early Popular Poetry of England* (London, 1866), IV, 179–226, "A merry Jeste of Shrewde and curste Wyfe lapped in Morrelles skin" [ca. 1550]. IIA1fi, CIa, IIIA2, B1, EO, IVA5, C2ai, f, VIO, (VIIA4).

GE Lit 5—Francis James Child, *The English and Scottish Popular Ballads* (The Folklore Press ed., New York, 1957), V, 104–107, number 277, "The Wife Wrapt in Wether's Skin" [Child's summary, page 104, is taken as a norm for this ballad which is related to literary forms of Type 1370]. IICIa, IIIA11, EO, IVA5, C2b, VIO.

RF Lit 3A—Thomas Frederick Crane, ed., *The Exampla of Jacques de Vitry* (The Folk-Lore Society: London, 1890), no. CCXXV, pp. 93–94, tr. and note, pp. 224–225 [From the 13th-century *Sermones Vulgares*]. IIIEO, IVA5, C3e, VIO.

RS Lit 4—Juan de Timoneda, *El Buen Aviso y Portacuentos*, I, no. 28 [First edition 1564; indexed as W111.3.4.1* in J. W. Childers, *Motif-Index of the Cuentos of Juan Timoneda*

Table I: The Versions of The Tale   29

(Indiana University Folklore Series, No. 5: Bloomington, 1948)]. IIA2a, IIIEO, IVA5, C6, VIO.

SR Lit 1—S. Drukovcov, ed., *Babuškiny* (Moscow, 1778), no. 24 [The New Year's gift book of the manufacturer "Demidov," Jan. 1, 1778]. IIA1g, 2a, (C1b), IIIA2a, C5a, EO, IVA5, C1a, VIO.

SR Lit 2—*Staričok vesel'čak Razskazy-vajuščij Davnija Moskovskija Byli* (Petersburg, 1790), pp. 8–9. ID5, IIIEO, IVA5, C1b, VIO.

SR LIt 3—D. Rovinskij, *Russkija narodnyja kartinki* (Petersburg, 1881), I, 381 [An 18th-century black-and-white print[6] with a poetic text]. ID5, IIIEO, IVA5, C1b, VIO.

Literary Forms of Tales Containing Miscellaneous Taming Devices[7]

GE Lit 6—W. Carew Hazlitt, ed., *Shakespeare Jest-Books* (London, 1864), II, 91–93, "How Scogin caused his wife to be let blood" [From *Jests of Scogin* (1565–66)]. IIIEO, IVA5, D1a, VIO.

GE Lit7—Joseph Ritson, ed., *Ancient Songs, from the time of King Henry the third to the Revolution* (London, 1790), pp. 215–220, "The Taming of a Shrew" [17th century]. IIIEO, IVA5, D1a, 3, 7, VIO.

GE Lit8—John Ashton, *Humor, Wit, and Satire of the Seventeenth Century* (London, 1883), pp. 82–84, "A Caution for Scolds or a True Way of Taming a Shrew." IIIEO, IVA5, D1a, VIO.

GE Lit9—*The Muse in Good Humour: A Collection of Comic Tales. By Several Hands* (8th ed.: London, 1785), II, 94–100, "The Taming of the Shrew. A tale." IB2, IIIEO, IVA5, (B1dii), VIO, VIIA1.

RF Lit4—Le Grand d'Aussy remarks in his note with RF Lit 2, pp. 356–357, "Among our French stories there is one of a husband who on the first day of his marriage breaks the arm of his wife. She hopes that the cost will cure him and make him more restrained. He must take her to a surgeon. He asks 100 pounds. 'Take 200,' says the husband. 'That's for the next arm that I will break.' One finds this story in a thousand places." IIIEO, IVA5, D2, VIO.

RF Lit5—*The Book of the Knight of La Tour-Landry*, ed. by G. S. Taylor (London, 1930), pp. 22–24 [Written 1371. This is a modernized text; Caxton's translation of 1484 is reproduced in the EETS edition by Thomas Wright, revised edition (London, 1906), pp. 26–28]. IIIEO, VIA2, 3, Bla, D15, 16.

RS Lit5—Juan de Timoneda, *El Buen Aviso y Portacuentos*, I, no. 15 [Childer's index, W111.3.5.*]. IIIEO, IVA5, D3a, VIO.

Iceland[8]

GI 1—Sigfús Sigfússon, Íslenzkar þjóð-sögur og-sagnir (Reykjavík, 1957), XIII, 169–172. IIAleii, B13, Cla, IIIB4, Elc, 3a, IVA4, Blbiv), cix, di, VIA2, Blb, D1, 9, 10, VIIA3, C3. Suður-Múlasýsla, ca. 1900–1920.

GI 2—Einar Ol. Sveinsson, Verzeichnis Isländischer Märchenvarianten, FFC 83 (1929), p. 137. IIIEO, IVAll, VIBla, VIIC3. Vestur-Skaftafellssýsla.

Norway

GN 1—Norsk Folkeminnesamling, A.E. Vang, II, 1. IIIAleii, Cla, IIIA2, B4, EO, IVA5, (6) Cla, VAlbiii, (IVBlciii), C2, VIal, B1, C3, D1. Valdres, ca. 1850.[9]

Sweden

GS 1—Waldemar Liungman, *Sveriges Samtliga Folksagor*, I (Stockholm, 1949), 361–363. IIIAl3, IIIA2, Bl, E2b, 3a, IVA4,

Table I: The Versions of The Tale

Blbiii, 2ai, VA3, Bl, C2aii, b, VIAl, Blb, C2, D5a, VIIC2. Bohuslän, 1925.

GS 2—Västsvenska Folkminnesarkivet, Liungman no. 138, pp. 92–99. IAl, IIAleii, Bll, Clf, IIIA2, E3a, IVA4, Blciii, di, 2biv, VIAl, 3, B2d, C5, D1, VIIbl, C3. Bohuslän, 1919.

GS 3—VF, Liungman, no. 488, pp. 4–6. IIAleii, Cla, IIIA2, Cl, Ele, 3b, IVA4, Blbiii, 2aviii, VAlbii, Cl, C2a, b, VIAl, B2e, C2, D1, VIIC2. Bohuslän, 1925.

GS 4—Richard Steffen, ed., *Svenska sagböcker efter berättarnes egna uppteckningar* (Stockholm, 1902), I, 8–14. IC3, IIIAlg, Cld, IIIE3a, IVA4, Bl, di, VIO, VIID2. Hägersta, before 1838.

GS 5—VF, Liungman, no. 481, p. 6 [Printed in Liungman, *Sveriges Samtliga Folksagor*, I, 454]. IB2, IIBl, IIIEO, IVA5, Clc, VIO. Halland, 1925.

GS 6—Sven Liljeblad, ed., *Svenska Folksagor* (Stockholm, 1943), III, 117–119. IIAlg, 2a, Cla, IIIA2, C3, EO, IVA5, D3a, VClb, VIO, VIIB2. Småland, ca. 1843–1844.

GS 7—Lund Univ. Folkminnesarkiv no. Luf M. 2995:6–8. IIAlei, Cla, IIIA2, Ela, c, e, 3b, IVA4, Blavi, 2aviii, VAlavi, Bl, C2aii, b, VIAl, B2d, Dl, VIIC2. Skåne, 1931.

GS 8—Eva Wigström, *Sagor och Äfventyr upptencknade i Skåne* (Stockholm, 1884), pp. 98–99. IIAleii, IIIA2, E3a, IVA4, Blbi, 2ai, VIAl, B2d, C1, D1. Skåne.

Swedes in Finland

GSF 1—Oskar Hackman, ed., *Finlands Svenska Folkdiktining* (Helsingfors, 1917), I.A. Sagor, Referatsamling, I. 459, no. 181, variant 1. IIAleii, B3, Clc, IIIE3a, IVA4, Blbi, di, 2bx, VIAl, Blb, C5, D5a. Österbotten, Nykarleby.

GSF 2—Hackman, I.A., I, 459–460, no. 181, variant 2. IIAlei, Clc, IIIE3a, IVA4, Blciii, di, 2biv, VIAl, Blb, C5, D5a, VIIC3. Österbotten, Vörå.

GSF 3—Hackman, I.A., II (Helsingfors, 1920), 107, no. 271, variant 2. IIA2a, IIIEO, IVA5, C2c, VIO. Finnby.

GSF 4—Hackman, I.A., II, 107, no. 271, variant 1. IIA2a, Bl, IIIA2, C5a, EO, IVA5, Clb, VIO. Nyland, Borgå.

GSF 5—Hackman, I.A., I, 460, no. 181, variant 3. IIAleii, B13, IIIEO, IVA5, Blbix, 3g, 5aii, VIBlb, C5, D5c. Nyland, Borgå.

Denmark

GE 1—*Nye Tobaks-Discourses* (København, 1818), pp. 27 f. IAl, IIAlh, IIIA4, C1, E2b, 3a, IVA4, Blbi, di, 2bi, VIO, VIIB5.

GD 2—Danske Folkemindesamling (Nordisk Institut for Folkdigtning), ETkr 2527. IIAlei, 2diii, B3, IIIA2, Ela, c, 2b, 3b, IVA4, Blbi, di, 2bii, (VBl), VIAl, B2d, D1. Slagelseegnen, ca. 1894.

GD 3—*Manuscript Collection of Danish Folktales Collected By Svend Grundtvig* (Mimeographed copy of originals in Danske Folkemindesamling, Copenhagen: Indiana University Library), no. 79d (DFS XVI, 147–148). IIAleii, Cla, IIIA2, Elb, 3b, IVA4, Blbiii, di, 2bi, VAlaiv, bii, B1, C2aii, b, VIal, B1, C2, D1, (VIIC2). Svendborg Bøstrup, 1861.

GD 4—O. L. Grønborg, *Optegnelser pa Vendelbomal* (København, 1884), pp. 116–121. IIAleii, 2diii, Cla, IIIEla, ci, e, f, 2b, 3b, IVA4, Blbv, di, ix, 2av, VAlai, bi, 2d, B1, C2aii, b, VIAl, B2d, C3, D1, VIIC2. Hjørring Børglum.

GD 5—Grundtvig MS., no. 79b (DFS XI, 97a–99b); reprinted in *Niels Levinsen, Folkeeventyr fra Vendsyssel* (*Danmarks Folkeminder*, No. 68: København, 1958), pp. 2–4. IIAleii,

Table I: The Versions of The Tale

IIIEla, ci, f, 3b, IVA4, Blbiii, di, VBl, C2ai, b, VIAl, B2e, D1, 14, VIIC2. Hjørring Furreby, 1854.

GD 6—E. T. Kristensen, *Aeventyr fra Jylland*, IV (*Jyske Folkeminder*, XIII: Aarhus, 1897), 8–10. IIAleii, IIIA2, Ela, c, 2b, 3b, IVA4, Blbiii, di, VAlai, bi, B1, C2aii, b, VIAl, B2, D1, VIIC2, 3. Tisted Sundby, 1889.

GD 7—Svend Grundtivig, *Gamle danske Minder i Folkemunde*, I (København, 1854), 88–90. IIAleii, IIIEla, b, ci, e, f, 2b, 3b, IVA4, Blai, 2aviii, VAlaii, laiii, 2a, B1, C2aii, b, VIAl, B2d, D1, VIIC2. Ålborg Åby, 1854.

GD 8—DFS 1929/12:II, 439b. IIAlh, IIIE3a, IVA2, B1, di, 2ciii, VIO, (VII5). Viborg Vindum, 1871.

GD 9—DFS Db 1793a = ETKr 864. IIAlei, 2diii, IIIEla, c, e, 2b, 3b, IVA4, Blbi, 2ai, VC2ai, b, VIAl, B2d, D1, VIIBl. Ringkøbing Mejrup, 1875.

GD 10—DFS DB 1994a = ETKr 953. IIAlei, B5, IIIA2, 8a, Ela, c, 3, 2b, 3b, IVA4, Blbi, di*, 2bi, VIAl, B2h, D1. Ringkøbing Borbjerg, 1875.

GD 11—DFS Db 1868b = ETKr 887. IIAleii, B5, IIIA2, 8a, Ela, c, 3, 2b, 3b, IVA4, B2ai, VIAl, B2h, D1. Ringkøbing Hodsager, 1875.

GD 12—DFS Db 1870b = ETKr 889. IIAlh, B3, IIIA4, E2b, 3a, IVA4, Blbi, di, 2lbi, VIO, VIIB5. Ringkøbing Hodsager, 1875.

GD 13—E. T. Kristensen, *Aeventyr fra Jylland*, III (*Jyske Folkeminder*, XII: Københaven, 1895), 255–256. IIAlh, k, B1, Clk, IIIAll, B2, EO, IVA5, Clc, VIA6, D1. Ringkøbing Nøvling, 1873.

GD 14—DFS Db 879b = ETKr 420. IIAlei, IIIA2, Ela, c, e, 3d, IVA4, Blbi, di, 2ai, VBl, C2ai, b, VIAl, B2d, C3, D1, VIIC2. Ringkøbing Simmelkjaer, 1873.

GD 15—DFS, DB 197b = ETKr 120. IIAlei, IIIA2, B1, Elcii, e, 2b, 3b, IVA4, Blbi, di, 2bx, VIAl, B2d, C1, D1, VIIBl. Ringkøbing Herning, 1871.

GD 16—DFS, Db 1335a = ETKr 627. IIAleii, B4, IIIAl, 2, Elc, 2c, 3b, IVA4, Blbi, di, 2ai, VAlav, 2g, (B1), C2ai, ii, b, VIAl, B2e, D5a. Ringkøbing Staby, 1874.

GD 17—DFS 1929/1 = ETKr 2352. IIAlei, IIIA2, E3b, IVA4, Blbi, VBl, VIAl, B2d, D1. Ringkøbing Hemmet, ca. 1890.

GD 18—DFS 1929/1 = ETKr 1829. IIAlei, B5a, Cla, IIIEla, c, e, 2b, 3d, IVA4, Blbi, di*, 2ai, VC2ai, VIAl, B2d, D1, VIIBl. Ribe Føvling, 1894.

GD 19—DFS 1906/16:II. IIAlg, 2a, b1, IIA2a, D1, (E3c), IVA4, 5, Blciv, Cla, D8c, VIO, (B2d). Tønder Nørreamt Hostrup, 1865.

GD 20—DFS, Db 10194a = ETKr 2559. IIAlei, IIIA2, Elci, 3a, IVA4, Blbi, VBl, C2ai, VIAl, B2c, C2, D1, VIIC2. Åbenrå, 1910.

GD 21—Svend Grundtvig, *Gamle danske Minder i Folkemunde*, III (København, 1861), 39–44. IC4, IIAleii, B5, III(A7), D6, EO, IVA4, VC2ai, b, VIAl, B2bi, D1, VIIBl.

Germany

GG 1—Archiv für Volkskunde, Marburg no. 74954. IIAlg, B7, IIIA2, 11, B2, EO, IVA5, D2, VIO. Petersdorf, 1909.

GG 2—AVM no. 74948. IIAlg, Clf, 2a, IIIA2, Ele, gii, 3b, IVA4, Blaiii, di, (ii), 2ax, 4c, VIO, VIIA4e. Petersdorf, 1909.

GG 3—Gustav Fr. Meyer, *Plattdeutsche Volksmärchen und Schwänke* (Neumünster, 1925), pp. 259–260. IIAlh, k, B7, Clk, IIIB2, EO, IVA5, D7b, VIA5, (B1), C6, D5f. Rondsburg, 1923.

Table I: The Versions of The Tale   35

GG 4—Folklore archives in Kiel, no. 6 A 24 (Gustav Fr. Meyer collection). IIAlh, k, B7a, Clk, IIIB2, EO, IVA5, D7b, VIA5, (B1), C6, D5f. Eutin, 1928 or 1929.

GG 5—AVM no. 75955-24 27 10cl [Printed in Wilhelm Wisser, *Plattdeutsch Volksmärchen* (Märchen der Weltliteratur: Jena, 1927), pp. 111–112]. IIAlh, k, B7a, Clk, IIIB2, EO, IVA5, D7b, VIA5, (B1), C6, D5f. Schleswig-Holstein, 1899.

GG 6—Meyer, pp. 214–217. IIAleii, B1, IIIEla, (B), ci, e, f, 2c, IVA4, Blai, 2aviii, VAlaii, cii, 2c, B1, C2aii, b, VIAl, B2d, D1, VIIC2. Schleswig-Holstein.

GG 7—AVM no. 75955-24 26 22 bd [Printed in Wisser, pp. 110–111]. IIAlh, B7a, IIIA4, EO, IVA5, D2, VIO. Klenzau, 1898.

GG 8—Richard Wossidlo, *Aus dem Lande Fritz Reuters: Humor in Sprache und Volkstum Mecklenburgs* (Leipzig, 1910), pp. 92–93. IIAlg, 2a, B1, IIIC3, EO, IVCla, VIO. Mecklenburg, after 1884.

GG 9—AVM no. 191004. IIAleii, Clf, IIIA2, CI, EO, IVA(6), 7, Blai, 2ai, VAlci, B1, C2ai, ii, VIAl, Blb, D1, VIIC2. Told by a Romanian (b. 1926) in Austria who heard it told in a Russian war prison by a man from Hamburg.

GG 10—A Brunk, "Volkskundliches aus Garzigar," *Blätter für pommersche Volkskunde*, IX (1901), 58–60. IC6, IIA2aii, diii, IIIEO, IVA5, Cla, D3a, VClb, VIO.

GG 11—*Blätter für pommersche Volkskunde.* X (1902), 21. IIAlg, B17, Cla, IIIA2, EO, IVA5, Blaxi, 2bi, 5b, VCld, VIO.

GG 12—*Blätter für pommersche Volkskunde*, VIII (1900), 101. IIAlg, B3, Cla, IIIA2, EO, IVA5, D1b, 3, VIO. Greifenhagen.

GG 13—"Schwank und Streich aus Pommern," *Blätter für Pommersche Volkskunde*, VI (1898), 6–7. IIAlg, B1, (Cla), IIIA4, 6, B4, C1, EO, IVA5a, Blbi (two horses), dxi, 2bii, VIO, VIIA4e. Falkenburg.

GG 14—Heinrich Pröhle, *Kinder-und Volksmärchen* (Leipzig, 1853), pp. 164-165. IIAlg, Clc, IIIA2, C3, EO, IVA5, Clb, VIO.

The Netherlands

GNE 1—*Volkskunde*, XVI, 98-100. ID1, IIAlg, B5, C2a, IIIA10, EO, IVA6. Blbi, div, 2ai, VIO, (VIICl). Broek, Waterland, 1901.

Anglo-Amerian[10]

GEAm 1—"Think and Grin" [Joke page], *Boys' Life*, 48 (October, 1958), 82. IIIE3c, IVA4, Blbi, VIO. Sent in by Maury Christensen of Minneapolis, Minnesota.

GEAm 2—Indiana University Folklore Archives, collected by Alysanne Dove, 1954. IBl, IIIE3c, IVA4, Blbi, VIO. Birmingham, Michigan, 1954.

GEAm 3—A text collected by Mrs. Marie Walter from Alfonse De Angelis, a student at Brooklyn College. IIIEO, IVA9, Blbvi, dv, VIO. Brooklyn, New York, 1960.[11]

GEAm 4—Private collection of Jan Brunvand [Hereafter referred to as JB], a text collected from Richard Vreeland, Evanston, Illinois, formerly from Michigan. IBl, IIIE3c, IVA4, Blbi, VIO. Evanston, Illinois, 1960.

GEAm 5—IU, turned in by Kathleen Brennan, 1959. IA3, B1, IIIEO, IVA5, Blaii, VIO. South Bend, Indiana, 1959.[12]

GEAm 6—JB, a text collected from Mrs. Gail Jones. IIEO, IVA12, (IIIE3c), Blavi, bi, VIO. Logansport, Indiana, 1959.

GEAm 7—A text collected by Prof. Jesse W. Harris from Larry Lynch, a student at Southern Illinois University. IA4, IIIA2, E3b, IVA4, Blbi, dv, VIO. Champaign, Illinois, 1959.

GEAm 8—IU, collected by Jean S. Harney, 1960. IB3, IIIEO, IVA5, Blbi, VIO. Elwood, Indiana, 1960.

Table I: The Versions of The Tale 37

GEAm 9—JB, a text collected from William Randall. IIBl, IIIE3c, IVA4, Blbi, VIO. Terre Haute, Indiana, 1960.[13]

GEAm 10—Una Keeling, "You Haven't Packed the Saddle," *Illinois Folklore*, I (1947), 17–19. IIAlj, IIIA2, Elc, e, f, 3b, IVA4, Blbi, di, 2bvi, (VIAl, D6), VIIC3. Pinckneyville, Illinois, 1947.

GEAm 11—A text collected by Prof. Jesse W. Harris from L. D. McCarty, a student at Southern Illinois University. IIIEO, IVA5, B5f, VIO. Carbondale, Illinois, 1960.[14]

GEAm 12—A text collected by Prof. Jesse W. Harris from David L. Rector, a student at Southern Illinois University. IA3, IIIE3c, IVA4, Blbi, VIO. Carbondale, Illinois, 1960.

GEAm 13—IU, collected by Janet Small, 1960. IA2, IIIE3b, IVA4, Blbi, viii, VIO. Bloomington, Indiana, 1960.

GEAm 14—IU, collected by Mrs. Ann F. Shields, 1960. IIIEO, IVAO, Blbi, VIO. Brownstown, Indiana, 1960.[15]

GEAm 15—IU, turned in by Ann Walls, 1959. IBl, IIBl2, IIIE3c, Blbi, VIO. Louisville, Kentucky, 1957 or 1958.[16]

GEAm 16—Jan Harold Brunvand, "Folktales by Mail from Bond, Kentucky," *Kentucky Folklore Record*, VI (1960), 69–76, "The Taming of the Shrew," pp. 70–71. IIIElc, 3b, IVA4, Blavi, vi, di, VIO.

GEAm 17—A text collected by Sidney Stewart and sent to me by Prof. Leonard Roberts of Morehead State College, Kentucky. IIBi, IIIE3b, IVA4, Blbi, VIO. Around Hindman, Kentucky, about 1952.

GEAm 18—Marie Campbell, *Tales from the Cloud Walking Country* (Bloomington, Ind., 1958), pp. 220–221. IIAleii, 2a, (B6), IIIA2, EO, IVA5, D3a, VIO, VIID3. Eastern Kentucky, between 1926–1934.

GEAm 19—JB, a text collected from S. N. Alger. IBl, IIIE3c, IVA4, Blbi, VIO. West Virginia, 1960.[17]

GEAm 20—Richard Chase, *American Folk Tales and Songs* (The New American Library: New York, 1956), pp. 226–227 [Also recorded by Richard Chase on his Tradition recording of the same title, TLP 1011, Side A, item 2]. IIA2b, IIIElci, 3b, IVA4, Blbi, ii, di, VIO. Clintwood, Virginia.

GEAm 21—JB, a text collected from Donald Manley. IIBl, IIIE3c, IVA4, Blbi, VIO. Topeka, Kansas, 1959.[18]

GEAm 22—JB, a text collected from Norman Crabtree. IIIE3c, IVA4, Blbx, VIO. Ridgeway, Missouri, 1959.[19]

GEAm 23—Vance Randolph, *Sticks in the Knapsack and other Ozark Folk Tales* (New York, 1958), pp. 71–73. IIIEO, IVA5, B2bix, VIO. Farmington, Arkansas, 1941.[20]

GEAm 24—*The Emancipator*, XV (San Antonio, Texas, Sept., 1952), 5 [Credited to *The Scandal Sheet*, Graham, Texas]. IBl, IIIE3a, IVA4, Blbi, VIO.

GEAm 25—JB, a text collected from Donald Winkelman from Ohio, who did not recall the source of his version. IBl, IIIE3b, IVA4, Blbi, di, VIO, (VIIA2a).

GEAm 26—Max Rezwin, ed., *Sick Jokes, Grim Cartoons & Bloody Marys* (The Citadel Press: New York, 1958), p. 14. IIIEO, IV(A4), Blbi, ii, VIO.

GEAm 27—IU, collected by Mrs. Doris Collester, 1960. IIIE3c, IVA4, Blbi, VIO. Bloomington, Indiana.

GEAm 28—IU, collected by Jack Osborne, 1960. IIBl, IIIE3c, IVA4, Blbi, (v), VIO. Bloomington, Indiana.

GEAm 29—IU collected by Jack Osborne, 1960. IA7, B1, IIBl, IIIE3c, IV(A4), Blbi, VIO. Learned in Formosa from an American soldier from Plymouth, Indiana, 1957.

Table I: The Versions of The Tale   39

GEAm 30—IU, collected by Alan R. Diodore, 1960. IIBl, IIIEO, IVA12, Blbvi, VIO. Marion, Indiana.

GEAm 31—IU, collected by Edith Ferber, 1960. IIBl, IIIE3c, IVA4, Blbi, VIO. Bloomington, Indiana, but learned in Iowa in 1950s.

GEAm 32—IU, collected by James Ruge, 1960. IIIEO, IV(A4), Blbi, ii, VIO. Bloomington, Indiana.

Scotland

CS 1—Folklore Archives of The School of Scottish Studies, University of Edinburgh, no. R.L. 1475 (B.4.). ID1, IIAlg, B1, C2b, IIIA2, EO, IVA6a, D7(b), VIO, VIIA4c, g. Haclate, Benbecula, 1958.

CS 2—John F. Campbell and John G. McKay, *More West Highland Tales* (Edinburgh and London, 1940), I, 149–167. IIAle, 2a, B17, IIIA2, EO, IVA5, D3a, VIO, VIID3. Between 1859 and 1885.

CS 3—SSS, collected by John Lorne Campbell from Angus MacLellan [English translation in Angus Maclellan, *Stories from South Uist* (London, 1961), pp. 65–69]. ID1, IIAlg, B15, C2aii, b, IIIA2, E(1c, e), 3b, IVA4, Blavi, di, 2bii, civ, VIA6, B1, D4b, VIIA4a, e, g, B1. South Uist, 1959.[21]

CS 4—SSS, no. RL. 1248 (B.1.). IIIAle, 2aii, B8, Clb, (2b), IIIEO, IVA5, 6a, D7, VIA6, B1, C1, D1. Ardnamurchan, 1958.

Ireland[22]

CI 1—Irish Folklore Commission Archives, MS. 223, pp. 3869–3875. IIAld, 2a, B1, IIIA2, EO, IVA5, D3a, (VCle), VIAl, 3, B1, C1, D1, VIIB3. Donegal, 1936.

CI 2—IFC MS. 233, pp. 4256–4261. IIAle, 2a, IIIEO, IVA4, 5, Blaiv, D3a, 9, VIAl, 3, B1, D4c, (ii). Donegal, 1936.

CI 3—IFC MS. 234, pp. 338–340. IIAleii, 2a, IIIBl, EO, IVA4, Bla, 2a, VClc, e, VIO. Donegal, 1936.

CI 4—IFC MS. 310, pp. 569–576. IIAleii, 2a, IIIA2, EO, IVA5, D3a, 9, VCle, VIAl, 3, B1, D1. Donegal, 1937.

CI 5—IFC MS. 348, pp. 274–275. IIA2a, IIIEO, IVA13, (D3a), VClb, e, VIO. Donegal, 1937

CI 6—IFC MS. 398. pp. 318–320. IIAle, B3, Cld, IIIBl, EO, IVA4, Blavi, dii, 2, VIAl, 3, B1, D3. Donegal, 1937.

CI 7—IFC MS. 454, pp. 351–360. IIAleii, 2ai, B17, IIIA2, EO, IVA4, Blavi, di, 2axi, 4bii, D3a, VClb, VIAl, 3, B1, C1, D1. Donegal, 1938.

CI 8—IFC MS. 477, pp. 122–129. IIAle, 2a, IIIB3, E3b, IVA4, Blavi, 2bii VIAl, 3, B1, C5, D1, 2. Donegal, 1938.

CI 9—IFC MS. 518, pp. 158–170. IIAle, B8, Cla, IIIAll, B3, EO, IVA5, D3, 9, VIAl, 3, Blb, C1, D1, VIIBla. Donegal, 1938.

CI 10—IFC MS. 590. pp. 547–588. IIAle, B8, IIIAll, B3, EO, IVA4, (5), Blavi, 2bii, D3, 9, VIAl, 3, B1, C5, D1, 2, VIIBla. Donegal, 1939.

CI 11—IFC MS. 837, pp. 92–102. IIEleii, IIIA4, ll, B1, D3, EO, IVA4, Blaiv, D3a, VB2, Clc, VIA2, 3, Blb, D1, VIIC2. Donegal, 1942.

CI 12—IFC MS. 846, pp. 393–405. IIAleii, 2aiii, IIID2, EO, IVA4, D6, VCle, VIAl, 3, B1, C1, D1. Donegal, 1942.

CI 13—IFC MS. 1043, pp. 184–185. IIAlg, 2a, B1, IIIA2, ll, B1, D2, Elci, e, f, IVAl, 4, Blaiv, 2a, D3a, 9, VClb, VIO. Donegal, 1938.

CI 14—IFC MS. 1047, pp. 384–386. IIAla, 2a, IIIElc, eii, f, IVA4, Blavi, 2bii, VIAl, 3, B2, D1. Donegal, 1938.

Table I: The Versions of The Tale 41

CI 15—IFC MS. 1050, pp. 1–3. IIAleii, IIIBl, Eleii, IVA4, B2bii, D3a, VClb, VIAl, 3, B1, D17, E. Donegal, 1934.

CI 16—IFC MS. 1064, pp. 193–199. IIEle, B16, Cld, IIIAll, B3, Elc, e, gi, IVA4, Blavi, bii, (iv), dv, 2bii, 4bi, VIAl, B2f, C1, D1. Donegal.

CI 17—IFC MS. 1120, pp. 445–450. IIAleii, B17, IIIA2, B1, D5, EO, IVA4, Blbiv, di, 2bii, 4bi, D3a, VIAl, 3, B1, C1, Donegal, ca. 1939.

CI 18—IFC MS. 1216, pp. 478–479. IIIAlg, IIIBl, E3c, IVA4, Blbiv, 2biii, VIO. Tyrone, 1950.

CI 19—IFC MS. 1017, pp. 227–228. IIIEO, IVA12, Blavi, di, VIA2, Blb, C1, D1. Cavan, 1938.

CI 20—Éamonn O'Tuathail, "Sgéal Na Dtrí Slat," *Béaloideas*, I (1927), 345–348. IIAleii, IIIA4, D2, EO, IVA4, Blbi, di*, D3a, VB2, Clb, VIA2, B1, C2, D1, VIIC2. Ulster, 1928.

CI 21—IFC MS. 1014, pp. 131–133. IIAleii, IIIB2, EO, IVA13, Bla, 2a, 5a, VIA2, 3, B1, C1, D1. Leitrim.

CI 22—IFC MS. 1429, pp. 99–102. IIAle, IIIE3b, IVA4, Blaiii, di, 2bi, D3a, VIAl, 3, Blb, C1, D1. Leitrim.

CI 23—IFC MS. 339, pp. 338–340. IIAleii, Cla, III(A4), EO, IVA5, D6, VIAl, 3, Blb, C1, D1. Sligo, 1937.

CI 24—IFC MS. 86, pp. 31–32. IIAleii, IIIEO, IVA13, B2axii, 5b, VIO. Mayo, 1938.

CI 25—IFC MS. 96, pp. 743–746. IIAle, B1, IIA2, ll, D3, Elci, e, f, IVA4, Blaiv, 2aii, D3a, VIA2, 3, B1, C1, D1. Mayo, 1938.

CI 26—IFC MS. 104, pp. 261–264. IIAleii, B17, Cla, IIIEO, IVA12, Blaiv, 2a, VIAl, B1, C1, D1. Mayo.

CI 27—IFC MS. 191, pp. 213–220. IIAleii, IIIBl, EO, (VIIDl), IVA7, Blaiv, 2axi, VIAl, 3, B1, C1, D1, VIIDl. Mayo, ca. 1936.

CI 28—IFC MS. 193, pp. 979–986. IIAle, C1a, IIIAll, B1, Elci, e, f, IVA3, Blaiv, 2bii, VIAl, B1, C1, D1. Mayo.

CI 29—IFC MS. 194, pp. 296–302. IIAlei, B6, C1d, IIIBl, EO, IVA6, Blaiv, 2axi, VIAl, 2, B2, C1, D1. Mayo.

CI 30—IFC MS. 227, pp. 319–324. IIAle, 2a, dii, IIIE3a, IVA4, B1(aiv), cii, 2(axi), ci, D3a, VC2d, VIO, VIIB4. Mayo, 1936.

CI 31—IFC MS. 258, pp. 363–369. ICl, IIAleii, IIEO, IV-none, VIA6, C1, D1. Mayo, 1936.

CI 32—IFC MS. 277, pp. 253–260. IIAleii, 2di, B1, IVAll, D2, (Elb, ci, e, 3b), IVA4, Blaiv, di, 2axi, D3a, VIAl, 3, B1, 2, C1, D1. Mayo, 1937.

CI 33—IFC MS. 625, pp. 170–173. IIAle, B13, IIIElcii, IVA4, Blaiv, di, VIA6, B1, C1, D1. Mayo, 1939.

CI 34—IFC MS. 662, pp. 255–257. IIAleii, IIIBl, Elci, 3b, IVA4, Blaiv, VIAl, 3, B1, C1, D1. Mayo 1939.

CI 35—IFC MS. 788, pp. 557–561. IIAle, IIIEO, IVA8, Blaiv, di, 2bii, VIA2, 3, B1, C1, D1. Mayo, 1941.

CI 36—IFC MS. 836, pp. 365–371. IIAlei, IIICl, D5, E3b, IVA4, Blaxiii, 2aii, VIAl, B1, D1, 4di. Mayo, 1942.

CI 37—IFC MS. 915, pp. 542–546. IIALei, 2diii, IIIA2, E3b, IVA4, Blaiv, VIAl, 3, B1, D1. Mayo, 1944.

CI 38—IFC MS. 1230, pp. 408–420. IIA2ai, B17, (IIIElci), IVA4, Blaxiii, 2bii, D3a, VIAl, 3, B1, C1, D1, VIIBl. Mayo, 1952.

CI 39—IFC MX. 1399, pp. 553–556. IIAlei, IIIA2, B1, D2, E3a, IVA4, Blaiv, di, VCle, VIAl, 3, V1, C1, D1. Roscommon.

Table I: The Versions of The Tale 43

CI 40—*An Claidheamh Solvis* (August 30, 1902), pp. 426–427 [an account of a storytelling competition won by a girl who told The Taming of the Shrew; text not given]. Title indicates IVBl only. Galway.

CI 41—Lady Gregory, *Poets and Dreamers* (Dublin and London, 1903), pp. 185–187. IIAle, B17, IIIEO, IVA4, Blbiv, 2bii, D3a, VIAl, Blb, C1, D1, (VIICl). Galway.

CI 42—IFC MS. 16, pp. 24–26. IIAlei, IIIEO, IVA5a, Blaiv, 2aii, IVAl, B1, C1, D1. Galway, 1937.

CI 43—IFC MS. 30, pp. 86–87. IIAle, IIIElc, e, IVA4, Blavi, 2a, VIO. Galway, 1936.

CI 44—IFC MS. 61, pp. 231–233. IIAlei, IIIEO, IVA4, Blavi, di, 2bii, VIAl, B1, C1, D1. Galway, ca. 1937.

CI 45—IFC MS. 61, pp. 471–475. IIAleii, IIIA2, C3, EO, IVA8, Blai, 2aii, IVAl, 3, B1, C1, D1. Galway, ca. 1938.

CI 46—IFC MS. 62, pp. 14–15a. IIAleii, IIIE3b, IVA4, Blaiv, 2aii, VIAl, 3, B2, C1, D1. Galway, ca. 1938.

CI 47—IFC MS. 72, pp. 275–280. IIAlei, B6, Cld, IIIC4a, E3b, IVA4, Blavi, di, 2aii, VIAl, B1, C1, D1. Galway.

CI 48—IFC MS. 75, pp. 58–61. IIAlei, IIIE3b, IVA4, Blaiv, 2bii, D3a, VIAl, 3, B1, C1, D1. Galway, 1935.

CI 49—IFC MS. 75, pp. 185–186. IIAle, IIIE3b, IVA4, Blaiv, di, D3a, VIA2, 3, B1, D1. Galway, ca. 1934.

CI 50—IFC MS. 80, pp. 40–43. IIAldii, Bl, IIIAll, D2, E3b, IVA4, Blaiv, di, 2bii, D3a, IVAl, B1, C1, D1. Galway, 1938.

CI 51—IFC MS. 90, pp. 28–33. IIAlei, B3, Clf, IIIB4, E3a, IVA4, Blaxiii, 2bx, D3a, VIAl, B1, C1, D1. Galway, 1930.

CI 52—IFC MS. 154, pp. 173–177. IIAlei, B3, Clf, IIIBl, EO, IVA5, Blaiv, 2a, 3d, VIAl, B1, C1, D1. Galway, ca. 1930.

CI 53—IFC MS. 157, pp. 649, 653. IIAle, Bl, IIA2, EO, IVA5, D2, VIA4, B1, C1, D1. Galway, 1935.

CI 54—IFC MS. 159, pp. 190–198. IIAlei, Bl, IIIA2, Blbv, div, 2bx, VIAl, 3, B1, C1, D1. Galway, 1936.

CI 55—IFC MS. 161, pp. 141–143. IIAlei, B1, IIIEo, IVA8, 12, Blaiv, 2axi, VIAl, B1, C1, D1. Galway, 1935.

CI 56—IFC MS. 182, pp. 701–722. IIAlei, B1, Cla, IIIAll, B1, C3, Elcii, e, f, IVA4, Blaiv, 2bii, D3a, VIAl, B1, C1, D1, 4, VIIBl. Galway, 1936.

CI 57—IFC MS. 182, pp. 814–822. IIAle, 2a, B1, IIIA2, 11, B1, EO, IVA4, Blaiv, 2axii, D3a, VIA2, 3, B1, C1, D1, 4, VIIBl. Galway, 1936.

CI 58—IFC MS. 271, pp. 437–440. IIAlei, Clf, IIIEO, IVA5, B7, VIA2, 3, Blb, C1, D1. Galway, 1936.

CI 59—IFC MS. 346, pp. 172–179. IIAle, 2a, Cla, IIIAll, B1, D2, Elc, e, f, IVA4, Blaxii, di, 2ax, VIAl, 3, Bl, C1, D1. Galway, 1937.

CI 60—IFC MS. 349, pp. 322–328. IIAlei, B1, IIIAll, D2, Elci, e, f, IVA4, Blavi, 2a, D3a, VCle, VIAl, 3, B1, C1, D1. Galway, 1937.

CI 61—IFC MS. 413, pp. 366–374. IIAlei, B1, IIIAll, B1, D2, EO, IVA5, 12, Blaxii, diii, 2ax, D3a, VIAl, 3, B1, C1, D1. Galway, 1937.

CI 62—IFC MS. 415, pp. 150–153. IIAlbi, IIIA2, a, EO, IVA12, B2aii, VIA2, 3, B1, C1, D1. Galway, 1937.

CI 63—IFC MS. 455, pp. 185–191. IIAle, IIA2, EO, IVA12, Blaiii, iv, VIAl, 3, B1, 2a, C1, D1. Galway, 1938.

Table I: The Versions of The Tale

CI 64—IFC MS. 487, pp. 180–184. IIAleii, iIIA2, C3, EO, IVA8, Blai, 2aii, VIAl, 3, B1, C1, D1. Galway, ca. 1937.

CI 65—IFC MS. 578, pp. 45–48. IIAle, 2a, B17, IIIA2, EO, IVA8, Blaxi, di, 2avi, VIA6, B1, C1, D1. Galway, 1938.

CI 66—IFC MS. 605, pp. 222–227. IIAle, B17, IIIA2, C3, EO, IVA12, Blaiv, di, xi, 2a, VIAl, 3, B1, C1, D1. Galway, 1939.

CI 67—IFC MS. 617, pp. 140–144. IIAle, B17, Cla, IIIA2, C3, EO, IVA12, Blbvi, 2bii, VIAl, 3, B1, C1, D1. Galway, 1939.

CI 68—IFC MS. 641, pp. 232–236. IIAlei, B1, IIElc, e, IVA4, Blaxi, 2a, D3a, VIAl, 3, B1, C1, D1. Galway, ca. 1939.

CI 69—IFC MS. 784, pp. 254–255. IIAle, 2a, B17, IIIA2, a, Elcii, IVA4, Blavi, VIAl, 3, Blb, C1, D1. Galway, 1941.

CI 70—IFC MS. 784, pp. 400–401. IIAle, B17, IIIA2, a, Elcii, IVA4, Blavi, VIAl, (3), Blb, C1, D1. Galway, 1941.

CI 71—IFC MS. 785, pp. 501–508. IIAleii, Cla, IIIA2, C3, EO, IVA8, Blaiv, 2aii, D3a, VIAl, 3, B1, C1, D1. Galway, 1941.

CI 72—IFC MS. 802, pp. 484–491. IIAlei, 2a, B1, IIIBl, D2, EO, IVA8, 12, Blaxii, diii, 2ax, D3a, VIAl, 3, B1, C1, D1. Galway, 1942.

CI 73—IFC MS. 851, pp. 37–40. IIAlei, B6, IIIC4, a, EO, IVA4, Blavi, 2bii, VIAl, B1, (2b), C1, D1. Galway, 1932.

CI 74—IFC MS. 1010, pp. 8–14. IIAlei, B1, IIIAll, D2, EO, IVA12, Blaiv, 2ax, D3a, VIAl, 3, Blb, C1, D1. Galway, 1946.

CI 75—IFC MS. 1235, pp. 455–457. IIAle, IIIEO, IVA8, Blaiv, 2axi, VIA2, B1, C1, D1. Galway, 1952.

CI 76—IFC MS. 1323, pp. 139–145. IIAldi, B17, IIIEO, IVA4, Blaiv, 2axii, D3a, VIA6, B1, C1, D1. Galway, 1953.

CI 77—IFC Oireachtas MS. 102, pp. 1–10. IIAle, B17, Cld, IIIB2, (C4), Elci, ei, IVA4, Blaxiii, 2aii, xi, D3, VIAl, 3, B1, 2f, C1, D1. Connacht.

CI 78—*Ireland's Own* (June 3, 1933), p. 710. IIAle, B1, IIID2, EO, IVA4, Blaiii, D3a, VB2, VIA2, 3, B1, D1. VIIC2. Connacht.

CI 79—*Irish Weekly Independent* (Sept. 19, 1936), IIAle, B1, IIIA2, EO, IVA5, D2, VIAl, 3, B1, C1, D1. Connacht.

CI 80—*Ar Aghaidh* (July, 1940), p. 2. IIAlei, III(C3), E3b, IVA4, Blavi, di, 2bii, VIAl, 3, B1, C1, D1. Connacht.

CI 81—Pádhraic O'Domhnelláin, *An t-Iolrach Mór,* p. 42. IIAlg, Cla, IIIA2, EO, IVA5, Blaxv, 2aix, (3), (D7), V(Cle), VIO, VLLA2a. Connacht.

CI 82—IFC MS. 719, pp. 188–190. IIAle, 2a, B1, Cla, IIIAll, B1, D2, E3b, IVA4, Blbii, (iv), di, VIA6, Blb, C1, D1. Westmeath, 1938.

CI 83—IFC MS. 866, pp. 53–55. IIAle, 2a, B1, Cla, IIIAll, (C2), D2, E3b, IVA4, Blbii, (iv), di, VIAl, B1, C1. D1. Kilkenny, ca. 1938.

CI 84—*Ireland's Own* (January 9, 1937), p. 32. IIAle, B1, IIIAll, D2, EO, IVA7, Blbii, (iv), di, VIA2, 3, Blb, C1, D1. Wexford.

CI 85—IFC MS. 642, pp. 165–174. IIAl38, 2a, IIIC3, EO, IVA12, Blaiv, D3a, VC1b, VIAl, 3, B1, C1, D1. Clare, 1939.

CI 86—IFC MS. 317, pp. 147–150. IB2, IIIA4, EO, IVA12, Blaiv, 5bi, VIO. Tipperary, 1937.

CI 87—IFC MS. 576, pp. 447–450. IIAlei, B1, Cla, IIIAll, B1, C3, EO, IVA4, Blaiv, bviii, di, 5a, VIAl, 3, B2, C1. D1. Tipperary, ca. 1938.

CI 88—*Béaloideas*, III (1931–1932), 261. IIAlei, B1, IIIA3, E3b, IVA4, Blaviii, 2a, 5ai, VIAl, 3, B1, C1, D1. Kerry, 1930.

Table I: The Versions of The Tale

CI 89—*Béaloideas*, III (1931–1932), 261–264. IIAlei, 2b, B5a, B8, IIIBl, EO, IVA4, Blavi, di, 2axi, VIAl, 3, B1, C1, D4b, E, VIIBlb. Kerry, 1930.

CI 90—Kenneth Jackson, "Scéalta ón mBlascaod," *Béaloideas*, VIII (1938), 23–25. IIAlei, B8, IIIAll, B1, EO, IVA4, Blaiv, VIAl, 3, B1, D4. Kerry, between 1932 and 1937.

CI 91—"Sgéal na mná Míreaírí," *Béaloideas*, XII (1942), 196–199. IIAlei, IIIA2, B1, D2, EO, IVA4, Blaiv, 2axi, D3a, VIAl, 3, B1, C1, D1. Kerry, 1928.

CI 92—*Béaloideas*, XVII (1947), 81–83. IIAlei, IIIA3, EO, IVA4, Blavi (two horses), dx, VIAl, 3, B1, D4, E. Kerry, between 1914 and 1916.

CI 93—*An Lóchrann* (April, 1930), p. 5. IIAlai, IIIA2, EO, IVA5, Blaxi, 2biii (kicked, but not killed), 4aii, 5bi, VIAl, 3, B1, D4. Kerry.

CI 94—*Ireland's Own* (Sept. 26, 1936), p. 12. IIAlai, IIIA2, EO, IVA5, Blaxi, 2biii (as in C193), 4aii, 5bi, VIAl, 3, B1, D4. Kerry.

CI 95—Séamus O'Duilearga, *Leabhar Sheáin I Chonaill* (Dublin, 1948), pp. 153–156. IIAlei, IIIEO, IVA13, Blaiv, 2axii, 5a, VIAl, 3, B1, C1, D1. Kerry, between 1923 and 1931.

CI 96—IFC MS. 21, pp. 22–25. IIAle, IIIEO, IVA4, Blbiv, 2axi, D3a, VIO. Kerry, 1929.

CI 97—IFC MS. 21, pp. 200–203. IIAleii, IIIEO, IVA4, Blbiv, 2axi, D3a, VIO. Kerry.

CI 98—IFC MS. 39, pp. 165–175. IIAlei, B1, IIIA2, 11, C1, D2, E1c, e, f, 3b, IVA4, Blaiv, di, 2bii, D3a, VIAl, 3, B1, 2h, C1, D1, 4b. Kerry, ca. 1931.

CI 99—IFC MS. 97, pp. 34–46. IIAlei, B1, IIIBl, C1, EO, IVA4, Blaiv, 2bi, 5ai, VIA2, 3, Bl, D4. Kerry, 1938.

CI 100—IFC MS. 126, pp. 180–186. IIAleii, B1, IIIBl, 2, EO, IVA12, Blaiv (two horses), VIA6, B1. Kerry, 1938.

CI 101—IFC MS. 217, pp. 55–61. IIAlei, B3, C1d, IIIEO, IVA6, Blb, VIAl, 3, B1, D4, E. Kerry, 1936.

CI 102—IFC MS. 267, pp. 267–273. IIAlci, III(Elci, 3, f), IVA4, Blaiv, 2bii, D3a, VIAl, 3, B1, C1, D1, VIIBl. Kerry, 1936.

CI 103—IFC MS. 269, pp. 181–186. IIAlei, B1, IIIElc, e, f, 3b, IVA4, Blavi, di, 2bii, D3a, VClb, VIAl, 3, B1, C1, D1, (4), cii, VIIBl. Kerry, 1936.

CI 104—IFC MS. 308, pp. 70–79. IIAlaii, IIEO, IVA5, Blaxi, 4aii, 5b, VIAl, 3, B1, D4, d. Kerry, 1936.

CI 105—IFC MS. 379, pp. 17–20. IIAle, IIIEO, IVA4, Blaiv, VIAl, 3, B1, C1, D1, (4). Kerry, ca. 1936.

CI 106—IFC MS. 386, pp. 350–358. IIAle, B1, IIIBl, E3b, IVA4, Blbiv, VIAl, B1, D4, E. Kerry, 1937.

CI 107—IFC MS. 402, pp. 772–774, continued in MS. 429, pp. 1–10. IIAle, B1, IIIAll, B1, D2, EO, IVA5, Blaiv, b, 2bii, VIA2, (3), B1, C1, D1, 4. Kerry. 1937.

CI 108—IFC MS. 417, pp. 164–165. IIAle, B1, IVEO, IVA5, Blaiv, VIAl, 3, B1, C1, D1. Kerry.

CI 109—IFC MS. 423, pp. 65–70. IIAle, B5a, IIIEO, IVA4, Blavi, 2bii, VIAl, 3, B1, C1, D4b. Kerry, 1935.

CI 110—IFC MS. 429, pp. 548–586. IIAlci, B6, Clc, IIIBl, EO, IVA5a, Blaiv, 2axi, VIAl, B1, C1, D1. Kerry, 1937.

CI 111—IFC MS. 444, pp. 91–92. IIAle, IIIE3b, IVA4, Blbi, di, VIAl, 3, B1, C1, D1. Kerry, ca. 1938.

Table I: The Versions of The Tale   49

CI 112—IFC MS. 446, pp. 154–159. IIAlaii, IIIA2, EO, IVA5, Blaxi, 2biii (kicked, not killed), 4aii, 5b, VIAl, 3, B1, D4. Kerry, ca. 1938.

CI 113—IFC MS. 446, pp. 189–191. IIAle, IIIA2, EO, IVA4, Blaiii, 2aii, VIAl, 3, B2h, C1, D1. Kerry, ca. 1938.

CI 114—IFC MS. 456, pp. 339–342. IIAlci, 2a, IIIElci, e, f, IVA4, Blavi, 2bii, VIAl, B1, C1, D1, 4, Kerry, 1938.

CI 115—IFC MS. 464, pp. 147–149. IIAlei, IIIBl, EO, IVA4, Blaiv, 2bii, VIO. Kerry.

CI 116—IFC MS. 533, pp. 33–43. IIAlei, B1, IIIAll, IVA4, Blaiv, dxiii, 2axi, D3a, VIAl, 3, B1, C1, D1, VIIBlb. Kerry, 1938.

CI 117—IFC MS. 587, pp. 506–510. IIAle, B1, IIIElc, 3, f, 3b, IVA4, Blavi, 2bii, VIAl, 3, B1, C1, D1. Kerry, 1939.

CI 118—IFC MS. 597, pp. 345–355. IIAle, 2a, B8, IIIA3, 4, 11, B1, 3a, IVA4, Blavi, VIA4, B1, C1, D1, 4. Kerry, 1939.

CI 119—IFC MS. 613, pp. 296–300. IIAlei, IIIVl, EO, IVA12, Blaiv, 2a, VIAl, 3, B1, C1, D1, VIIBlb. Kerry, 1939.

CI 120—IFC MS. 658, pp. 496–498. IIAlei, IIIE3b, IVA4, Blaiv, VIA6, B1, C1, D1, (VIICl). Kerry, 1939.

CI 121—IFC MS. 658, pp. 165–169. IIAle, B1, IIID4, Elc, eii, f, IVA4, Blaiv, 2bii (two dogs), VIAl, 3, B1, C1, D1. Kerry, 1939.

CI 122—IFC MS. 968, pp. 208–210. IIAle, IIIEO, IVA4, Bla, 2axi, VIA2, 3, B1, C1, D1. Kerry, 1945.

CI 123—IFC MS. 1007, pp. 258–260. IIAle, IIIBl, E3b, IVA4, Blavi, VIAl, B1, D4. Kerry, 1947.

CI 124—IFC MS. 1114, pp. 169–170. IIAlg, 2a, B1, Cla, IIIAll, EO, IVA5, D2, VIO. Kerry.

CI 125—IFC MS. 1199, pp. 355-364. IIAlei, 2a, B8a, IIIAll, (Elci), IVA4, 5, Blaiv, 2axi, VIAl, 3, B1, C1, D1. Kerry, 1951.

CI 126—IFC MS. 1278, pp. 603-607. IIAleii, IIIA2, EO, IVA5, B2biii, 5bi, VIA6, B1, D5b. Kerry, ca. 1950.

CI 127—IFC MS. 259, pp. 660-661. IIIC2a, EO, IVA12, Blaiv, 2axii, 5bi, VI(O). Waterford, 1936.

CI 128—*An Lóchrann* (February, 1909), p. 8 [also in *An Seanchaidhe Muimhneach* (Dublin, 1932), p. 243]. IIIEO, IVA12, Blaiv, 5bi, VIO. Cork.

CI 129—C. O. Muimhneacháin, *Béaloideas Bhéal Atha an Ghaorthaidh*, pp. 136-140. IIAlaii, IIIA2, EO, IVA5, B2biii (kicked, not killed), 4aii, 5b, VCle, VIAl, B1, D4. Cork.

CI 130—IFC MS. 283, pp. 409-417, 450-451. IIAlbii, B1, Cla, IIIA2, 11, EO, IVA5, Blaxi, 2biii (kicked, not killed), 4aii, 5b, VIAl, (3), B1, D4, E. Cork.

CI 131—IFC MS. 311, pp. 241-243. IIAlei, IIIBl, EO, IVA5a, Blaiv, 2aii, 5bi, VCle,VIO. Cork.

CI 132—IFC MS. 358, pp. 160-163. IIAlci, B1, IIID2, EO, IVA4, Blaiv, di, 2bii, D3a, VIAl, 3, B1, C1, D1. Cork.

CI 133—IFC MS. 516, pp. 104-112. IIAle, 2a, B1, Cla, IIIAll, B1, EO, IVA12, Blaiv, 2axi (two dogs), xvi (two dogs), 5b, VIAl, 3, B1, C1, D1. Cork.

CI 134—IFC MS. 612, pp. 449-464. II2a, B1, IIIAll, D2, EO, IVA8, Blaiv, di, 2axi, D3a, VIAl, 3, B1, D4. Cork, ca. 1939.

CI 135—IFC MS. 660, pp. 60-102. IIAleii, 2a, B1, IIIA2, a, C3, EO, IVA8, 12, Blaiv, di, 2axi, D3a, VCle, VIA2, 3, B1, C1, D1, 4. Cork, 1939.

CI 136—IFC MS. 807, pp. 42-47. IIAlei, B1, IIIA2, Elci, e, f, IVA4, Blaiv, di, 2axi, D3a, VIAl, 3, B1, C1, D1, VIIBlb.

Table I: The Versions of The Tale   51

CI 137—IFC MS. 1165, pp. 92–102. IIAle, B1, IIIEO, IV(A3), 4, Blaxi, di, 2a, 4aii, 5b, D3a, VIAl, 3, B2b, C1, D1. Cork, 1944.

CI 138—*Fáinne An Lae* (May 6, 1899), p. 139. IIIEO, IVa8, Blaxi, 2aii, bv, VIA6, B1, C1, D1. Munster.

CI 139—*An Sguab* (November, 1925), p. 469. IIAle, 2a, IIIBl, (Elci, ei, f,), IVA4, Blbiv, 2axi, D3a, VIO. Munster.

CI 140—*Ireland's Own* (October 31, 1953), p. 3. IA5, B1, IIIE3a, IVA4, Blbv, VIO.

Finland

FF 1—Folklore Archives of the Finnish Literary Society, Leppänen, K.V., 4. IIAleii, B2, IIIEO, IVA6, Blciii, dxi, 2cii, (Clc), VC2a, VI(Al), D18, VIIC4. Pori(b), 1890.

FF 2—FLS, Helsingin Suomalaisen Alkeisopiston Konventti, XXXIX. IIAlg, 2a, B1, Cla, IIIA2, 11, B1, EO, IVA5, C2e, VIO. Tuusula (c), 1886.

FF 3—FLS, Alava, V. 80. IIIEO, IVA12, Blbvi, div, 2axi, VIO. Vehkalahti (c).

FF 4—FLS, Tolonen, V., 7. IIAlg, B2, Cla, IIIEO, IVA5, 12, Blbi, 4aii, VIO. Joutsa (d), 1886.

FF 5—FLS, Jäntti, A., 13. IIAlg, B2, Cld, IIIA2, C3, E3c, IVA4, Blciii, dvii, VIO. Korpilahti (d), 1894.

FF 6—FLS, Lindquist, A., 37. IC5, IIAlg, Cla, III(A2), EO, IVA5, B2axiv, 3b, 4aiv, VIO. Tammela (d), 1886.

FF 7—FLS, Rytkönen, Al., 41. IIIA4, C1, EO, IVA5, 6, Blbvi, (div), 3d, VIO. Joroinen (f), 1888.

FF 8—FLS, Väätanen, A., n.258. IIAlg, 2a, B17, Cla, IIIA2, C3a, EO, IVA5, 6, Blbvi, div, 2axvii, 4ai, VIO. Juva (f), 1896.

FF 9—FLS, Kuopienlyseon Toverikunta, XVIII:2. ID3, IIB8a, IIIA2, CI, EO, IVA5, 6, Blbvi, div, 3g, 4aii, 5aii, VIO. Rantasalmi (f), 1886.

FF 10—FLS, Vesterlund, A., 8. IIAle, IIA2, C3, EO, IVA5, 6, Blbvi, di, 3e, 4aii, VIAl, Blb, D4a, VIIC3. Rantasalmi (f), 1888.

FF 11—FLS, Hautala, 54. IIIEO, IVA6, Blbvi, div, 2bx, VCle, VIO, VIIB2. Sääminki (f), 1938.

FF 12—FLS, Savokarj. Osakunta, 46. IIAlg, B2, Cld, IIIA2, 11, C4b, E3c, IVA4, 5, Blax, 2bx, 4aii, VIO. Sääminki (f), 1887.

FF 13—FLS, Krohn, K., 13765. IIAle, B2, IIEO, IVA2, B1, di, VC2c, VIAl, Blb, C4, D3, VIIC3. Paloistenkylä (g), 1885.

FF 14—FLS, Krohn, K., 15123. IIAlg, B2, Clc, IIIEO, IVA13, B1, 2, (C2a), F, VIAl, D2. Iisalmi (g), 1885.

FF 15—FLS, Teräksinen, 32315. IIAlg, IIIA2a, EO, IVA5, 6, Blaii, div, 3d, 5b, VIO. Juankoski (g), 1944.

FF 16—FLS, Tikkanen, KRK, 121:50. IIIEO, IVA5, 6, Bla, div, 2axvii, 3a, VIO. Nilsiä (g), 1935.

FF 17—FLS, Poutanen, H., 24. IIAlcii, IIIA5, E3c, IVA4, 5, Blaii, div*, 4aii, VIAl, Blb, D5a. Parikkala (h), 1916.

FF 18—FLS Krohn, K., 10383. IIAlg, Cla, IIIA2, 3, EO, IVA3, 5, (11), Blci, div, 3e, 4aii, VIO. Rautu (h), 1884.

FF 19—FLS, Kaarama, KT 127:36. IIAlg, IIIA2a, EO, IVA5, 6, Blaii, div, 2bx, 4aii, VIO. Impilahti (i), 1936.

FF 20—FLS, Aalto, KT 122:2. IIAlei, IIIEO, IVA5, 6, Blaii, div, 2axiv, 3b, 4aiv, VIAl, B2, C2, D1. Sortavala (i), 1937.

FF 21—FLS, Jerkkola, K. J., 33:14404. IA6, IIAlg, B17, Cla, IIIA2, EO, IVA6, Blaii, div, VIO. Suojärvi (i), 1957.

Table I: The Versions of The Tale 53

FF 22—FLS, Krohn, K., 5905. IIAlg, 2a, IIIA2, EO, IVA5, Blaiii, div, ix, 2av, VIO, VIIA5a, bi, A5, a, g. Suojärvi (i), 1884.

FF 23—FLS, Krohn, K., 7148. IIIEO, IVA5, C1, VIO, VIID5. Tsokki (i), 1884.

FF 24—FLS, Krohn, K., 7670. IIAle, IIIEO, IVA5, 6, Blaii, div, ix, 2av, xiv, 3b, VIO. Äimäjärvi (i), 1884.

FF 25—FLS, Polviainen, J., 7. IIA2a, IIIEO, IVA5, 6, Blaiii, div, 2bvii, 3e, 4avi, VIO. Äglöjärvi (i), 1914.

FF 26—FLS, Turunen, A., 75. IIAlg, IIIA2, EO, IVA5, 6, Blaii, div, 2axvii, VIO. Eno (j), 1909.

FF 27—FLS, Krohn, K., 6780 [only bare essentials of tale were collected]. IIIEO, IVA13, B1, 2, 3, VIO. Ilomantsi (j), 1884.

FF 28—FLS, Krohn, K., 6856 [only bare essentials of tale were collected]. IIIEO, IVA13, B1, 2, 3, VIO. Ilomantsi (j), 1884

FF 29—FLS, Krohn, K., 10058. IIIEO, IVA13, Blb, div, 2axvii, 3j, VIO. Nurmes (j), 1885.

FF 30—FLS, Nurmio, M., 176. IIIEO, IVA6, Blaiii, div, VIO. Nurmes (j), 1891.

FF 31—FLS, Kallio, P., 2. IIAlg, Cla, IIIEO, IVa5, 6, Blaix, div, 2aii, 3a, VIO. Pielinen (j), 1892.

FF 32—FLS, Kärki, F., 3. IIAlg, B17, Cla, IIIA2, 7, IVAl, (5), Blaiii, 2aii, 3a, VIO. Polvijärvi (j), 1906.

FF 33—FLS, Krohn, K., 11370b. IIIEO, IVA5, D4, VIO. Rautavaara (j), 1885.

FF 34—FLS, Krohn, K., 11370a. IIAlg, IIEO, IVA5, 6, Blaii, div, 4aii, 5bii, VIO. Säynäinen (j), 1885.

FF 35—FLS, Brandt, H., 219. IIAlg, B2, Clg, IIIA2, C1, EO, IVA5, D3, 4, VIA6, Blb, C6, D1. Laihia (k), 1889.

FF 36—FLS, Brandt, H., 238. IIIEO, IVa5, Clc, VIO. Laihia (k), 1889.

FF 37—FLS, Brandt, H., 847. IIB2, IIEO, IVA13, D6, VIA6, B1, C6, D1, 9. Laihia (k), 1891.

FF 38—FLS, Brandt, H., 1041. IIB2, IIIEO, IVA5, D6, (Bldi), VIO. Laihia (k), 1893.

FF 39—FLS, Krohn, K., 1826. IIAlg, B6, IIIA2, EO, IVA5, 6, B(ldiv), 2bx, 4aii, VIO. Lapua (k), 1884.

FF 40—FLS, Krohn, K., 11310. IIAleii, B2, IIIA2, a, EO, IVA5, D4, VIA2, Bla, C4, D3. Finnish-Swedish border (o), 1885.

FF 41—FLS, Meriläinen, H., 60. IIClc, IIIEO, IVA6, Blaii, div, VIO. Häme, Karelia (p), 1889.

FF 42—FLS, Waronen, M., 125. IIAleii, B2, Cle, IIIAll, EO, IVA5, D4, VIAl, B2h, D5d, VIIB2. Jyskyjarvi (p), 1897.

FF 43—FLS, Krohn, K., 6240. IIAlg, IIIEO, IVA5, 6, Blaiii, div, 2bx, 4aii, V(bl), VIO, VIIC2. Korpijärvi (q), 1884.

FF 44—*Suomi*, II, 14 as summarized in Hanna Lindberg, *"The Shrew" Argbiggans Typ i den Engelska Literaturen intill Shakespere* (Tavastehus, 1901), p. 144n. IICla, IIIE3c, IVA2, 5, Blavi, D6, a, 7a, VIAl, B1, D4. Aunus (q).

FF 45—FLS, Saxbäck, F. A., 13. IIIEO, IVA6, Blaiii, div, 2aii, VIO. Inkeri (s), 1859.

Estonia

FE 1—Folklore Archives of the Kirjandusmuuseum, Tartu, H III 28, 951/4. IIAlh, B3, IIIA4, (D6), E3a, IVA4, Blaiv, di, xi, xiv, 2axv, VIO. Kroonlinn, 1896.

Table I: The Versions of The Tale 55

FE 2—KMT H II 8, 286/93 (2). IIAleii, B17, C2aiii, IIIA10, EO, IVA6, a, (11), Blaxiv, 3e, 4aii, VIO. Johvi, Vaivara, 1889.

FE 3—KMT H II 8, 351/9 (14). IIAleii, 2a, C1a, IIIEO, IVA6, Blaiii, div, VIAl, B2h, C2, D1, VIIB3. Vaivara, 1889.

FE 4—KMT H II 9, 393/5 (4). IIAlg, 2a, IIIA2, C5a, EO, IVA5, C1b, V(B1), C1e, VIO, VIIC2. Haljala, 1889.

FE 5—KMT E 15544 (10). IIAlh, IIIEO, IVAl, B1bvii, VIO. Haljala, 1895.

FE 6—KMT H III 12, 591/3 (1). IIAlj, C2a, IIIA10, EO, IVA5, (VIA4), 6, Blav, 4aii, VIO. Tallinn, 1893.

FE 7—KMT H II 57, 182-2a (33). IIC2ai, IIIEO, IVA6b, B1bvi, div, 2aiv, VIO. Kose, 1897.

FE 8—KMT H II 57, 228/30 (18). IIAlg, 2a, IIIA2, C5a, EO, IVA5, C1b, VIO. Kose, 1897.

FE 9—KMT ERA II 148, 449/52 (13). IIIA4, C1, EO, IVA5, 6, Blax, div, 2b, 4aii, VIO. Märjamaa, 1937.

FE 10—KMT ERA II 251, 525/9 (16). IIC2a, IIIEO, IVA5 (VIA4), 6, B1bvi, div, 4aii, VIO. Karuse, 1938.

FE 11—KMT E 16799/800 (11). IIIEO, IVAll, B1bvi, VIO. Pärnu-Jaagupi, 1895.

FE 12—KMT H II 20, 47/9 (15). IIAlh, IIIA4, EO, IV(A7), B1bvi, div*, 2bx, VIO, VIIb6. Pärnu, 1888.

FE 13—KMT E 38610/1. IIIE(1d), 3c, IVA4, B1bvi, 2aiv, VIO. Tõstamaa, 1899.

FE 14—KMT ERA II 22, 580/2. IIAlg, IIIEO, IVA5, 6, B1biv, div, vi, 5aiii, VIO, VIIA4bi, (5). Põltsamaa, 1930.

FE 15—KMT E StK 34, 228/9 (1). IIAlg, 2a, IIIA2, a, EO, IVA5, C1, D9, VIO. Kursi, Kodavere, 1926.

FE 16—KMT H II 28, 122 (4). IIA2a, IIEO, IVA5, Clb, VIO. Äksi, 1889.

FE 17—KMT H II 29, 256/9 (3). IIAlh, IIIA4, (E3c), IVAl, Blbvi, 2aiii, VIO, VIIA4a, bii, 5, d, g. Tartu. 1889.

FE 18—KMT H III 15, 245/7 (1). IIA2a, IIIC5a, EO, IVA5, Clb, VIO. Võnnu, 1893.

FE 19—KMT H I 6, 242/3 (2). IIA2a, IIIEO, IVA5, Clb, VIO. Vastseliina, 1894.

FE 20—KMT H I 8, 451/3 (5). IIAldii, IIIEO, IVA5, 6, Blaiii, div, viii, 4aii, 5di, VIAl, B1, C4, D2. Vastseliina, 1896.

FE 21—KMT H III 30, 765/72 (6). IIA2a, IIIEO, IVA6, Blaiii, div, vi, VIO, VIIA4a, bi, 5, a, g, B2. Vastseliina, 1902.

FE 22—KMT H II 73, 126/8 (17). IIB17, IIIEO, IVAl, 5, Blax, 2bi, VIO, VIIB6. Vastseliina (?), 1906.

FE 23—KMT S 39939/51 (11). IIAleii, B8, IIIA2, 11, B4, EO, IVA5, B3g, 4aii, 5bii, VIAl, B1, D4e, VIIA4, (IVBlbvi, div), b, (5), c. Setu, 1932.

FE 24—KMT S 45285/8 (19). IIIEO, IVA5, Clb, VIO. Setu, 1932.

FE 25—KMT ERA II 144, 507/13 (3). ID2, IIA2a, IIIA2a, EO, IVA5, Blcviii, VCle, VIO. Setu, 1937.

FE 26—KMT ERA II 194, 296/7 (25). IIAlg, 2a, diii, IIIA2a, C1, EO, IVA5, C3c, D3a, VIO, VIIA4a, f, 5. Setu, 1938.

FE 27—KMT ERA II 209, 253/4 (5). IIAlg, 2a, IIIA2b, C5a, EO, IVA5, Clb, VIO. Setu, 1939.

Table I: The Versions of The Tale 57

FE 28—Andres Pranspill, comp. and tr., *Estonian Anthology* (Milford, Conn., 1956), "A Contrary Wife, A Folk Tale," by M. I. Eisen, pp. 211–215. IIBl, (C2b), IIIEO, IVA5, D11, VAlciii, VIO.

Hungary

FH 1—A text sent to me by Professor Dr. Béla Gunda, Ethnological Institute of the University, Debrecen, collected by Imre Ferenczi of the Institute; unpublished. IIAlg, 2a, CIa, IIIA(2), 11, C3, EO, IVA5, Clb, VIO. Mogyoróska, 1955.

FH 2—W. Henry Jones and Lewis L. Kropf, *The Folk-Tales of the Magyars* (The Folk-Lore Society: London, 1889), pp. 23–25 [original text printed in Kriza János, *Vadróssák*, II (Magyar Népköltési gyüjtemény, XII: Budapest 1911), 137–139; also translated in Gyula Ortutay, *Ungarische Völksmarchen* (Berlin, 1957), 405–407]. IIA2a, CIa, IIIAll, C3, EO, IVA5, Clb, VIO. 1863.

FH 3—Dégh Linda, *Kakasdi Népmesék*, II (Budapest, 1960), 253. IIA2, IIIEO, IVA5, Clb, VIO. Tolna, Kakasd, 1950.

FH 4—Kovács Agnes, *Kalotaszegi Népmesék*, I (Budapest, 1944), 190–196. (IC5), IIAlg, B1, 17, Clb, IIIEO, (IV no taming), VIO, VIIA4a, b, 5, c, g. Ketesd, Kalotaszeg.

Lithuania[23]

BLi 1—Jonas Balys, *Lietuvių Samojus* (Sakalas, 1937), pp. 13–14. IIAlg, IIIA2a, EO, IVA5, 6, Blbvi, div, 4aiii, 5ai, VIO, VIIB2. Baisogala, 1936.

BLi 2—Balys, pp. 14–15. IIIEO, IVA5, 12, Blaii, div, xii, 5ai, VC2c, VIA6, B1, D4. Šventežris.

BLi 3—J. Basanavičius, *Lietuviškos Pasakos Ivairios*, II (Chicago, 1904), pp. 268–269. IIIEO, IVA5, 12, Blbiv, (div), 3d, rai, VIO. Kaunas.

BLi 4—Jonas Balys, *Lithuanian Folklore from the Territory of Vilnius; Folklore Studies*, IV (Lithuanian Folklore Archives: Kaunas, 1938), pp. 260–261. IIAle, BlO, IIIA2, B1, C5, EO, IVA5, 6, (a), Blaiii, div, 3a, 4aiii, 5ai, VIAl, B2a, C4, Dc. Gaveikiškė, Daugėliškis, 1936.

BLi 5—Balys (1930), pp. 261–262. IIAle, IIIA2, b, B1, EO, IVA5, 6, Blaiii, div, 4ai, ii, 5aii, VIAl, B1, C4, D3. Rizgúnai, Paringis, 1935.

BLi 6—Balys (1937), p. 18. IIA2dii, IIIA2a, C1, EO, IVA5, C4, VIO. Kabeliai, 1935.

BLi 7—Balys (1937), pp. 19–20. IIAlg, IIIA2, a, C5a, EO, IVA5, (C1), D3a, 9, VClb, VIO. Linkuva.

BLi 8—Jonas Balys, *Lietuviškos Pasakos* (Chicago, 1951), IIAleii, IIIA2, EO, IVA5, 6, Blaviii, div, 4aiii, 5ai, VIAl, B2h, C4, D3.

Poland

SP 1—"The Whipping Bag: A Tale Traditional in the Family of Anne H. Sidwa," *Polish Folklore*, V (1960), 2–4 [Mrs. Sidwa's mother told this to her family as she had learned it from her father in Poland]. (IB2), IIA2a, IIIEO, IVA5, C3, VIO. Kęty (near Kraków).

SP 2—Mieczyslaw Karaś *Powieści Dudu Rzeszowskiego* (Krakow, 1956), pp. 53–54 [from A. Salon, *Lud rzeszowski material etnograficzne* (1908)]. IIAlg, 2a, IIIEO, IVA5, C3d, VIO. Rzeszow.

White Russia

SRW 1—V. N. Dobrovol'skij, *Smolenskij etnografičeskij sbornik*, I (Petersburg, 1891), pp. 359–361. IIAlcii, 2a, Cla, IIIA2, C3, D2, 4, EO, IVA5, D10, VIAl, B1, (2h), C5, D1, 2. Berdebjaki in Jel'nja.

Table I: The Versions of The Tale 59

SRW 2—Lauri Kettunen, *Näytteitä Etelävepsästä*, II (Helsinki, 1925), pp. 11–14. IIAleii, 2a, Cla, IIIAll, EO, IVA5, 6, Blbvi, div, Clb, VIAl, (3), B1, D4b. Arskaht, 1918.

SRW 3—Kettunen, II, pp. 118–122. IC2, IIAld, Cla, IIIAll, EO, IVA5, 6, Blbvi, div, 4aii, 5di, VIAl, 3, B1, D10, 11. Kortlaht, 1918.

The Ukraine

SRUk 1—*Trudy etnografičesko-statističeskoj ekspediciju y sapadno-russkij kraj*, II (Petersburg, 1878), 546–548 [Summarized also in M. Dragomanov, "Taming of the Shrew, in the Folk-Lore of the Ukraine,"[24] *The International Folk-Lore Congress of the World's Columbia Exposition. Chicago, July, 1893* (Chicago, 1898), p. 370, summary no. 2]. IIAlg, IIIA2, C5a, EO, IVA5, Cla, VIO, VIIA4a, b, 5. Nokopol.

SRUk 2—I. Rudčenko, *Narodnyja juźnorusakija skazki*, I (Kiev, 1869), 179–181 [Also in Dragomanov, p. 370, summary no. 1]. IIAlg, IIIA2, C5a, EO, IVA5, Cle, VIO, VIIA4b. Cernjachov.

SRUk 3—Rudčenko, pp. 181–183 [Also in Dragomanov, pp. 370–371, summary no. 4]. IIIEO, IVA6, Blcvii, div, xii, 2aii, VIO, VIIA4a, b, 5a, g. Near Kiev.

SRUk 4—Dragomanov, p. 370 [summary no. 3]. IIIEO, IVA5, Cld, VIO, VIIA4b.

SRUk 5—Dragomanov, pp. 372–373 [full text]. IIAlg, 2a, B8, Cla, IIIAll, D1, EO, IVA5, D3a, 9, VClb, VIO, VIIB2.

Karelia, Great Russia, and Siberia

SR 1—O. E. Ozarovskaja, *Pjatireč'e* (Leningrad, 1931), pp. 93–101. IIAlg, Cla, IIIEld, 3c, IVAl, Blbvi, div, VIO, VIIA4a, bii, 5, a, g. Collected on the banks of the river Pinega while waiting for a steamer to the settlement Ust-Ezhuga, 1916.

SR 2—M. K. Azadovskij, *Russkije Skazki y Karelii* (Petrozavodsk, 1947), pp. 131–133. IIAlg, B1, IIIA4, Cl, E3c, IVA4, Blaii, (cv), VIO, VIIA4a, b, 5. Sumskij; first pub., 1911.

SR 3—N. V. Novikov, *Skazki Filippa Pavloviča Gespodrajova* (Petrozavodsk, 1941), pp. 419–422. IIAlei, Cla, IIIA2, 11, EO, IVA5, 6, Blbix, div, 4aii, 5ci, VIAl, B1, D12, VIIB2. Petrozavodsk, 1938.

SR 4—Boris M. and Iu. Sokolov, *Skazki i Piesni Bielozerskago Kraia* (Moskva, 1915), p. 63. IIAle, B9, IIIAll, B1, EO, IVA5, B4ai, 5b, VIAl, B1, D4.

SR 5—*Zivaja Starina*, XXI (1912), 236–238. IIAleii, IIIEO, IVA5, B4av, 5c, dii, VIAl, B1, D4, 13, VIIA4a, b, 5, a, d, g. Town of Kostenskaja, Spassskaja, Tot'ma, Vologda, 1905–1908.

SR 6—V. I. Černyšev, *Skazki i Legendy Puškinskich Mest* (Moskva and Leningrad, 1950), pp. 223–225. IIAlg, IIIA2b, C5a, EO, IVA5, Clb, D8e, VIO, VIIA4a, b, 5, a, c, g. Lomy, Aševskaja, Novoržev, 1929.

SR 7—A. N. Afanasiev, *Russian Fairy Tales*, trans. by N. Guterman (New York, 1945), pp. 161–162. IIAlg, Clc, IIIA2, EO, IVA5, 6, Blbvi, div, 5diii, D8e, VIO. Osinsk, Permsk.

SR 8—D. Zelenin, *Velikoruskija skazki Vjatskoj gubernii* (Petersburg, 1915), pp. 73–76. IIAleii, B1, II(A2), B2, EO, IVA5, 6, Bldiv, D6, a 7, a, VIAl, 3, B2g, D11, 13, VIIA4a, b, 5, a, g.Ključeskaja, Vjatka, 1908.

SR 9—J. A. Čudinskij, *Russkije narodnyje skazki, pribautki pobasenki* (Moskva, 1864), p. 102 [referred to also in W. R. S. Ralston, *Russian Folk-Tales* (London, 1873), p. 38]. IIAlg, IIIA3, B1, EO, IVA5, D4, VIO. Moscow.

SR 10—*Zapiski Krasnojarskago Pod'otdela vostočno-sibirskago otdela Imp. Russkago Geografičeskago Obščestva po etnografii*, I:1 (Krasnojarsk, 1902), 123–125. I(C4), IIAlg, IIIA2, EO, IVA5, 6, Blbi, div, xii, 3g, 4aii, VIO, VIIA4a, b, 5,

Table I: The Versions of The Tale

a, e, g, B2. Borovskoje Kurgansk, Tobolsk, Siberia, before 1900.

SR 11—*Narodnopisnů Věstnik Českoslovanský* XXI (Praha, 1928), 211–213 and 245. IIAlg, 2a, B1, IIIA2, EO, IVA5, B3b, (C1), D7, 8e, VIO, VIIA4a, b, 5, a, d, g. Upper reaches of the Lena, Siberia, 1915.

SR 12—A. M. Smirnov, *Sbornik Velikorusskikh Skazok arkhiva russkago geograficeskago obščestva* (Petersburg, 1917), pp. 901–910. IIAlg, 2a, B8, Cla, IIA4, 11, Eld, 3c, IVAl, Blbv, vi, div, VIO, VIIA4a, bii, 5, a, g. Zabikalsk Oblast, Siberia.

Yugoslavia

SY 1—Boduen-de-Kurtene, *Materialy dlja južnoslavjanskoj dialektologii i Etnografii*, II (Petersburg, 1904), 149–151. IIAlg, 2a, IIIEO, IVA5, D3a, 9, VClb, e, VIO. Slovenians in Torre, northern Italy, 1873.

SY 2—Maja Bošković-Stulli, *Istarske narodne priče* (Zagreb, 1959), pp. 101–102. I(D1), IIAlg, C2c, IIIEO, IVA5, B4a, VIO, VIIA4a, di, 5. Istra.

SY 3—*Evolucija*, II:8 (Zagreb, 1933), 400–401. IIAlg, IIIEO, IVAl, Blaiii, 2bii, VIO, VII(4a), b, 5. Virje.

SY 4—*Zbornik za narodni život i običaje Juznih Slavena*, XXXII (Zagreb, 1940), 175–176. IDi, IIAlg, 2a, IIIEO, IVA5, D3a, 9, VClb, VIO, VIIA4b, 5. Dakavo.

SY 5—INU MS. 273, pp. 68–69, no. 38. ID1, IIAlg, C2b, c, IIIEO, IV (completely unspecified), VIO, VIIA4c, di, (5), f, g. Palanka, Zrmanja, 1957.

SY 6—INU MS. 273, pp. 25–27, no. 13. IIAlg, 2a, C2b, IIIEO, IVA5, C5, VClb, VIO, VIIA4c, d, 5, b, g. Zrmanja, 1957.

SY 7—INU MS. 180, pp. 40–41, no. 30. IIIEO, IVA5, Cla, VIO. Near Lovinac in Lika, 1955.

SY 8—*Venac*, XVI (Beograd, 1931), 524–526. IIAlg, IIIEO, IVA5, B3c, 5aiv, ci, VIO, VIIA4a, b, 5, b, g. Glumač.

SY 9—*Zbornik za narodni život i običaje Južnih Slavena*, XIII (Zagreb, 1908), 216–218. IIAlg, C2b, c, IIIEO, IVA5, C5, VIO, VIIA4b, d, ii, (5), b, g, D4. Bukovica, Dalmatia.

SY 10—INU MS. 102, pp. 93–94, no. 20. ID1, IIAlg, C2b, c, IIIEO, IVA5, C5, VIO, VIIA4c, (5), b, g. Gornje Danilo, Šibenik, 1952.

SY 11—*Venac*, XIV (Beograd, 1929), 530–531. IIIEO, IVA5, B5e, D8a, b, VCle, f, VIO. Užice. 1880.

SY 12—INU MS. 189, pp. 147–148 (from the Bogišić library MSS.). ID1, IIAlg, 2a, C2b, IIIEO, IVA5, C2b, VIO, VIIA4c. Cavtat, Dubrovnik, 1884.

SY 13—*Bosanska vila*, III (Sarajevo, 1888), 77. IIAlg, 2a, C2b, IIIEO, IVA5, C5, VIO, VIIA4b, d, 5.

SY 14—*Bosanska vila*, XIV (Sarajevo, 1899), 316–317. IIAlg, 2a, IIIEO, IVA5, C5, VIO, VIA4a, b, 5, (c).

SY 15—*Bosanska vila*, XXIII (Sarajevo, 1908), 286. IIAlg, C2b, IIIE3d, IVA4, B1bi (three horses), dii, 2bx, (three dogs), VIO, VIIA4b, d, (5), b, g. Lipovo Polje, 1907.

SY 16—J. Miodragović, *Narodna pedogogija u Srba* (Beograd, 1914), p. 339. IIIEO, IVA12, B1, div, 2, VIO.

SY 17—Veselin Čajkanović, *Srpske narodne pripovetke* (Beograd, 1927), no. 105. IIAlg, 2a, IIIEO, IVA5, C2d, VIO.

SY 18—*Venac*, XIV (Beograd, 1929), 531–532 [reprinted from the newspaper *Vila*]. IIAlg, C1a, IIIEO, IVA5, B4aii, 5bii, VIO, VIIA(4d), 5.

Table I: The Versions of The Tale 63

SY 19—*Novica Šaulić Srpske narodne priče*, I (Beograd, 1931), 140-141. IIIEO, IV (completely unspecified), VIO, VIIA4d, (5b, g).

SY 20—Peter Ž. Petrović, "Život i običaje naroda u Gruži," *Srpski etnografski zbornik*, LVIII (Beograd, 1948), 429-430. IIAlg, C2b, IIIEO, IV (completely unspecified), VIO, VIIA4, (5), b, g

France

RF 1—Jean-François Bladé, *Contes Populaires de la Gascogne*, III (Les Littératures Populaires de Toutes les Nations: Paris, 1886), 287-288. IIAlh, IIIE3a, IVA4, Blavi, di, 2ai, VIO, VIIB5. Pergain-Taillaz, Gers.

French-America

RFAm 1—Archives de Folklore de l'Université Laval (Québec), Coll. J. Dominique Gauthier, Enreg. G-242. IIAle, B1, Cld, IIIA2, 8, 11, Elb, ci, 3c, IVA4, 5, Blaiv, D3b, VIAl, B1, C1, D1. Evangéline (Gloucester), New Brunswick, 1953.

RFAm 2—AF, Luc Lacourcière, MS. 120. IIAle, B1, Cld, IIIA2, 8, 11, D2, Elb, d, 3c, IVA4, 5, Blaiv, 5g, D3b, VIAl, Blb, C1, D1. Tracadie (Gloucester), New Brunswick, 1955.

RFAm 3—AF, Luc Lacourcière, Enreg. 3269. IIAle, B1, Cld, IIIA2, 8, 11, B2, D2, Eld, 3c, IVA4, 5, Blaiv, dvii, D3b, VIAl, B1, D1, 4d. Tracadie (Gloucester), New Brunswick, 1957.

RFAm 4—AF, Coll. Conrad Laforte, Enreg. L-448. I(B3), D6, IIIEO, IVA12, Blaiv, VIO. Saint-Joseph-d'Alma (Lac Saint-Jean), Québec, 1956.

RFAm 5—AF Luc Lacourcière, 2084-2084A. IIAleii, 2a, B1, IIIA2, C3, EO, IVA5, Clc, VA1, B1, C1, D1. Paul-Baie-Nord, Saguenay, P. Q., 1954.

Portugal

RP 1—F. Xavier D'Athaide Oliveira, *Contos Tradicionaes do Algarve*, I (Tavira, 1900), 184–185. IIAlg, 2a, IIIA2, EO, IVA5, D3a, VClb, 3, VIO. S. Lourenço D'Almancil.

RP 2—D'Athaide Oliveira, II (Porto, 1905), 502–504. IIAlg, IIIA2, EO, IVA5, 6, Blavi, di, 6a, b, VIO, VIIA2a.

Spain

RS 1—Aurelio de Llano Roza de Ampudia, *Cuentos Austurianos Recogidos de la Tradición Oral* (Madrid, 1925), no. 123. IIA2a, B9, IIIA4, C1, EO, IVA5, (C3a), VIO. Moru, Ponga, 1920.

RS 2—Ampudia, note to no. 123 [summary]. IIIO, IVA5, C3a, VIO. San Roman de Candamo.

RS 3—José A. Sánchez Pérez, *Cien cuentos populares* (Madrid, 1942), pp. 213–218. IIAlh, B17, IIIA4, C1, E3b, IVA4, Blaxi, V(A2h), VIO, VIIBla, C1. Known in Léon, Salamanca and Zamora.

RS 4—Aurelio M. Espinosa, *Cuentos Populares de Castilla* (Buenos Aires-México, 1946), pp. 74–75. IIAlh, IIIA4, EO, IVA5a, Blaxiv, di, VIO. Valladolid.

RS 5—Aurelio M. Espinosa, *Cuentos Populares Españoles*, 2nd ed. (Madrid, 1946–47) I, 159–160. IIAlh, IIIA4, C2, EO, IVA5a, Blaxi, VA2h, VIO, VIICl. Zamora, Zamora.

RS 6—Espinosa (1946–1947), I, 160–62. IIA2a, IIIEO, IVA5, D2, VIO, VIIC5. Zamora, Zamora.

Spanish America[25]

RSAm 1—Juan B. Rael, *Cuentos Españoles de Colorado y Nuevo Méjico* (Stanford, California, 1957), II, 563–565. IIAlg, IIIAl,

EO, IVA6b, Blaiii, bix, 4aii, VCldi, VIO. Española, New Mexico, ca. 1940.

RSAm 2—A text sent to me by Professor Américo Paredes of the University of Texas, who heard it told in Matamoros, Mexico by Manfred del Castillo from Brownsville, Texas, who had heard it from a Mexican citizen who spoke no English. IBl, IIIE3b, IVA4, Blbi, VIO. 1959.

Romania[26]

RR 1—*Revistă Pentru literatură si traditiuni populare*, Fălticeni, V (1898), no. 1, 83–85 [FFC 78, Type 1370, var. la]. IIAlg, 2aiv, dii, B9, IIIEO, IVA5, C3a, VIO.

RR 2—*Revistă Pentru*, XIII (1913), no. 1, 165–166 [FFC 78, Type 1370, var. lb]. IIIEO, IVA5, C2b, VIO.

RR 3—*Revistă folcloristică*, Balota-Doljiu, I (1912), 12 [FFC 78, Type 1370, var. 2]. IIA2a, IIIAll, (C5), EO, IVA5, C2b, VIO.

RR 4—I. A. Candrea, *Graiul nostru*, II (1908), 183 [FFC 78, Type 1370, var. 4]. IIAle, 2a, B17, IIIEO, IVA5, D3a, VIO.

Greece

Gre 1—Dimitris Loukopoulos (Folklore collection from Aetolia), *Laographia*, VIII (1921–1925), 15–16. IIAlf, B17, IIIA4, EO, IVA5, D8a, VIO, VIIA2b. Lambri.

Gre 2—Dimitrios S. Loukatos, ed., *Neoellinika Laographika Keimena* (Athens, 1957), 277–278. IIIEO, IVA5, B3g, (VIA2, D13a), VIIA2b. Ithaca, 1956.

Gre 3—*Neoellinika Analekta*, II (1874), 16–17. IIA2a, IIIEO, IVA5, C2b, VIO. Naxos.

Gre 4—Folklore Archives, Academy of Athens, No. 184–44 D. IB2, IIIEO, (IVA5, B3), VIO, VIIA2b. Thrace.

Gre 5—Folklore Archives, Academy of Athens, No. 672, p. 35. IIAlg, 2a, Cld, IIIDla, EO, IVA5, (C5), VClc, VIO, VIIA4. Megara.

Persia

Per 1—*Sketches of Persia, from the Journals of a Traveler* in the East [Sir John Malcolm] (London, 1827), II, 54–58 [also summarized in Karl Simrock, *Die quellen des Shakespeare in Novellen. Märchen und Sagen* (Bonn, 1831), I, 327–354, and in the translation *The Remarks of M. Karl Simrock on the Plots of Shakespeare's Plays* (London, 1850), 80–93; the summaries are based on *Kisseh-kuhn, der Persische Erzähler* (Berlin, 1829) which I have not seen]. I(B1), IIAlg, (B2, Clg), IIIAll, EO, IV(Aba), B3, VIO, VIIA2b.

India

Ind 1—*North Indian Notes and Queries*, V (May, 1895), 33 (note 37). IIAlg, IIIEO, IVA4, B2bx, 3ci, 4d, VCla, VIO, VIIC2a. Told by Madho Brashad, Khattri, of Mirzapur.

Ind 2—M. N. Ventakaswami, *Folktales from India* (Diocesan Press: Madras, 1923), No. 67, "The Young Man and Hazari Ial of Baidars' Daughter," pp. 135–157. IIAlg, 2ci, Cla, IIIAll, EO, IV(A6a), B2bviii, 3(e), g, D3, VIO.

Folk Sayings Analogous to the Taming of the Shrew

Sweden—"För säkerhets skull drar jag val katten en gång till, sa gubben, när han dragit katten över ryggen på käringen." ("Just to be sure, I'd better pull the cat one more time," the fellow said when he dragged the cat over his old lady's back.)

"För säkerhets skull skall jag ta en gäng till, sa gubben, när han rev gumman med katt-tassen i ansiktet." ("Just to be sure, I'll do it once again," the fellow said when he scratched his old lady in the face with the cat's claws.)

Table I: The Versions of The Tale

Dr. Carl-Martin Bergstrand, Västsvenska Folkminnesarkivet, informs me that these and similar sayings have been widely collected in Sweden. The saying occurs also in text GS 5 above.

Morocco—"When you beat the dog, the bride takes care." Mr. Ghoulem Berrah from Morocco, a student at Indiana University, gave me this saying in Arabic; it rhymes as a couplet in that language. Mr. Berrah says that he has never seen the saying in a book, but he has heard many people use it in any situation in which they cannot directly attack a person who is at fault. The referent of the saying is this story: "A man is recently married. He wants to teach a lesson to his wife. She has made some mistakes and he cannot do anything to her for she is a bride. So he beats his dog. The conclusion of the story is the saying, 'When you beat the dog, the bride takes care.'" [The only similar expression in E. A. Westermarck's *Wit and Wisdom in Morocco* (London, 1930), is #1264, "Beat the dog, the other dogs will run away," p. 232.]

Turkey—"Tear off a cat's legs on the first night." Professor Pertev Boratav, Paris, France, sent me this Turkish popular saying with the explanation that, "one considers that this expression has its origin in the act of a husband, who, on the first night of his wedding, finds some pretext to kill a cat, by tearing off its legs. Thus he intimidates his future spouse and shows that she will be mistreated in the same way if she disobeys thereafter.

Burma—"For the newlywed, the cat has to die" or "At the beginning of taking a wife, the cat has to die." Mr. Maung Than Sein from Burma, a student at Indiana University, reports that this saying rhymes in Burmese. He dictated the following story to explain the saying: "The man is expected to be superior to his wife, and once a man married a girl and all his friends and relatives expected him to beat his wife. But he's a coward, and they are eavesdropping, so he beats the cat instead of his wife. Hence the saying, 'The cat has to suffer for a newly married man.'" [I am indebted to Alan Dundes of Bloomington, Indiana, for supplying me with this reference.]

NOTES TO TABLE I

1. The earliest known translations of Shakespeare's play, into German and Dutch, cannot be treated as separate versions here, but may be briefly characterized as follows. *De dolle bruyloft* (1654), by Abraham Sybant of Amsterdam, was discussed by Johannes Bolte in "Eine holländische Uebersetzung von Shakespeare's *Taming of the Shrew* vom Jahre 1654,"*Shakespeare Jahrbuch*, XXVI (1891), 78–86; this, the oldest known inclusive translation of a play by Shakespeare, was rendered in alexandrines and followed the plot of the original closely. A play called *Die wunderbare Heurath Petruvio mit der bösen Catharine*, it is known from a program, was performed by the young students of the Zittau rector Christian Keinmann on March 7, 1658. The transmission of Sybant's translation to Germany is suggested by the production of a play called *Die tolle Hochzeit* in Dresden in 1663. A program from 1676 reveals that a play by the Görlitz rector Christian Funcke, *Der Wunderbahren Heyrath Petruvio mit der bosen Katharinen* was also performed by shoolboys. Bolte discussed all of these titles in "Der Widerspenstigen Zähmung als Görlitzer Schulkomodie (1678),"*Shakespeare Jahrbuch*, XXVII (1892), 124–129. The first printed German version of a play by Shakespeare which survives is *Kunst über alle Künste: Ein bös Weib gut zu machen* (1672) which was published by Reinhold Köhler in a parallel text edition (Berlin, 1864). *Kunst* derives both from Shakespeare and, probably, from the earlier German derivatives of *The Shrew*. Christian Weise's *Komödie von der bösen Catherine* (1705) is a free version based on the earlier Geman plays with the addition of the motifs of rocking the wife in a cradle and having her beaten on the soles of her feet. Bolte (*Jahrbuch* [1892], 128) suggested the following scheme for the relationship of all of these plays:

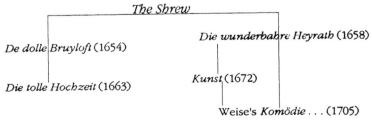

Table I: The Versions of The Tale

Köhler thought (*Kunst*, pp. xvi–xvii and note) that Weise borrowed the cradle episode from *Cunae*, a comedy in Latin by the Harlem schoolmaster Cornelius Shonaeus (d. 1611); from *Cunae*, as Köhler demonstrated, this motif can be traced back to older jest collections, of which he gave a French and an Austrian example.

2. This version was first pointed out by Samuel Johnson in the notes to his edition of Shakespeare; he regarded it merely as a retelling of *The Shrew*. I quote his note from Johnson and Steevens edition (4th ed.: London, 1793), VI: 565–567, where *The Tatler* story was reprinted: "It cannot but seem strange that Shakespeare should be so little known to the author of *The Tatler* that he should suffer this story to be obtruded upon him; or so little known to the publick, that he could hope to make it pass upon his readers as a real narrative of a transaction in Lincolnshire; yet it is apparent, that he knew not himself whence the story was taken, or hoped that he might rob so obscure a writer without detection." (I was able to see an original of *The Tatler* for September 30, 1710 in the Lilly collection at Indiana University.) Dr. Johnson's opinion persisted, and the version from *The Tatler* has been ignored. The following traits from this version, however, are not in Shakespeare but are found in folktales: The Shrew is the youngest of four daughters; the bridegroom is followed by a dog and he carries a gun; his horse stumbles and he shoots it and forces his wife to carry the saddle home; he also shoots the dog; when the wives are called, they had been playing cards. Further discussion of this important version will be found in Chapter IV.

3. *Conde Lucanor* XXXV has had wide circulation in textbooks for teaching Spanish and in anthologies of various sorts. Commonly some general statement has been appended to these reprintings to the effect that the story was used by Shakespeare in *The Shrew*. It is difficult to judge what influence, if any, these printed appearances might have had on oral traditions in different countries. Three recent American printings of the story are in Milton Rugoff, ed., *A Harvest of World Folk Tales*, (New York, 1949), pp. 712–716; Harriet de Onis, ed., *Spanish Stories and Tales*, Pocket Library PL-40 (New York, 1956), pp. 142–146; and Angel Flores, ed., *Spanish Stories/Cuentos Españoles*, Bantam Dual-Language Book, S1994 (New York, 1960), pp. 2–11. *Conde Lucanor* XXVII (RS Lit 2), although not about a tamed shrew, is included here because it contains the important element of the husband's deliberately making absurd statements with which the wife agrees; this is combined with Type 901 in *The Shrew* as well as in a number of folktales. The fact that two modern Spanish tales are among these combined versions lends support to believing that such a form of the tale was current in Manuel's time, but this possibility is not insisted upon by the mere

inclusion of both of his stories here. The latter tale, to my knowledge, has had no printed circulation comparable to the former.

4. Casona's farce, though agreeing in all basic traits with *Conde Lucanor* XXXV, has been included as a separate version because it gave the old Spanish tale new currency in a new genre. Furthermore, his manner of rendering certain elements of the tale into drama is interesting to compare with Shakespeare's techniques in *The Shrew*.

5. The play's title page, reproduced by Seelmann, contains a woodcut showing a man and woman holding something between them (perhaps a pair of breeches) and with their other hands beating each other with clubs.

6. The print to which this text is appended shows a rather well-dressed couple standing on a checker-patterned courtyard with trees, houses, and sky in the background. The back of the woman's blouse is torn open, and a cat is perched on her bare and scratched back. The man is on a backswing with his three-tailed whip. The whole scene has very much the appearance of a stage setting.

7. Several miscellaneous literary taming tales which do not seem to be closely related to the folktales here examined may be briefly noted. The battle between husband and wife over the wearing of the breeches, which occurs in Straparola (RI Lit 1) and in a sixteenth-century Dutch version of Type 1370 (GNe Lit 1), and which is represented as trait IVD5 in Table II, can be found in several other printed sources that are not otherwise related to the Taming of the Shrew. The fabliaux *De Sire Haine et de Dame Anieuse* tells of a tailor who proposes the fight to his wife when she angers him; the text is given in Le Grand d'Aussy (see RF Lit 2), II, 323–329. Franco Sacchetti made the incident the subject of number 138 of his *Novelle* (ca. 1388); it is contained in *Raccolta de' Novellieri Italiani*, XXI (Milano, 1815), 327–239. Hans Sachs' Shrovetide play *Der böse Rauch* (1551) is about a husband unsuccessful in a fight over the breeches (see the F. von Jäger ed. [Nürnberg, 1908], pp. 233–245). Finally, I have noted "How Eulenspiegel Wore the Breeches" as Chapter XXII of *The German Rogue* (1720) described by Friedrich W. D. Brie in *Eulenspiegel in England* (Berlin, 1903), p. 120. Expressions about "wearing the pants in the family" crop up frequently in many of the versions of The Taming of the Shrew, but have not been studied here.

Boccaccio's tale nine of the ninth day belongs to an apparently chiefly literary cycle of taming stories which deserves separate investigation. Here a man learns from seeing a muleteer beating his mule so it will cross a bridge that he ought to beat his wife to make her behave. Parallels for this tale are provided by A. C. Lee, *The Decameron, its Sources and Analogues* (London, 1909), pp. 289–291.

Table I: The Versions of The Tale 71

An English play, one of many similar generalized taming farces that might be mentioned—*Tom Tyler and his Wife* (1661)—again has the shrew tamed with a beating. Here, however, a friend has dressed in the husband's clothes to tame the wife, and when the woman learns of the trick, she becomes as bad as before, though eventually they make peace with one another. The play is edited in John S. Farmer, *Six Anonymous Plays, Second Series* (London, 1906), pp. 289–321.

Immediately following the text labeled here as GE Lit 9, in *The Muse in Good Humour* (1785), is a rhymed tale, "A New Receipt to Tame a Shrew" (pp. 101–105), which commences, "Shakespear's receipt to tame a shrew/ May sometimes, but won't always do." The method here is for the husband to "withhold something she must have," namely (though it is *not* named), himself; the wife, named Kate, soon becomes tractable.

Crabbe's poetic tale "The Wager" is another minor literary effort inspired by Shakespeare, and quotations from *The Taming of Shrew* adorn its title page (see *The Poetical Works of the Rev. George Crabbe*, V [London, 1834], 183–196). Two friends wager on which of them can stay in Newcastle away from his wife the longer; the loser's wife will not let him go in the first place. (There are, of course, many revisions, answers, continuations and reworking of Shakespeare's play in England and elsewhere. A study of these texts would be a problem in literary history beyond the scope of this study.)

The Low-German writer Fritz Reuter probably made use of an acquaintanceship with folktales in a story told by "Unkel Matthies" in "Woans ich tau'ne Fru kamm"—part of the first section of his *Olle Kammellen (Sämmtliche Werke*, IV [Wismar, 1890], 29–34). The taming method here is generally that of outdoing the wife in shrewishness—ruining her nice things and making light of these "accidents." The story ends with an unsuccessful attempt at repeating the device by another husband (see element VIIA2a in Table II) and the proverbial advice (paralleled in the folktales which end this way): "Vör de Hochtid möst du s' wen'n/Nah de Hochtid is't tau En'n."

8. Knut Liestøl suggested in *The Origin of the Icelandic Family Sagas* (Oslo, 1930), p. 169, that an incident in the *Svarfdaelasaga* could have been borrowed from Type 901; he referred to a summary of the incident in Sveinsson's *Verzeichnis*, pp. xx-xxi. The taming device—selling a woman as a slave—does not correspond to any versions considered here.

Dr. Bo Almqvist, who sent me a translation of GI 1, mentioned in a letter of June, 1960, that he heard another version of Type 901 told on the radio some months before during a program about Eyjafjöll, a district in southern Iceland. A copy of this text is not available.

9. This text, according to Prof. Dr. Reidar Th. Christiansen, who wrote me on January 2, 1960, was printed "in some kind of curiosity-bibliophile publication," but is a rarity in this form. I have found no reference to this printing.

10. I have secured a number of passive reports of the Taming of the Shrew in the United States from people who have heard or read the story but who do not themselves tell it to others. Some of these reports came to me as a result of correspondence with folklorists, but most were more or less direct results of samples of the story (GEAm 21) which I posted on two bulletin boards in an Indiana University dormitory housing thirty-five married couples for two months in the Fall of 1959. Versions GEAm 6, 9, and 22 were direct and immediate results of this technique; GEAm 21 itself, my sample tale, was from another student in the dormitory. A record of all these passive reports will serve further to document the vitality of the tradition, both orally and through mass communications, in the United States. Notes to versions GEAm 14, 15, 21, and 23 cite further such reports from informants.

James D. Studebaker, student, from Dayton, Ohio, heard the Taming of the Shrew told during a sermon about marriage delivered in the Church of the Brethern, North Manchester, Indiana. He also heard it, he believed, told in his home church. The tale, he recalled, had a western setting with the couple riding out to a homestead on a buckboard. Mr. Studebaker's wife, from Elkhart, Indiana, heard the story told in Bloomington at a Youth Fellowship meeting of the Church of the Brethern; here the married couple were riding home in a buggy. Mrs. Studebaker also remembered once witnessing a dramatic reading based on Shakespeare's play in which the heroine was asked to take off her clothes as a finale to the wager scene.

Robert Orth, student, from Evansville, Indiana believed he had heard the story told on television, he guessed by Groucho Marx. Ray Richardson, another student at Indiana University, commented, "Oh, this is an old story. I heard it a long time ago and hundreds of times since—possibly on TV or radio."

An anonymous informant told me that he had read the story in *Playboy* magazine about 1956.

Mrs. Marie Walter, who sent me version GEAm 3, wrote me on May 6, 1960, the following report of a classroom query, "Of the forty-five to fifty students in my two classes, no one had heard the story in true oral transmission, though many recognized it as a joke which various radio and TV comedians are passing off as their own material. One said someone on the Jack Paar show had told it in a New England dialect. A radio 'raconteur'—William B. Williams—was also mentioned as having used it. One girl said it was in her Spanish textbook."

Table I: The Versions of The Tale

Dr. Marie Campbell, who collected the fragment of the Taming of the Shrew listed below as GEAm 18, wrote me on December 6, 1959, that she believed she had collected two Negro versions, but that these were not transcribed and available yet.

Prof. Leonard Roberts, who supplied me with version GEAm 17, wrote on January 13, 1960, "about a year or two ago T. Ernie Ford told the 'That's once' version."

11. The informat gave the following account of the situation when he learned this text: "While I was in the Army, I heard what I thought was a funny story. It was a hot day and the officer in charge led us on a long hike. After walking about two miles, one of the men became so exhausted that he was forced to stop and sit down. Seeing this, the officer approached the soldier and told him the story."

12. Miss Brennan reported, "This joke was told by the main speaker at the School City of South Bend's orientation week program for teachers in the Fall of 1959."

13. At the time I posted my query in the Indiana University dormitory (see not 10 above) I did not realize that Mr. Randall had spontaneously told his version of the story only the night before during a bridge game in the lounge, not twenty feet from my own room. He wrote it out for me later.

14. The informant commented, "Right before I got married my father told me that if I wanted to have a successful marriage I should keep this story in mind."

15. Mrs. Shields collected her husband's version of the Taming of the Shrew as he told it to her shortly after their marriage, but she also had known it from her own mother and then, in 1960, heard the tale from an Indiana University acquaintance who had proudly proclaimed it as "a new joke."

16. The informant said that she learned the tale, probably, from her father, but she also recalled seeing it printed "two or three years ago in the Sunday *Courier-Journal* [Louisville, Ky.]."

17. Mr. Alger, a student, learned his version from an Economics professor who told it in class.

18. Mr. Manley had heard the story told several times, and remembered that the first time was in a sermon by a young Baptist minister in Topeka about 1951. He thought that the occasion might have been Father's Day and the message was to the effect that wives ought to obey their husbands. Mrs. Manley had heard her own father tell the story but had never repeated it or heard her husband tell it before I collected it from him.

19. Mr. Crabtree's mother learned this version from a female friend who came to their farm to help pick strawberries. Mrs. Crabtree found the version to be embarrassing, but did pass it on to her son.

20. Baughman in his note to this version (pp. 152–153) mentions that he heard a version of the story told in the spring of 1954 by a colleague at the University of New Mexico who had heard it on television the night before.

21. The text of MacLellan's version which I secured from the School of Scottish Studies does not contain the wager on the wives' obedience, but the collector, John Lorne Campbell, wrote me on October 12, 1960, that he had heard it from his informant told both ways and that the wager was part of the text to be published in *Stories from South Uist*. I have included the wager in my summary.

22. Mr. Seán Cronin, student of University College, Dublin, who prepared English summaries of all of the Irish versions for me, also sent me the following notes on the nature of the periodicals in which the Taming of the Shrew has appeared in Ireland: "*Ireland's Own*, a popular magazine, started 1902, still running. Contains reading matter mainly for rural readers—jokes, serial stories, poetry, competitions, etc. The matter is often repeated after a number of years, and the jokes recur monotonously often. This magazine had some matter in Irish occasionally. Present circulation 45,000. *Fáinne an lae*, a weekly journal of the Gaelic League, the Irish language revival movement. *An Claidhamh Solvis*, as above, at different periods. To my knowledge, neither of these is published at present. *Ar Aghidh*, a monthly journal, published in Galway in the Irish language. Linguistic and cultural. *An Lóchrann*, a monthly journal, published in either Cork or Tralee (Co. Kerry), at various times. Mainly cultural with much folklore. *An Sguab*, a literary journal in the Irish language, now extinct. *Irish Weekly Independent*, a weekly newspaper, with news of the week summarised. Had a column in the Irish language, which often contained folktales." Mr. Cronin also wrote that he felt sure that the Taming of the Shrew had been included in radio broadcasts of folktales, but he could cite no specific occurrences.

23. Jonas Balys, "Motif-Index of Lithuanian Narrative Folk-Lore," *Tautosakos Darbei*, II (Kaunas, 1936) lists eight versions of Type 901, eight of Type 1370 and four of 1370A which would be of interest to this study. However, my query to the Keeper of Collections at the Lithuanian Academy of Sciences in Vilnius has not been answered. Only three of the Lithuanian versions available to me from print are among those mentioned in Balys' index.

24. Dragomanov's paper was reprinted in *The Annals of the Ukrainian Academy of Arts and Sciences in the U.S.*, II (1952), 214–218.

25. Two suggested Spanish-American variants of the Taming of the Shrew were found after comparison with other texts not to belong to the group studied here. These versions are in Howard T. Wheeler, *Tales from Jalisco, Mexico*, Memoirs of the American Folklore Society, XXXV

Table I: The Versions of The Tale

(Philadelphia, 1943), 91–92; and Franz Boas, "Tales of Spanish Provenience from Zuñi," JAF, XXXV (1922), 74–76.

26. Adolf Schullerus, *Verzeichnis der rumanischen Märchen*, FFC 78 (1928) lists five versions of a Type 902 and five of Type 1370. I secured translations of most of these texts from the Institutul de Folclor in Bucharest, but found that only the four versions included here belong to the Taming of the Shrew.

TABLE II
The Elements of the Tale

I. SPECIAL INTRODUCTIONS

A. *The scene of the story (when remote from the storyteller)*

A1. France
   GS 2, GD 1.
A2. Italy
   GEAm 13.
A3. The Ozarks
   GEAm 5, 12 ("hills of Arkansas").
A4. Two hundred years ago
   GEAm 7.
A5. America
   CI 140.
A6. Russia
   FF 21.
A7. Vermont
   GEAm 29.

B. *The setting for the story's being told*

   B1. *Person explains secret of his long and happy marriage*
   GEAm 2, 4, 5, 15, 19, 24, 25, 29, CI 140, RSAm 2, (Per 1).
   B2. *A man advises another how to tame a shrew*
   GE Lit 9, GS 5, CI 86, (SP 1), Gre4.
   B3. *A husband tells his shrewish wife the story to tame her*
   GEAm 8, (RFAm 4).
   B4. *Taming is a play within a play or a story within a story*
   GE Lit 1, 2, RS Lit 1–3, RI Lit 1.

C. *Introductions drawn from other Tale Types*

   C1. *"The Search for the Lost Husband" (Type 425)*
   CI 31.
   C2. *"Open Sesame" (Type 767—the borrowed measure, Motif N478.)*
   SRW 3.
   C3. *"King Thrushbeard" (Type 900)*
   GS 4.
   C4. *"Wise Through Experience, The Precepts" (Type 910A)*
   GD 21, (SR10).
   C5. *"The Slovenly Fiancée" (Type 1453*)*
   FF 6, (FH4).
   C6. *"The Unwilling Suitor Advised from the Tree" (Type 1461*)*
   GG 10.

D. *Miscellaneous Introductions*

   D1. *Suitor comes, meets henpecked father of Shrew outside working*
   (RF Lit 1), GNe 1, CS 1, 3, SY (2),4, 5, 10, 12.
   D2. *Husband kills his first wife (then tames second)*
   FE 25.
   D3. *Hero inherits poor things (rooster, cat, pig, old horse), kills them to tame wife.*
   FF 9.
   D4. *A father tames his son*
   RF Lit 2.

Table II–The Elements of the Tale 79

  D5. *Wife spoils dinner and lies to her husband—blames the cat*
  /SR Lit 2, 3/.
  D6. *Man and woman each marry for a second time; each has 6 children from first marriage. New father lectures the children and tames the wife*
  RFAm 4.

II. THE MAJOR ACTORS

A. *The Shrew*

  A1. *Her position in the family (when specified)*
  1a. *One of seven daughters*
   CI 14.
    ai. *The oldest*
     CI 93, 94.
    aii. *The youngest*
     CI 104, 112, 129.
  1b. *One of six daughters*
   bi. *The oldest*
    CI 62.
   bii. *The youngest*
    CI 130.
  1c. *One of five daughters*
   ci. *The oldest*
    CI 132.
   cii. *The youngest*
    FF 17.
  1d. *One of four daughters*
   CI 1, SRW 3.
    di. *The oldest*
     CI 76.
    dii. *The youngest*
     GE Lit 3, CI 50, FE 20.
  1e. *One of three daughters*
   GS 1, CS 2, 4, CI 2, 6, 8–10, 16, 22, 25, 28, 30, 33, 34, 41, 43, 49, 53, 57, 59, 63, 65–67, 69, 70, 75, 77–79, 82–84, 96, 105–

109, 111, 113, 117, 118, 121–123, 133, 137, 139, FF 10, 13, 24, BLi 4, 5 SR4, RFAm 1–3, RR 4.

   ei. The oldest
GE Lit 1, GS 7, GSF 2, GD 2, 9, 10, 14, 15, 17, 18, 20, CI 29, 36, 37, 39, 42, 47, 48, 51, 52, 54–56, 58, 60, 61, 68, 72–74, 80, 85, 87–92, 95, 98, 99, 101–103, 110, 114–116, 119, 120, 125, 131, 136, FF 20, SR3.

   eii. The youngest
RS Lit 2, GI 1, GN 1, GS 2, 3, 8, GSF 1, 5, GD 3–7, 11, 6, 21, GG 6, 9, GEAm 18, CI 3, 4, 7, 11, 12, 15, 17, 20, 21, 23, 24, 26, 27, 31, 32, 34, 45, 46, 64, 71, 97, 100, 126, 135, FF 1, 40, 42, FE 2, 3, 3, BLi 8, SRW 1, 2, 5, 8, RFAm 5.

1f. One of two daughters
RI Lit 1, Gre 1.

   fi. The older
GE Lit 2, /GE Lit 4/.

1g. An only child
GG Lit 1, 2, RF Lit 1, RS Lit 1, 3, /GG Lit 3, 4, SR Lit 1/, GS 4, 6, GD 19, GG 1, 2, 8, 11–14, GNe 1, CS 1 3, CI 13, 18, 81, 124, FF 2, 4–6, 8, 12, 14, 15, 18, 19, 21, 22, 26, 31, 32, 34, 35, 39, 3, FE 4, 8, 14, 15, 26, 27, FH 1, 4, BLi 1, 7, SP 2, SRUk 1, 2, 5, SR 1, 2, 6, 7, 9–12, SY 1–6, 8–10, 12–15, 17,18, 20, RP 1, 2, RSAm 1, RR 1, Gre 5, Per 1, Ind 1, 2.

1h. She is a widow
RF Lit 3, GD 1, 8, 12, 13, GG 3–5, 7, FE 1, 5, 12, 17, RF 1, RS 3–5.

1j. Youngest daughter (total not stated)
GEAm 10, FE 6.

1k. She is a servant on a farm
GD 13, GG 3–5.

A2. Her character (shrewishness understood for all heroines)

   2a. She is lazy (Motif W111)
/GG Lit 3, RS Lit 4, SR Lit 1/, GS 6, GSF 3, 4, GD 19, GG 8, GEAm 18, CS 2, CI 1–5, 8, 13, 14, 30, 57, 59, 65, 69, 72, 82, 83, 85, 114, 118, 124, 125, 133–135, 139, FF 2, 8, 22, 25, FE 3, 4, 8, 15, 16, 18, 19, 21, 25–27, FH 1–3, SP 1, 2, SRW 1, 2, SRUk 5, SR 11,12, SY 1, 4, 6,12–14, 17, RFAm 5, RP 1, RS1, 6, RR 3, 4, Gre 3, 5.

Table II—The Elements of the Tale

    ai. So lazy she must be dressed
        CI 7, 38.
    aii. So lazy she eats and drinks in bed
        GG 10, CS 4.
    aiii. So lazy she will not wash herself
        CI 12.
    aiv. So lazy she will not move away from the hearth when she is too warm
        RR 1.
  2b. *She is industrious*
    GEAm 20, CI 89.
  2c. *She has demands for her future husband*
    ci. Certain punishments]
        Ind 2.
  2d. *Other elements*
    di. She was put on an island by her father in an attempt to cure her
        CI 31.
    dii. She is an ash-sitter (Motif L131.1.)
        CI 30, Bli 6, RR 1.
    diii. She bears a nickname referring to her temperament
        /GG Lit 7/, GD 2, 4, 9, GG 10, CI 37, FE 26.

B. *The husband (when his status is specified)*

  B1. *A farmer or peasant*
    /GG Lit 3/, GS 5, GSF 4, GD 13, 19, GG 6, 8, 13, GEAm 9, 17, 21, 28–31, CS 1, CI 1, 13, 25, 32, 50, 53–57, 60, 61, 68, 72, 74, 78, 79, 82–82, 87, 88, 98–100, 103, 106–108, 116, 117, 121, 124, 130 132–137, 140, FF 2, FE 28, FH 4, SR 2, 8, 11, RFAm 1–3, 5.
  B2. *A soldier*
    RF Lit 3, RI Lit 1, FF 1, 4, 5,12–14, 35, 37, 38, 40, 42, (Per 1).
  B3. *A knight or minor nobility*
    GG Lit 1, 2 RF Lit 1, /GG Lit 8/, GSF 1, GD 2, 12, GG 12, CI 6, 51, 101, FE 1.
  B4. *A huntsman or gamekeeper*
    /GG Lit 7, 9/, GD 16.

4a. A forester
  GD 18.
B5. A horse or cattle dealer
  /GG Lit 4/, GD 10, 11, 21, GNe 1.
  5a. Stockdealer as matchmaker
    CI 89, 109.
B6. A prince
  (GEAm 18), CI 29, 47, 73, 110, FF 39.
B7. A coachman
  GG 1, 3.
  7a. A servant
    GG 4, 5, 7.
B8. A poor widow's son
  CS 4, CI 9, 10, 89, 90, 118, FE 23, SRUk 5, SR 12.
  8a. A poor widower's son
    CI 125, FF 9.
B9. A shepherd
  SR 4, RS 1, RR 1.
B10. A shoemaker
  BLi 4.
B11. A Spaniard
  GS 2.
B12. A Quaker
  GEAm 15.
B13. Three brothers marry three sisters
  GI 1, GSF 5, CI 33.
B14. A tanner
  /GNe Lit 1/.
B15. A joiner
  CS 3.
B16. A working man
  CI 16.
B17. A "gentlemen" or other general designation of high status and/or wealth.
  GE Lit 1, 2, 3 RS Lit 1, 2, 3, GG 11, CS 2, CI 7, 17, 26, 38, 41, 65–67, 69, 70, 76, 77, FF 8, 21, 32, FE 2, 22, FH 4, RS 3, RR 4, Gre 1.

Table II–The Elements of the Tale 83

C. *The parents of the Shrew*

C1. *Her father*

1a. A wealthy man (often a farmer or a merchant)
GG Lit 2, GE Lit 1, 2, RS Lit 1, 3, /GE Lit 4, 5/, GI 1, GN 1, GS 3, 6, 7, GD 3, 4, 18, GG 11, 12,(13), CI 9, 23, 26, 28, 56, 59, 67, 71, 81–83, 87, 124, 130, 133, FF 2, 4, 6, 8, 18, 21, 31, 32, 44, FE 3, FH 1, 2, SRW 1–3, SRUk 5, SR 1, 3, 12, SY 18, Ind 2.

1b. A poor man
GG Lit 3, /(SR Lit 1)/, CS 4, FH 4.

1c. A churchman
GSF 1, 2, GG 14, FF 14, 41, SR 7.

1d. A king
GS 4, CI 6, 16, 29, 47, 77, 101, 110, FF 5, 12, RFAm 1–3, Gre5.

1e. The Czar
FF 42.

1f. A knight or nobleman
GG Lit 1, 3, RF Lit 1, RS Lit 2, /GG Lit 4/, GS 2, GG 2, 9, CI 51, 52, 58.

1g. A governor
FF 35, (Per 1).

1k. No father, but instead the master of farm on which the Shrew is a servant
GD 13, GG 3–5.

C2. *Her mother (when described as a shrew herself)*

2a. Instructs her daughter to be shrewish
GG Lit 1, RF Lit 1, RS Lit 3, /GG Lit 5, 6, GNe Lit 2/, GG 2, GNe 1, FE 6,10.

  ai. Tells her always to say "No" to her husband
  FE 7.

  aii. Gives daughter a bundle of sticks with which to beat her husband
  CS 3.

  aiii. Sisters instruct the Shrew to act badly
  FE 2,6.

2b. Must be asked the opposite of what her husband wants
RF Lit 1, CS 1, 3,(4), (FE 28), SY 5, 6, 9, 10, 12, 13, 15, 20.

2c. *Has belled her husband to be sure that he works*
SY 2, 5, 9, 10.

III. THE ENGAGEMENT AND MARRIAGE OF THE SHREW

A. *Factors discouraging the marriage*

A1. Shrew's father posts a warning for possible suitors
GD 16, RSAm 1.

A2. Shrew's father personally warns suitors
GE Lit 2, GG Lit 1, RS Lit 1, 3, /GG Lit 4, GE Lit 4/, GN 1, GS 1–3, 6–7, GSF 4, GD 2, 3, 6, 10, 11, 14–17, 20, GG 1, 2, 9, 11, 12, 14, GEAm 7, 10, 18, CS 1–3, CI 1, 4, 7, 13, 17, 25, 37, 39, 45, 53, 54, 57, 62–67, 68–71, 79, 81, 91, 93, 94, 98, 112, 113, 126, 129, 130, 135, 136, FF 2, 5,(6), 8–10, 12, 18, 21, 22, 26, 32, 35, 39, 40, FE 4, 8, 15, 23, (FH 1), BLi 4, 5, 7, 8, SRW 1, SRUk 1, 2, SR 3, 7,(8), 10,11, RFAm 1–3, 5, RP 1, 2.

2a. Shrew's mother warns suitor
/SR Lit1/, GD 19, CI 62, 69, 70, 135, FF 15, 19, 40, FE 15, 25, 26, BLi 1, 6, 7.

2b. The girl herself warns suitor
FE 27, BLi 5, SR 6.

A3. Suitor's father or mother warns him
RS Lit 1,3, CI 88, 92, 118, FF 18, SR 9.

A4. Friends of suitor warn him
GE Lit 2, GD 1, 2, GG 7, 13, CI 11, 20,(23), 86, 118, FF 7, Fe 1, 9, 12, 17, SR 2, 2, RS 1, 3–5, Gre 1.

A5. Husbands of Shrew's sisters warn him
FF 17.

A6. Warning against the future mother-in-law, who is a shrew
GG 13.

A7. Suitor visits Shrew in disguise and observes her behavior
(GD 21), FF 32.

A8. Father insists that Shrew be married first or at the same time as her sister(s)
Ge Lit 1, 2, RFAm 1–3.

8a. Custom—eldest marries first
GD 10, 11.

Table II—The Elements of the Tale

A10. *Suitor overhears bride's mother or sisters advising her to rule her husband*
GNe 1, FE 2, 6.

A11. *The Shrew's greater wealth and/or higher social standing than her husband's gives her a prerogative to rule him*
RS Lit 1, 3, /GG Lit 3, 4, 7, 9, GE Lit 5/ GD 13, GG 1, CI 9–11, 13, 16, 25, 28, 32, 50, 56, 57, 59–61, 74, 82–84, 87, 90, 98, 107, 116, 118, 124, 125, 130, 133, 134, FF 2, 12, 42, FE 23, FH 1, 2, SRW 2, 3, SRUk 5, SR 3, 4, 12, RFAm 1–3, RR 3, Per 1, Ind 2.

B. Factors encouraging the marriage

B1. *Father offers a large dowry*
GE Lit 1, 2, RF Lit 1, /GE Lit 4/, GS 1, GD 15, CI 3, 6, 11, 13, 15, 17, 18, 27–29, 34, 39, 52, 56, 57, 59, 61, 72, 82, 87, 89, 90, 91, 99, 100, 106, 107, 110, 115, 118, 119, 123, 131, 133, 139, FF 2, BLi 4, 5, SR 4, 9.

B2. *Father offers a farm or other lands or a prize as dowry*
GD 13, GG 1, 3–5, CI 21, 77, 100, SR 8, RFAm 3.

B3. *Father offers his daughter's weight in gold as dowry*
CI 8–10, 16.

B4. *Large dowry or inheritance expected by suitor from wealthy father*
RS Lit 1,3, GI 1, GN 1, GG 13, CI 51, FE 23.

C. The suitor's claims for his taming ability or his work-free household

C1. *He says that he can tame a shrew*
GE Lit 1, 2, /GG Lit 3, 4,/ GS 3, GD 1, GG 9, 13, CI 36, 98, 99, FF 7, 9, 35, FE 9, 26, BLi 6, SR 2, RS 1, 3.

C2. *He lays a bet that he can tame the Shrew*
CI 67, (83), RS 5.

2a. *Bets he can tame her in one day*
CI 127.

C3. *He promises to tame her without beating her*
GS 6, GG 8, 14, CI 45, 56, 64, 66, 71,(80), 85, 87, 135, FF 5, 10, FH 1, 2, SRW 1, RFAm 5.

> *3a. Says he can tame her without saying one word*
> FF 8.
> *C4. He is to have no dowry until she is tamed*
> CI 73,(77).
>> *4a. Horse, hound and (sometimes) gun as dowry*
>> RF Lit 1, CI 47, 73.
>> *4b. Horse and carriage as dowry*
>> FF 12.
> *C5. He has something at home to do all of the work*
> BLi 4, (RR 3).
>> *5a. A cat*
>> /SR Lit 1/, GSF 4, FE 4, 8, 18, 27, BLi 7, SRUk 1, 2, SR 6.

D. Demonstrations of the suitor's ability in taming (often used as an introduction)

> *D1. He succeeds in plowing with an unmatched team*
> GD 19, SRUk 5.
>> *1a. Plows with a lazy ox*
>> Gre 5.
> *D2. Induces a stubborn animal to work by leading it with food*
> CI 12, 13, 20, 32, 39, 50, 59–61, 72, 74, 78, 82–84, 91, 98, 107, 132, 134, SRW 1, RFAm 2, 3.
> *D3. Breaks an unruly horse*
> CI 11, 25.
> *D4. As a test he tames an unruly horse for the Shrew's father*
> (CI 121), SRW 1.
> *D5. He advises the Shrew's father how to tame a stubborn horse*
> CI 17, 36.
> *D6. His servants work at top speed and obey him without question*
> GD 21, FE 1.

E. The wedding

> *E1. The groom's arrival*
>> *1a. Arrives late*
>> Ge Lit 1, 2, GS 7, GD 2, 4–7, 9–11, 14, 18, GG 6.

Table II—The Elements of the Tale

    1b. Dressed poorly
    GE Lit 1, 2, (GD 3, 7), (GG 6), (CI 32), RFAm 1, 2.
    1c. On horseback
    GI 1, GS 7, GD 2, 6, 9–11, 14, 16, 18, GEAm 10, 16, (CS 3), CI 14, 16, 43, 59, 68, 98, 103, 117, 121.
        ci. Rides an old nag or a sick horse
        GG Lit 1, GE Lit 2,(3), GD 4, 5, 20, GG 6, GEAm 20, CI 13, 25, 28,(32), 34, (38), 60, 77,(102), 114,(125), 136,(139), RFAm 1.
        cii. Rides a fine horse
        GD 15, CI 33, 56, 69, 70.
    1d. In a horse-drawn conveyance which is pulled by an old nag (or nags)
    CI 54, (FD 13), SR 1, 12, RFAm 2, 3.
    1e. Followed by a dog
    GG Lit 1, (GE Lit 3), GS 3, 7, GD 4, 5, 7, 9–11, 14, 15, 18, GG 2, 6, (GNe 1)m GEAm 10, (CS 3), CI 13, 16, 25, 28,(32), 43, 56, 59, 60, 68, 98,(102), 103, 114, 117, 136.
        ei. A blind dog
        CI 77,(139).
        eii. More than one dog
        CI 14, 15, 121.
    1f. Carries a gun (or guns)
    GE Lit 3, GD 4, 5, 7, GG 6, GEAm 10, CI 13, 14, 25, 28, 54, 56, 59, 60, 98, (102), 103, 114, 117, 121, 136,(139).
    1g. Has a bird
        gi. Falcon
        GG Lit 1, CI 16.
        gii. Raven
        GG 2.
E2. The groom's behavior
    2a. Boorish behavior at wedding
    GE Lit 2.
    2b. Refuses to stay for a celebration
    GE Lit 1, 2, RF Lit 1, GS 1, GD 1, 2, 4, 6, 7, 9–12, 15, 18, GG 6.
    2c. Refuses to stay overnight before beginning long trip home
    GD 16.

E3. *The married couple's departure*
   3a. *They ride horses*
      Ge Lit 1, 2, GI 1, GS 1, 2,4, 8, GSF 1, 2, GD 1, 8, 12, 20, GEAm 24, CI 30, 39, 51, 118, 140, FE 1, RF 1.
   3b. *Both ride on one horse*
      GG Lit 1, GE Lit (2, 3), RF Lit 1, GS 3, 7, GD 2–7, 9–11, 15–17, GG 2, 6, GEAm 7, 10, 13, 16, 17, 20, 25, CS 3, CI 8, 16, 22, 32, 34, 36, 37, 46–49, 50, 80, 82, 83, 88, 98, 103, 106, 111, 117, 120, 123, RS 3, RSAm 2.
   3c. *Ride in a horse-drawn conveyance*
      GD 19, GEAm 1, 2, 4,(6), 9, 12, 15, 19, 21, 22, 27, 28, 29, 31, CI 18, 54, FF 5, 12, 17, 44, FE 13,(17), SR 1, 2, 12, RFAm 1–3.
   3d. *Husband rides and wife walks*
      GD 14, 18, SY 15.
E0. *Trait is absent or unspecified*
   GG Lit 2, RF Lit 2, 3, RS Lit 1–3, RI Lit 1, /GG Lit 3–9, GNe Lit 1, 2, GE Lit 4, 5, RF Lit 3A, RS Lit 4, SR Lit 1–3/, GE Lit 6–9, RF Lit 4–5, RS Lit 5, GI 2, GN 1, GS 5, 6, GSF 3–5, GD 13, 21, GG 1, 3–5, 7–14, GNe 1, GEAm 3, 5, 6, 8, 11, 14, 18, 23, 26, 30, 32, CS 1, 2, 4, CI 1–7, 9–12, 17, 19–21, 23, 24, 26, 27, 29, 31, 34, 41, 42, 44, 45, 52, 53, 55, 57, 58, 61–67, 71–76, 78, 79, 81, 84–87, 89–97, 99–101, 104, 105 107–110 112, 113, 115, 116, 119, 122, 124, 126–135, 137, 138, FF 1–4, 6–11, 13–16, 18–31, 33–43, 45, FE 2–12, 14–16, 18–28, FH 1–4, BLi 1–8, SP 1, 2, SRW 1–3, SRUk 1–5, SR 3–11, SY 1–14, 16–20, RFAm 4, 5, RP 1, 2, RS 1, 2, 4–6, RSAm 1, RR 1–4, Gre 1–5, Per 1, Ind 1, 2.

IV. THE TAMING OF THE SHREW

A. *When the taming occurs*

   A1. *On the way to the wedding*
      CI 13, FF 32, FE 5, 17, 22, SR 1, 12, SY 3.
   A2. *Between the church and the wedding celebration*
      GD 8, FF 13, 44.
   A3. *At the wedding celebration*
      CI 28,(137).

Table II–The Elements of the Tale

A4. On the trip home after the wedding
GG Lit 1, GE Lit 2, 3, RF Lit 1, GI 1, GS 1–4, 7, 8, GSF 1, 2, GD 1–7, 9–12, 14–21, GG 2, 6, GEAm 1, 2, 4, 7, 9, 10, 12, 13, 16, 17, 19–22, 24, 25,(26), 27, 28, (29), 31,(34), CS 3, CI 2, 3, 6–8, 10–18, 20, 22, 25, 30, 32–34, 36–39, 41, 43, 44, 46–51, 54, 56, 57, 59, 60, 68–70, 73, 76–78, 80, 82, 83, 87–92, 96–99, 102, 103, 105, 106, 109, 111, 113–118, 120–123, 125, 132, 136, 139, 140, FF 5, 12, 17, FE 1, 13, SR 2, SY 15, RF 1, RFAm 1–3, RS 3, RSAm 2, Ind 1.

A5. At the couple's home
GE Lit 1, 2, RS Lit 1, 3, RI Lit 1, /GG Lit 3–9, GNe Lit 1, 2, GE Lit 4, 5, RF Lit 3A, RS Lit4/, SR Lit 1–3, GE Lit 6–9, RF Lit 4, RS Lit 5, GN 1, GS 5, 6, GSF 3–5, GD 13, 9, GG 3–5, 7, 10–12, 14, GEAm 5, 8, 11, 18, 23, CS 2, 4, CI 1, 2, 4, 9,(10) 23, 52, 53, 58, 61, 79, 81, 93 94, 104, 107, 108, 112, 124–126, 129, 130, FF 2, 4, 6–10, 12, 15–17, 19, 20, 22–26, 31,(32), 33–36, 38–40, 42–44, FE 4, 6, 8–10, 14–16, 18–20, 22–28, FH 1–3, BLi 1–8, SP 1, 2, SRW 1–3, SRUk 1, 2, 4, 5, SR 3–6, 7–11, SY 1, 2, 4, 6–14, 17, 18, RFAm 1–3, 5, RP 1, 2, RS 1, 2, 6, RR 1–4, Gre 1–5.

   5a. Inspecting husband's lands
      GG 13, CI 42, 110 131, RS 4,5.

A6. On a trip to visit the wife's parents
(GN 1), (GG 9), Gne 1, CI 29, 101, FF 1, 7–11, 15, 16, 19–21, 24–26, 30, 31, 34, 39, 41, 43, 45, FE 2, 3, 6, 9, 10, 14, 20, 21, BLi 1, 4, 5, 8, SRW 2, 3, SRUk 3, SR 3, 7, 8, 10, RP 2.

   6a. While visiting wife's parents
      CS 1, 4, (BLi 4), (Per 1, Ind 2).

   6b. On a trip to visit the husband's parents and during this visit
      FE 7, RSAm 1.

A7. After a visit to the wife's parents
GG 9, CI 27, 84, FE (12).

A8. On a hunting trip
GG Lit 2, CI 35, 45, 55, 64, 65, 71, 72, 75, 134, 135, 138.

A9. On a shopping trip
GEAm 3.

A10. On a date
GEAm 14.

A11. On the way to church
GI 2, GSF 5, (FF 18), FE (2), 11.

A12. Simply "on a trip" or "out driving"
GG 1, GEAm 6, 30, CI 19, 26, 55 61–63, 66, 67, 72, 74, 85, 86, 100, 119, 127, 128, 133, 135, FF 3, 4, BLi 2, 3, SY 16, RFAm 4.
A13. Unspecified
CI 5, 21, 24, 95, FF 14, 27–29 37.

B. *Husband kills or tortures recalcitrant animal(s)*

B1. Horse, burro, mule, or donkey (Motif T251.2.3)
RF Lit 3, GS 4, GD 8, CI 40, FF 13, 14, 27, 28, SY 16.
1a. Animal ignores a command
GG Lit 1, CI 3, 21, 122.
ai. To come
GD 7, GG 6, 9, CI 45, 64.
aii. To start going
GEAm 5, FF 15–17, 19, 21, 24, 26, 34, 41, BLi 2, SR 2.
aiii. To move faster
GG 2, CI 22, 63, 78, 113, FF 22, 25, 30, 32, 43, 45, FE 3, 20, 21, BLi 4, 5, SY 3, RSAm 1.
aiv. To jump a fence, wall, gate, or hedge
CI 2, 11, 13, 25–29,(30), 32–35, 37, 39, 31, 42, 46, 48–50, 52, 55–57, 63, 66, 71, 74–76, 85–87, 90, 91, 95, 98–100,(two horses), 102, 105, 107, 108, 110, 115, 116, 119–121, 125, 127, 131–136, FE 1, RFAm 1–4.
av. To turn a corner
FE 6.
avi. To cross a marsh, stream, river, bridge, etc.
GS 7, GEAm 6, 16, CS 3, CI 6–8, 10, 14, 16, 19, 43, 44, 47, 60, 69, 70, 73, 80, 89, 92(two horses), 103, 10 114, 117, 118, 123, FF 44, RF 1, RP 2.
avii. To enter a gate
CI 88.
aviii. To slow down
BLi 8.
aix. To move to the side of the road
FF 31.
ax. To halt
FF 12, FE 9, 22.

Table II—The Elements of the Tale

 axi. To stand still
  RF Lit 1, GG 11, CI 65, 68, 93, 94, 104, 112, 130, 137, 138, RS 3, 5.
 axii. To drink some water
  CI 59, 61, 72.
 axiii. To stop drinking water
  CI 36, 38, 51, 77.
 axiv. Not to eat
  FE 2, RS 4.
 axv. To go away from the window of the house
  CI 81.
 axvi. To bring some water
  RS Lit 1, 3.
1b. Animal commits a displeasing action
 CI 101, 107, FF 29.
 bi. Stumbles or balks
  GG Lit 2, Ge Lit 3, RI Lit 1, GS 8, GSF 1, GD 1, 2, 9, 10, 12, 14, 15–18, 20, GG 13(two horses), GNe 1, GEAm 1, 2, 4, 6–10, 12–17, 19–21, 24–27, 28, 29 31, 32, CI 20, 111, FF 4, SR 10, SY 15, RSAm 2.
 bii. Throws rider(s)
  GE Lit 2, GEAm 20, 26, 32, CI 16, 82–84.
 biii. Splashes the rider(s)
  GS 1, 3, GD 3, 5, 6.
 biv. Gets itself stuck in bog etc.
  GE Lit 2, GI (1),2, CI (16, 17,(82–84), 96, 97, 106, 139, FE 14, BLi 3.
 bv. Falls
  GD 4, (GEAm 28), CI 54, 140, SR 12.
 bvi. Stops
  GEAm 3, 30, CI 18, 67, FF 3, 7–11, FE 7, 10–13, 17,(23), BLi 1, SRW 2, 3, SR 1, 7, 12.
 bvii. Pulls crookedly: riders tipped out
  FE 5.
 bviii. Drinks water or grazes
  GEAm 13, CI 87.
 bix. Neighs or brays
  GSF 5, SR 3, RSAm 1.
 bx. Breaks wind
  GEAm 22.

1c. Other taming devices involving a horse etc.
   ci. Weak horse driven to death
      FF 18.
   cii. Disobedient horse transformed to hare
      CI 30.
   ciii. Horse killed when wife disobeys
      (GN 1), GS 2, GSF 2, FF 1,5.
   civ. Servant obeys orders to drive horse through an obstruction
      GD 19.
   cv. Servant beaten when horse misbehaves
      GE Lit 2, (SR 2).
   cvii. Wife has hitched horse backwards; horse killed for not pulling forwards
      SRUk 3.
   cviii. Horse and wife hitched together; both beaten
      FE 25.
   cix. Husband causes wife's saddle girth to break; she must walk
      GI 1.
1d. Results of the horse's being killed
   di. Wife must carry the saddle
      GG Lit 2, GE Lit 3, GI 1, 2, GS 2,4 , GSF 1, 2, GD 1–6, 8, 12, 14–16, GG 2, GEAm 10, 16, 20, 25, CS 3, CI 7, 17, 19, 22, 32, 33, 35, 39, 44, 47, 49, 50, 59, 65, 66, 80, 82–84, 87, 89, 98, 103, 111, 132, 134–137, FF 10, 13,(38), FE 1, RF 1, RP 2, RS 4.
   di.* Husband carries saddle and sometimes wife also
      GD 10, 18, CI 20.
   dii. Wife must carry husband on her own back (Motif Q493.)
      GG Lit 1, (GE Lit 9), (GG 2), CI 6, SY 15.
   diii. Wife must carry wagon harnesses
      CI 61,72.
   div. Wife must pull buggy or sleigh
      GNe 1, CI 54, FF 3,(7), 8, 9, 11, 15, 16, 18–22, 24–26, 29–31, 34,(39), 41, 43, 45, FE 3, 7, 9, 10, 14, 20, 21,(23), BLi 1, 2,(3), 4, 5, 8, SRW 2, 3, SRUk 3, SR 1, 3, 7, 8, 10, 12, SY 16.

Table II—The Elements of the Tale

      div.* Husband pulls sleigh
        FF 17, FE 12.
      dv. Wife must carry baggage
        GEAm 3, 7, CI 16.
      dvi. Wife must skin the horse
        FE 14, 21.
      dvii. Wife must carry the dead horse's skin
        FF 5, RFAm 3.
      dviii. Wife must neigh like a horse
        FE 20.
      dix. Dog harnessed to pull load or made to carry saddle
        GD 4, FF 22, 24.
      dx. Bride is sent back to her parents for one day
        CI 92.
      dxi. Husband rides wife's horse; wife must walk
        GG 13, CI 66, (FF 1), FE 1.
      dxii. Wife put into stable or hitched to post after trip
        BLi 2, SRUk 3, SR 10.
      dxiii. Wife forced to walk home over rough ground; spoils her clothes
        CI 116.
B2. Dog killed
  RF Lit 3, FF 14, 27, 28, SY 16.
    2a. Dog ignores a command
      RF Lit 2, CI 3, 13, 21, 26, 43, 52, 60, 66, 68, 88, 119, 137.
      ai. To follow closely
        GG Lit 1, 2, GS 1, 8, GD 9, 11, 14, 16, 18, GG 9, GNe 1, RF 1.
      aii. To go where directed or come on call
        CI 25, 36, 42, 46, 62, 64, 71, 77, 113, 131, 138, FF 31, 32, 45, SRUk 3.
      aiii. To drag horse's severed head away
        FE 17.
      aiv. To eat horse's corpse
        FE 7,13.
      av. To pull horse's load or carry the saddle
        GD 4, FF 22, 24.
      avi. To jump up on horseback
        CI 65.

avii. To open a gate
GE Lit 3.
aviii. To retrieve a dropped glove or other object
GS 3, 7, GD 7, GG 6.
aix. To fetch a stick
CI 81.
ax. To retrieve game that was killed
GG 2, CI 59, 61, 72, 74.
axi. To catch a hare, fox, or squirrel
RF Lit 1, CI 6, 7, 27, 29,(30), 32, 55, 75, 77, 89, 91, 96, 97, 110, 122, 125, 132 (two dogs), 134–146, 139, FF 3.
axii. To herd sheep or cattle
CI 24, 57, 76, 95, 127.
axiii. To bring some water
RS Lit 1, 3.
axiv. To do housework
FF 6, 20, 24.
axv. To jump over a grave
FE 1.
axvi. To catch a cat
CI 133(two dogs).
axvii. To get out of the house
FF 8, 16, 26, 29.
2b. Dog commits a displeasing action
bi. Jumps up on a person
GD 1, 3, 10, 12, GG 11, CI 22, 99, FE 22.
bii. Chases after a hare
GD 2, GG 13, CS 3, CI 8, 10, 14–17, 28, 35, 38, 41, 44, 48, 50, 56, 67, 73 80, 98, 102, 103, 107, 109, 114, 115, 117, 121(two dogs), 132, SY 3.
biii. Gets into master's way
CI 18, 126, (kicked, but not killed in 93, 94, 112, 29,130).
biv. Must be carried when tired
GS 2, GSF 2.
bv. Loses scent of game
CI 138.
bvi. Trees falsely
GEAm 10.

Table II—The Elements of the Tale

      bvii. Begs at the table
        FF 25.
      bviii. Comes to eat unbidden
        Ind 2.
      bix. Bites husband
        GEAm 23.
      bx. Barks
        GSF 1, GD 15, CI 51, 54, FF 11, 12, 19, 39, 43, FE 9, 12, SY 15, Ind 1.
   2c. *Other taming devices involving a dog*
      ci. Disobedient dog transformed to stone
        CI 30.
      cii. Dog shot when wife disobeys
        FF 1.
      ciii. dog that wife admired is killed
        GD 8.
      civ. Dog killed and wife drops bundle of sticks brought for beating husband
        CS 3.
B3. *Cat killed*
  (CI 81), FF 27, 28, Gre 4, Per 1.
   3a. *For not moving on command*
      FF 16, 31, 32, BLi 4.
   3b. *For not doing housework*
      FF 6, 20, 23, SR 11.
   3c. *For not chasing mice*
      SY 8.
      (*ci. Cat catches rat on command*)
        Ind 1.
   3d. *For getting on the table*
      CI 52, FF 7, 15, BLi 3.
   3e. *For begging at the table*
      FF 10, 18, 25, FE 2, (Ind 2).
   3g. *For mewing*
      GSF 5, FF 9, FE 23, SR 10, Gre 2, Ind 2.
   3h. *For not bringing some water*
      RS Lit 1 3.
   3j. *For not leaving house*
      FF 29.

B4. *Bird killed*
   4a. *Cock or hen*
      SY 2.
         ai. *For getting on the table or bed*
            FF 8, BLi 3, 5, SR 4.
         aii. *For crowing*
            CI 93, 94, 104, 112, 129, 130, 137, FF 4, 9, 10, 12, 17–19, 34, 39, 43, FE 2, 6, 9, 10, 20, 23, BLi 5, SRW 3, SR 3, 10, SY 18, RSAm 1.
         aiii. *For getting in master's way*
            BLi 1, 4, 8.
         aiv. *For not doing housework*
            FF 6, 20.
         av. *For eating when commanded not to eat*
            SR 5.
         avi. *For not leaving house*
            FF 25.
   4b. *Falcon*
         bi. *For going after a bird (or trying to)*
            GG Lit 1, CI 16, 17.
         bii. *For not going after a bird on command*
            CI 7.
         biii. *For pecking at man's finger*
            GG Lit 2.
   4c. *Raven does not sing on command*
      GG 2.
   4d. *Parrot chatters*
      Ind 1.
B4. *Other animals killed*
   5a. *Pig*
      CI 21, 87, 95.
         ai. *Gets in master's way*
            CI 88, 99, BLi 1, 2, 4, 8.
         aii. *Is noisy*
            GSF 5, FF 9, BLi 5.
         aiii. *Several pigs annoy man, are killed.*
            FE 14.
         aiv. *Man breaks pig's leg for no apparent reason*
            SY 8.

Table II–The Elements of the Tale

    5b. *Cow or bull*
      GG 11, CI 24, 104, 112, 129, 130, 133, 137, FF 15, SR 4, SY 2.
        bi. Will not enter field on command
          CI 86, 93, 94, 126–128, 131.
        bii. Moos
          FF 34, FE 23, SY 18.
    5c. *Ox*
        ci. Bellows
          SR 3, SY 8.
        cii. Eats when commanded not to eat
          SR 5.
    5d. *Sheep*
        di. Bleats
          FE 20, SRW 3.
        dii. Eats when commanded not to eat
          SR 5.
        diii. Lamb torn apart for no apparent reason
          SR 7.
    5e. *Disobedient goat skinned alive*
      SY 11.
    5f. *Fly killed when buzzing around plate of food; food scattered*
      GEAm 11.
    5g. *Servants ordered to kill livestock which fails to come or wake up on command*
      RFAm 2.
  B6. *Analogous tamings involving objects*
    6a. *Lamp shot out when it does not extinguish on command*
      RP 2.
    6b. *Door split with ax when it does not open on command*
      RP 2.
  B7. *Generalized trait: gun is kept handy "to shoot disobedient people"*
      CI 58.

C. *Husband "punishes" animal or object; wife, however, suffers*

  C1. *Cat (Motif W 111.3.2.)*
    FF 23, FE 15, (BLi 7), (SR 11).
      1a. *Wife must hold disobedient cat while it is beaten*
          /GG Lit 4, SR Lit 1/, GN 1, GD 19, GG 8,10, SRUk 1, SY 7.
      1b. *Cat put on wife's back while it is beaten*
          /GG Lit 3, SR Lit 2, 3/, GSF 4, GG 14, FE 4, 8, 16, 18, 19, 24, 27, FH 1–3, SRW 2, SR 6.
      1c. *Disobedient cat drawn across wife's bare back*
          GS 5, GD 13, FF (1),36, RFAm 5.
      1d. *Wife is beaten with cat*
          SRUk 4.
      1e. *Cat in bag put on wife's back and beaten*
          SRUk 2.
  C2. *Animal hide put on wife's back and beaten*
    2a. *Horse hide*
        FF (14).
          ai. *Wrapped around wife after she is beaten*
              /GG Lit 5, 6, GNe Lit 1, 2, GE Lit 4/.
    2b. *Sheep hide*
        /GE Lit 5/, SY 12, RR 2 3, Gre 3.
    2c. *Cow or calf hide*
        /GG Lit 9/, GSF 3.
          ci. *Wrapped around wife after she is beaten*
              /GG Lit 7/.
    2d. *Ox hide*
        /GG Lit 8/, SY 17.
    2e. *Goat hide*
        FF 2.
    2f. *Hide is salted and/or peppered*
        /GG Lit 6–8, GNe Lit 1, 2, GE Lit 4/, FF 14.
    2g. *Wife rubbed with ashes after beating; then wrapped in hide*
        /GG Lit 5/.
  C3. *Bag on wife's back*
    SP 1.

Table II–The Elements of the Tale

    3a. Leather bag
        RS (1), 2, RR 1.
    3b. Bag full of shoes
        BLi 4.
    3c. Sandals leap out of bag to beat lazy wife (Motif D1401.7., Cf. Type 563)
        FE 26.
    3d. Knapsack
        SP 2.
    3e. Plowshare in bag
        RF Lit 3A.
C4. Basket on wife's back
    BLi 6.
C5. Stick, ax, or poker beaten on wife's back to punish it
    SY 6, 9, 10, 13, 14, (Gre 5).
C6. Picture of servant on wife's back
    /RS Lit 4/.

D. Other taming devices

    D1. Bogus surgery
        1a. Her "hot blood" must be let
            GE Lit 6–8.
        1b. Wife forced to get on table where she is cut, salted and peppered
            GG 12.
    D2. Husband breaks wife's arm and pays the doctor in advance for the next arm he will break
        RF Lit 4, GG 1, 7, CI 53, 79,124, RS 6.
    D3. Wife deprived of food or served bad food
        GG Lit 2, GE Lit 1, 2, 7, GG 12, CI 9, 10 77, FF 35, Ind 2.
        3a. "Who will not work, shall not eat" (Motif W111.3.4) [Sometimes only bad food is served]
            RS Lit 5, GS 6, GG 10, GEAm 18, CS 2, CI 1, 2, 4,(5), 7, 11, 13, 15, 17, 20, 22, 25, 30, 32, 38, 41, 48–51, 56, 57, 60, 61, 68, 71, 72, 74, 76, 78, 85, 91, 96–98, 102, 103, 116, 132, 134–137, 139, FE 26, BLi 7, SRUk 5, SY 1, 4, RP 1, RR 4.
        3b. Locked in room without food all day when she does not get up at husband's first call in the morning
            RFAm 1–3.

D4. *Wife rocked in a cradle*
/GG Lit 8/, FF 33, 35, 40, 42, SR 9.
D5. *Husband and wife fight over right to wear the breeches*
(RI Lit 1), /GNe Lit 1/.
D6. *Wife threatened with ax, gun, injury, etc.*
CI 12, 23, FF 37, 38, 44, SR 8.
    6a. *Ax and block thrown into room at husband's command*
FF 44, SR 8.
D7. *Wife beaten until she surrenders her will*
GE Lit 7, CS 1, 4, (CI 81), FF 44, SR 8,11.
    7a. *Stick or whip falls from ceiling at husband's command*
FF 44, SR 8.
    7b. *Bundle of sticks cut and kept ready to beat wife with*
GG 3–5, (CS 1).
D8. *Husband acts a tyrant's part*
    8a. *Throws food from the table*
GE Lit 1, 2, SY 11, Gre 1.
    8b. *Throws bedding to the floor*
GE Lit 2, SY 11.
    8c. *Mistreats his servants*
GE Lit 1, 2, RF Lit 1, GD 19, SY 11.
    8d. *Refuses to accept wife's new clothing*
GE Lit 1, 2.
    8e. *Pretends to get drunk on water*
SR 6, 7, 11.
D9. *Bride tamed wholly or partly by her mother-in-law*
CI 2, 4, 9, 10, 13, FE 15, BLi 7, SRUk 5, SY 1,4.
D10. *Wife put on anthill to be bitten*
SRW 1.
D11. *Stubborn wife pretends to be dead and husband arranges funeral*
FE 28.

V. THE SHREW'S OBEDIENCE

A. She must agree to absurd statements which her husband makes (Cf. Motif H386.)

    A1. About birds
        ai. Doves called ravens
           GD 4, 6.
        aii. Storks called ravens
           GD 7, GG 6.
        aiii. Hens called ravens
           GD 7.
        aiv. Swans called black birds
           GD 3.
        av. White ducks called spotted birds
           GD 16.
        avi. Geese called black birds
           GS 7.
    1b. Black birds called white
        bi. Ravens called doves
           GD 4, 6.
        bii. Ravens called swans
           GS 3.
        biii. Ravens called white birds
           GN 1, GD 3.
    1c. Species of birds disregarded
        ci. Ravens called swallow
           GG 9.
        cii. Chicks called goslings
           GG 6.
        ciii. Swans called wild geese
           FE 28.
    A2. About other animals
        2a. Sheep called wolves
           GD 7.
        2c. Sheep called dogs
           GG 6.
        2d. Foxes called lambs
           GD 4.

2e. *Cows called mares*
   RS Lit 2.
2f. *Mares called cows*
   RS Lit 2.
2g. *Red oxen called spotted*
   GD 16.
2h. *Lean calves or bulls called fine animals*
   RS (3), 5.
A3. About other aspects of nature
   3a. *Sunshine called rain*
      GS 1.
   3b. *Sun called moon*
      GE Lit 1, 2.
   3c. *Time wrongly stated*
      GE Lit 1, 2.
   3d. *Direction of stream's flow reversed*
      RS Lit 2.
   3e. *Man called a woman*
      GE Lit 1, 2.

B. *She must keep a bent green branch until her husband asks for it*

   B1. *A branch is cut, wound into a ring, tied (sometimes around wife's neck or arm)*
      GS 1, 3 ,7, GD (2), 3–7, 14, (16), 17, 20, GG 6, 9, (FF 43), FE 4.
   B2. *Several branches cut; one bent and tied*
      CI 11, 20, 78.

C. *She must behave herself during visits*

   C1. *When the wife's parents or friends visit the couple*
      1a. *She admits them only on husband's command*
         Ind 1.
      1b. *She warns them that only those who work may eat*
         GS 6, GG 10, CI 5, 7, 13, 15, 20, 85, 103, BLi 7, SRUk 5, SY 1, 4, 6, RP 1.

Table II–The Elements of the Tale   103

      1c. *She warns that visitors must work or face husband's anger*
         CI 3, 11.
      1d. *She warns visitors not to talk loudly*
         RS Lit 1, 3, GG 11.
        di. *She warns them not to complain*
           RSAm 1.
      1e. *Parents are surprised to find their daughter at work when they come*
         CI (1, 3),4, 5, 12, 39, 60,(81, 29), 131, 135, FF 11, fe 4, 25, SY 1, 11, RP 1, Gre 5.
      1f. *Daughter advises mother to go and eat hay with the goats*
         Sy 11.
    C2. *When the couple visit the wife's parents*
      2a. *Husband repeatedly turns back home on the trip*
         GS 23, (FF 1).
        ai. *Because wife is too slow dressing*
           GD 5, 9, 14, 16, 18, 20, 21, GG 9.
        aii. *Because wife disagrees with his absurd statements*
           GE Lit 1, 2, GN 1, GS 1, 7, GD 3, 4, 6, 7, 16, GG 6, 9.
      2b. *Wife either agrees with absurdities or dresses on the wagon for the sake of the trip*
         GE Lit 1, 2, GS 1, 3, 7, GD 3–7, 9, 14, 16, 21, GG 6.
      2c. *Wife enters house on visit only upon husband's command*
         FF 13, BLi 2.
      2d. *Wife remains seated at table until husband's command to get up*
         CI 30.

VI. THE TESTING OF THE WIVES' OBEDIENCE (MOTIF N12.)

A. *The place or occasion for the test (when specified)*

    A1. *Father-in-law's house*
      GE Lit 1–3, GN 1, GS 1–3, 7, 8, GSF 1, 2, GD 2–7, 9–11, 14–18, 20, 21, GG 6, 9, (GEAm 10), CI 1, 2, 3, 6–10, 12, 14–17,

22, 23, 26–29, 32, 34, 36–39, 41, 42, 44–48, 50–52, 54–56, 59–61, 63, 64, 66–74, 77, 79, 80, 83, 85, 87–95, 98, 101–106, 108–114, 116, 117, 119, 121, 123, 125, 129, 130, 132–134, 136, 137, FF (1), 10, 13, 14, 17, 20, 42, 44, FE 3, 20, 23, BLi 4, 5, 8, SRW 1–3, SR 3–5, 8, RFAm 1–3, 5.

A2. *Husband's house*
RF Lit 5, GI 1, CI 1 19–21, 25, 35, 49, 57, 58, 62, 75, 78, 84, 99, 107, 122, 135, FF 40, (Gre 2).

A3. *Testing in above two categories occurs after dinner*
GE Lit 1, 2, (RF Lit 5), GS 2, CI 1, 2,4, 6–12, 14, 15, 17, 21–23, 25, 27, 29, 32, 34–39, 45, 46, 48, 49, 54, 57–64, 66–69,(70), 71, 72, 74, 77–80, 84, 85, 87–95, 98, 99, 101–105,(107), 108, 109, 11–113, 116, 117, 119, 121, 122, 125,(130), 132–137, SRW (2), 3, SR 8.

A4. *At a baptismal celebration in another house*
CI 53, 118, (FE 10).

A5. *At a smithy*
GG 3–5.

A6. *Elsewhere or unspecified*
GD 13, CS 3, 4, CI 31, 33, 65, 76, 82, 100, 120, 126, 138, FF 35 37, BLi 2.

B. **The reward for the husband with the most obedient wife**

B1. *A cash wager*
GE Lit 1, 2, GN 1, GD 3, (GG 3–5), CS 3, 4, CI 1, 2, 4, 6–8, 10, 12, 15, 17, 20, 21, 25–28, 32, 39, 42, 44, 45, 47–57, 59–68, 71–73, 75–80, 83, 85, 88–95, 98–112, 114, 116–123, 125, 126, 129, 130, 132–136, 138, FF 37, 44, FE 20, 23, BLi 2, 5, SRW 1, 3, SR 3–5, RFAm 1, 3, 5.

1a. Wager for other stakes or unspecified stakes
RF Lit 5, GI 2, FF 40.

1b. No wager; simply a test of the wives
GE Lit 3, GI 1, GSF 1, 2, 5, GG 9, CI 9, 11, 19, 22, 23, 41, 58, 69, 70, 74, 82, 84, FF 10, 13, 17, 35, RFAm 2.

B2. *A prize offered by the father-in-law*
GD 6, CI 14, 29, 32, 46, 87, FF 20.

2a. Doubling the dowry
CI 63, BLi 4.

Table II—The Elements of the Tale

    2b. *Larger share of dowry than others have*
        CI 137.
        bi. *Whole dowry*
            GD 21, (CI 73).
    2c. *Larger share of his property than others*
        GD 20.
    2d. *A purse or canister full of money*
        GS 2, 7, 8, GD 2, 4, 7, 9, 14, 15, 17, 18,(19), GG 6.
    2e. *A silver cup or bowl*
        GS 3, GD 5, 16.
    2f. *His kingdom*
        CI 16 77.
    2g. *A horse and wagon*
        SR 8.
    2h. *Cash*
        GD 10, 11, CI 98, 113, FF 42, FE 3, BLi 8, (SRW 1).

C. *The wives' actions at time of the test (when specified)*

    C1. *Playing cards, dice, or chess*
        GE Lit 3, GS 8, GD 15, CS 4, CI 1, 7, 9, 12, 16, 17, 19, 21–23, 25–29, 31–35, 38, 39, 41, 42, 44–48, 50–77, 79, 80, 82–85, 87–89, 91, 95, 98, 102, 103, 105, 107–111, 113, 114, 116–122, 125, 132, 133, 135–138, RFAm 1, 2, 5.
    C2. *Working in the kitchen*
        GS 1, 3, GD 3, 20, CI 20, FF 20, FE 3.
    C3. *Looking over some new clothes*
        GN 1, GD 4, 14.
    C4. *In the steam bath*
        /(GG Lit 7)/, FE 13, 40, FE 20, BLi 4, 5, 8.
    C5. *In bed*
        GS 2, GSF 1, 2, 5, CI 8, 10, SRW 1.
    C6. *Wife at home*
        GG 3–5, FF 35, 37.

D. The husbands' command for the test

D1. Come in at once when called
GE Lit 1–3, GI 1, GN 1, GS 2, 3, 7, 8, GD 2–7, 9–11, 13–15, 17, 18, 20, 21, GG 6, CS 4, CI 1, 4, 7–12, 14, 16, 17, 19–23, 25–29, 31–19, 41, 42, 44–80, 82–85 87, 88, 91, 95, 98, 102, 102, 105, 107, 108, 110, 111, 113, 114, 116–122, 125, 132, 133, 135–138, FF 20, 35, 37, FE 3, SRW 1, RFAm 1–3, 5.

D2. Enter in nightdress
CI 8, 10, FF 14, SRW 1.

D3. Enter naked
/(GG Lit 7)/, CI 6, FF 13, 0, FE 20, BLi 4, 5, 8.

D4. Disrobe
CI 56, 57, 90, 92–94, 99, 101,(103), 104,(105), 106, 107, 112, 114, 116, 118, 123, 129, 130, 134, 135, FF 44, BLi 2, SR 4, 5.

    4a. Disrobe and then embrace husband
    FF 10.

    4b. Disrobe and burn clothes
    CS 3, CI 89, 98, 109, SRW 2.

    4c. Remove cap and throw to floor
    GE Lit 2, CI 2.

        ci. Throw cap to floor and step on it
        GE Lit 1.

        cii. Throw cap into fire
        CI (2),103.

    4d. Remove her shoe(s)
    CI 104, RFAm 3.

        di. Remove shoes and warm feet at fire
        CI 36.

    4e. Lift her skirt
    FE 23.

D5. Wait on her husband
    5a. Fill and light his pipe
    GS 1, GSF 1, 2, GD 16, FF 17.

    5b. Pull off his boots and clean them
    CI 126.

    5c. Bring water to him
    GSF 5.

    5d. Wash his hair
    FF 42.

Table II–The Elements of the Tale

    5e. Place her hand under his foot
       GE Lit 1,(2).
    5f. Bring more money for husband to gamble with
       GG 3–5.
D6. *Go home*
   (GEAm 10).
D7. *Bring the other wives in and lecture them*
   GE Lit 1, 2.
D8. *Swear her husband never beat her*
   CI 116.
D9. *Sit on husband's lap*
   GI 1, FF 37.
D10. *Kiss husband*
   GE Lit 2, GI 1, SRW 3.
D11. *Dance and/or sing*
   SWR 2, SR 8.
D12. *Drink a glass of vodka*
   SR 3.
D13. *Serve drinks to the men*
   SR 5, 8.
    13a. Serve the same food to the men five times
       Gre 2.
D14. *Answer husband's call politely*
   GD 5.
D15. *Jump into a container set before her*
   RF Lit 5.
D16. *Wife misunderstands command (in French) to place salt on the table; jumps on table herself*
   RF Lit 5.
D17. *"Do something shameful"*
   CI 15.
D18. *Wife asks husband's permission before acting*
   FF 1.

E. Others concede Shrew's husband the victory; prevent her from carrying out command

   CI 15, 89, 92, 101, 106, 130.

0. Trait is absent

GG Lit 1, 2, RF Lit 1–3, RS Lit 1–3, RI Lit 1, /GG Lit 3–6, 8, 9, GNe Lit 1, 2, GE Lit 4, 5, RF Lit 3A, RS Lit 4, SR Lit 1–3/, GE Lit 6–9, RF Lit 4, RS Lit 5, GS 4–6, GSF 3, 4, GD 1, 8, 1 19, GG 1, 2, 7, 8, 10–14, GNe 1, GEAm 1–9, 11–32, CS 1,2, CI 3, 5, 13, 18, 24, 30, 43, 81, 86, 96, 97, 115, 124,(127), 128, 131, 139, 140, FF 2–9, 11, 12, 15, 16, 18, 19, 21–34, 36, 39, 41, 43, 45, FE 1, 2, 4–19, 21, 22, 24–28, FH 1–4, BLi 1, 3, 6, 7, SP 1, 2, SRUk 1–5, SR 1, 2, 6, 7, 9–12, SY 1–20, RF 1, RFAm 4, RP 1, 2, RS 1–6, RSAm 1, 2, RR 1–4, Gre 1, 3–5, Per 1, Ind 1, 2.

VII. SPECIAL CONCLUSIONS

A. The taming device is repeated on or by another character

A1. A man successfully tames his wife
GE Lit 9.
A2. A man unsuccessfully tries to tame his wife (Motif T251.23.1.)
　2a. Shrew's father and mother
　　RS Lit 1 (kills horse, cock), 3 (kills cock), (GEAm 25 [says "that's the first time"]), CI 81 (punishes dog), RP 2 (leaves light burning at night with intention of shooting it out).
　2b. Friend of husband
　　RI Lit 1 (kills horse), Gre 1 (throws food from table), 2 and 4 (kills cat), Per 1 (kills cat).
A3. The Shrew's sister(s) tamed
GI 1.
A4. The Shrew's mother is tamed by son-in-law
/(GE Lit 4)/, SY 20, Gre 5.
　4a. Mother gives daughter bad counsels; overheard by son-in-law, who then tames her too
　　CS 3, FF 22, FE 17, 21, 26, FH 4, SRUk 1, 3, SR 1, 2, 5, 6, 8, 1–,12, SY 2,(3), 8, 14.

Table II—The Elements of the Tale

> 4b. *Mother must pull plow*
> FE 23, FH 4, SRUk 1–4, SR 2, 5, 6, 8, 10, 11, SY 3, 4, 8, 9, 13–15.
>> bi. *Daughter and mother hitched to plow together*
>> FF 22, FE 14, 21.
>> bii. *Mother threatened with plowing; escapes*
>> FE 17, SR 1, 12.
> 4c. *Mother is beaten*
> CS 1, SY 5, 6, 10, 12.
> 4d. *Mother tied in stable, fed hay or straw*
> SY 6, 9, 13, 15,(18), 19.
>> di. *Mother tied to a tree or hitching post*
>> SY 2, 5.
>> dii. *Bell hung on mother's neck*
>> SY 9.
> 4e. *Bogus surgery on mother*
> GG Lit 1, RF Lit 1, GG 2, 13, CS 3.
> 4f. *Mother is beaten by magic sandals*
> FE 26.
> 4g. *Mother rejoices to husband: "You never did that to me"*
> CS 1, 3.

A5. *The Shrew's father gives daughter good counsels; overheard by son-in-law, who entertains him richly*
FF 22, FE (14), 17, 21,(23), 26, FH 4, SRUk 1, SR 1, 2, 5, 6, 8, 10–12, SY 2–4,(5), 6, 8,(9), (10), 13, 14,(15), 18,(20).
> 5a. *Gets father-in-law drunk*
> FF 22, FE 21, SRUk 3, SR 1, 5, 6, 8, 10–12.
> 5b. *Gives him a red cloak*
> SY 6, 8–10, 15,(19), 20.
> 5c. *Gives him a cake or bread as a present; hung around neck for trip home*
> FE 23, FH 4, SR 6, (SY 14).
> 5d. *Gives him bottles of wine; hung around neck*
> FE 17, SR 5, 11.
> 5e. *Gives him cask of wine*
> SR 10.
> 5f. *Gives him an ox hide*
> SY 5.

5g. Mother sees father coming home; thinks he too was mistreated (cf. Motif W111.3.1)
FF 22, FE 17, 21, FH 4, SRUk 3, SR 1, 5, 6, 8, 10–12, SY 5, 6, 8–10, 15,(19), 20.

B. Concluding action of taming story

B1. Winnings are given to the wife
GS 2, GD 9, 15, 18, 21, CS 3, CI 38, 56, 57, 102, 103.
  1a. Other reward from husband to his wife
  CI 9, 10, RS 3.
  1b. Wife rewarded by her father
  CI 89, 116, 119, 136.
B2. Reward given husband for having tamed the Shrew (not as payment for wager)
GE Lit 1, 2, GS 6, FF 11, 42, FE 21, BLi 1, SRUk 5, SR 3, 10.
B3. Husband is given a horse to tame; he leads it with food
GG Lit 3, CI 1, FE 3.
B4. The tamed Shrew is sent back to her family
CI 30.
B5. Wife pulls off husband's boots and husband wife's. They reach an understanding that he will give back in future whatever treatment she gives him
GD 1, 8, 12, RF 1.
B6. Tamed Shrew must accompany husband when he goes out to relieve himself
FE 12, 22.

C. Concluding motto

C1. Reference to the killing of an animal
(GNe 1), (CI 41, 120), RS 3, 5.
C2. Reference to the green branch
GS 1, 3, 7, GD (3), 4–7, 14, 20. GG 6, 9, CI 11, 20, 78, FF 43, FE 4.
  2a. Demonstration of the principle, "Tame your wife young," with soft clay and a brick
  Ind 1.
C3. Reference to carrying the saddle
GI 1, 2, GS 2, GSF 2, GD 6, GEAm 10, FF 10, 13.

Table II–The Elements of the Tale

    C4. *Reference to scratching with the cat*
       FF 1.
    C5. *Reference to breaking wife's arm*
       RS 6.

D. *Continuation as another Tale Type*

    D1. "The Animal Languages" (Type 670)
       CI 27.
    D2. "King Thrushbeard" (Type 900)
       GS 4.
    D3. "The Clever Maiden Alone at Home Kills the Robbers" (Type 956B)
       GEAm 18, CS 2.
    D4. "The Evil Woman Thrown into the Pit" (Type 1164)
       SY 9.
    D5. "The Woman Does Not Know Herself" (Type 1383)
       FF 23.

CHAPTER II
Summary of the Combinations of Narrative Elements in the Versions

Numerous varied combinations of Types 901, 901B, and 1370; parts of these and other types; separate motifs, and miscellaneous other narrative elements appear in versions from the Taming of the Shrew Complex. The following summary indicates which combination of elements each version contains; it can be used in conjunction with the tables of data to help clarify the structure of the Taming of the Shrew Complex and to help place the various versions within that tradition. A brief explanation of each type, motif, or catchword title for a miscellaneous element is given only with the first appearance of that unit in the list. Combinations with tale types which are not regularly part of the Taming of the Shrew Complex are shown in parentheses after the number of the version in which they occur.

FREE–FLOATING ELEMENTS

The Wager (2 versions)

(A wager between husbands on whose wife is most obedient. Won by husband of former shrew.)
RF Lit 5, CI 31(Type 425 + wager).

Type 901B (4 versions)

(Taming the mother-in-law by making her pull a plow.)
FH 4 (Type 1453* + 901B), SY 5, 19, 20.

TYPE 901 WITHOUT A WAGER

The Basic Tale (99 versions)

(Husband slays recalcitrant animal or animals as an example to tame his bad wife.)
GG Lit 2, RF Lit 2, 3, GD 1, 8, 12, GS 4 (Type 900 + 901), GG 11, GNe 1, GEAm 1–9, 11–17, 19–24, 26–32, CI 3, 18, 24, 40, 43, 86, 115, 128, 131, 140, FF 3–5, 7–9, 11, 12, 15, 16, 18, 19, 21, 25–32, 34, 39, 41, 43, 45, FE 1, 2, 5–7, 9–13, 22 BLi 1, 3, SR 7, SY 11, 16, RF 1, RFAm 4, RS 3-5, RSAm 1, 2, Ind 1, 2.

Type 901 + Unsuccessful Repetition (10 versions)

(Another husband unsuccessfully attempts to apply the same taming method to his wife.)
RS Lit 1, 3, RI Lit 1, (GEAm 25), CI 81, RP 2, Gre 1, 2, 4, Per 1.

Type 901 + Type 901B (18 versions)

(The shrew-tamer also tames his mother-in-law.)
Plowing: FF 22, FE 14, 17, 21, SRUk 3, SR 1, 2, 10, 12, SY 2, 3, 8, 15, 18.
Anger Moles: GG Lit 1, RF Lit 1, GG 2, 13.

Type 901 + Motif W111.3.6. (5 versions)

(The shrew-tamer also tells his wife, "Who will not work, shall not eat.")
CI 13, 30, 96, 97, 139.

Summary of The Combinations of Narrative Elements 115

TYPE 901 INCLUDING A WAGER

The Basic Tale (122 versions)

    GE Lit 1–3, GI 1, 2, GS 1–3, 7, 8, GSF 1, 2, 5, GD 2–7, 9–11, 14–18, 20, 21 (Type 910A + 901 + wager), GG 6, 9, GEAm 10, CI 6, 8, 14, 16, 19, 21, 26, 27, (Type 901 + 670 + wager), 28, 29, 33–37, 39, 42, 44–47, 52, 54, 55, 58, 59, 62–67, 69, 70, 73, 75, 80, 82–84, 87–90, 92–95, 99–101, 104–106, 108–114, 117–123, 125–127, 129, 130, 133, 138. FF 10, 13, 17, 44, FE 3, 20, BLi 2, 5, 8, SRW 3, SR 3, 4, RFAm 1–3.

Type 901 + Type 901B + wager (4 versions)

    Plowing: FE 23, SR 5, 8.
    Anger Moles: CS 3.

Type 901 + Motif W111.3.6. + wager (39 versions)

    CI 2, 7, 10, 11, 15, 17, 20, 22, 25, 32, 38, 41, 48–51, 56, 57, 60, 61, 68, 71, 72, 74, 76–78, 85, 91, 98, 102, 103, 107, 116, 132, 134–137.

SEPARATED ELEMENTS OF TYPE 901 (3 versions)

Absurd statements

    RS Lit 2, FE 28.

Riding the wife

    GE Lit 9.

TYPE 1370

The Lazy Cat Is Punished (31 versions)

GG Lit 3, 4, SR Lit 1–3, GS 5, GSF 4, GG 8, 14, FF 23 (Type 1370 + 1383*), 36, FE 4, 8, 15, 16, 18, 19, 24, 27, FH 1–3, SY 7.
Type 1370 (cat) + wager
GD 13, RFAm 5.
Type 1370 (cat) + Motif W111.3.6.
GG 10 (Type 1461* + 1370 + Motif W111.3.6), BLi 7.
Type 1370 (cat) + Type 901B
SRUk 1, 2, 4, SR 6.

An Animal Hide Is Punished (16 versions)

GG Lit 5, 6, 8 (Type 1370 + cradle), 9, GNe Lit 2, GE Lit 4,5, GSF 3, FF 2, SY 17, RR 2, 3, Gre 3.
Type 1370 (hide) + wager
GG Lit 7.
Type 1370 (hide) + Type 901B
SY 12.

Another Object Is Punished (15 versions)

RF Lit 3A, RS Lit 4, BLi 6, SP 1, 2, RS 1, 2, RR 1.
Type 1370 (other object) + Type 901B
SY 9 (Type 1370 + 901B + 1164), 10, 13, 14, Gre 5.
Type 1370 (other object) + Motif W111.3.6. + Type 901B
FE 26 (Type 1370 + W111.3.6. + D1401.7. + 901B), SY 6.

TYPE 901 COMBINED WITH TYPE 1370 (10 versions)

Cat Punished

FF 6(Type 1453* + 901 + 1370), 24.
+901B
SR 11.
+ wager
GN 1, GD 19, FF 1, 20, SRW 2.

Hide Punished + wager

>FF 14.

Object Punished + wager

>BLi 4.

MOTIF W111.3.6. AS A SEPARATE TALE (13 versions)

The Basic Tale

>RS Lit 5, GS 6, GEAm 18 (Type 956B + W111.3.6.), CS 2 Type 956B + W111.3.6.), CI 5, SRUk 5, SY 1, RF 1, RR 4.

Motif W111.3.6. + Type 901B

>SY 4.

Motif W111.3.6. + wager

>CI 1, 4, 9.

MISCELLANEOUS TAMING DEVICES

The Broken Arm (7 versions)

>(Husband breaks his wife's arm and pays the doctor double his fee for "the next time.")
>RF Lit 4, GG 1, 7, CI 124, RS 6.

Broken Arm + wager

>CI 53, 79.

The Cradle (5 versions)

(Husband treats his wife like a baby—rocks her in a cradle to tame her.)
FF 33, SR 9.

Cradle + wager

FF 35, 40, 42.

Miscellaneous Cruelty (15 versions)

(Husband physically tortures his wife—beats her, lets blood, cuts her and so forth.)
GE Lit 6–8, GG 12, CS 1, FF 38, FE 25.
Cruelty + wager
GG 3–5, CS 4, CI 12, 23, FF 37, SRW 1.

Total 418

FOLK SAYINGS ANALOGOUS TO THE TAMING OF THE SHREW

There are Swedish folk sayings which allude to Type 1370 (cat form) and which, thus, further document the existence of that type in Sweden. There are also folk sayings from the southern and eastern periphery of the area of distribution of Type 901 which indicate that this type must have been known there. Sayings from Morocco, Turkey, and Burma have been collected and are listed at the end of Table I. All three of these sayings refer to killing or punishing an animal on the wedding day; in the Moroccan saying it is a dog, and in the Turkish and Burmese a cat.

CHAPTER III

Type 901: Historic-Geographic Study

FREE-FLOATING ELEMENTS

Two narrative elements, the wager on the wives' obedience and the taming of the mother-in-law, seem to be free-floating in this tradition; that is, they occur widely in combination with a number of different tales in the Taming of the Shrew Complex. They must be examined first to determine to which type, if any, they seem to have been attached originally.

The Wager on the Wives' Obedience

The following list of the total number of versions of Type 901 in each national group shows how many of them conclude with a wager on the obedience of the wives, and also (in parentheses) the occurrences of similar wagers in combination with other tale types. Two variations of the wager incident are in square brackets. Totals are given below the lists of figures.

Number of versions of Type 901	National group	Versions of Type 901 with wager	Wagers in other types
2	GG Lit	0	(1)
0	GNe Lit	0	
3	GE Lit	3	

119

3	RF Lit	0	(1)
3	RS Lit	0	
1	RI Lit	0	
0	SR Lit	0	
2	GI	2	
1	GN	1	
6	GS	5	
3	GSF	3	
20	GD	17	(1)
5	GG	2	(3)
1	GNe	0	
31	GEAm	1	
1	CS	1	(1)
130	CI	114	(8)
36	F F	7	(4)
16	F E	3	
0	F H	0	
6	BLi	4	
0	S P	0	
2	SRW	2	(1)
1	SRUk	0	
10	S R	4	
7	S Y	0	
1	R F	0	
4	RFAm	3	(1)
1	R P	0	
3	R S	[1]	
2	RSAm	0	
0	R R	0	
3	Gre	[1]	
1	Per	0	
2	Ind	0	
307		172 [2]	(21)

Three facts about the distribution of the wager element strike one immediately: (1) There is a strong attachment of the wager and Type 901; (2) The wager is lacking in older literary sources; and (3) The wager is concentrated in Scandinavia and Ireland, and it is scattered in the rest of northern Europe; but it is lacking in the Romance language area and in the East. Primarily, the wager on the wives' obedience belongs to Type 901 in northern Europe and to fairly recent times. More detailed examination of the data serves to amplify these generalizations.

In the usual form of this incident in the tales, the husbands come together and compare their wives; they lay a bet on who has the most obedient wife. The wives are called to come one at a time and each may be ordered to obey another command. Only the reformed shrew obeys. Thus, she wins the wager for her husband. There is no close analogue for such a scene in the versions from southern Europe or the East. The Canadian versions, though they may appear to contradict this pattern of distribution, do not really seem to be Romance in origin. As will be shown in more detail later, these French-American texts correspond closely to Celtic versions rather than to the continental French tradition; thus, they seem to be derived ultimately from Scotch or Irish sources in the Maritime Provinces where they were collected. In version RS 5 the husband bets *before* the wedding that he will be able to tame the Shrew, but he does not demonstrate his success before others later; in Gre 2 the husband forces his wife to carry out absurd commands in order to demonstrate her obedience, but no wager is laid and there is no contrast between disobedient and obedient wives. No clear traces can be shown in southern Europe, therefore, either of borrowing or of a possible survival of an original from of the wager incident.

The wager is found in about fifty-six per cent of the versions of Type 901 and also occurs in about eighteen per cent of the versions of other types. All of the occurrences of the wager apart from Type 901, however, are in countries where Type 901 including the wager is a common tale. The indication is strong that this concluding episode from a rather popular jest has sometimes simply been transferred to other jests about bad wives. It must have originally been invented and attached to Type 901 in northwestern Europe. The wager is found with most of the versions of Type 901 in all of the Germanic countries, except that it has not been transplanted to the United States. It is equally popular as part of Type 901 in Ireland, but thins out sharply in the groups of versions from Finland, Estonia, Lithuania, and the Slavic countries, here progressively dropping away as one looks to the south.

The oldest literary appearance found of a wager on the obedience of wives is in version RF Lit 5, *The Book of the Knight of La Tour-Landry*, a book which goes back to fourteenth-century France and was known at least in manuscripts in Germany, and, after Caxton's translation in 1484, in England. An examination of the summary of this version in Table I compared with the elements outlined in Table II, however, shows how far removed the version is from usual forms of the wager in Type 901. There is no previous taming of the wife; the command to the wives (to jump into a basin) is unique; the stakes for the wager (a dinner) are unusual, and the whole story depends on a French pun. It would seem highly unreasonable to see this version as an original form of the wager incident of the Taming of the Shrew. It seems to be strictly a literary invention. A second tale from the same collection in which version RF Lit 5 occurs has been suggested by Shroeder[1] as a possible original for Shakespeare's wager scene; the contradiction of this argument is presented in Chapter IV. It is sufficient to say here that in this latter version not only is no wager laid, but no other wives are on the scene. Version GG Lit 7, which is a form of Type 1370, ends with a demonstration of the wife's reform that is known in eastern European forms of the wager—she is called away naked from a bath. This isolated appearance in a printed text of one trait of the wager element must be a chance borrowing in the late seventeenth century from a popular tale.

Shakespeare's comedy and the other two literary versions of Type 901 from England are, thus, the only printed examples of the wager in the form in which we find it in folktales. The question immediately arises, then, whether folktales have derived the trait from Shakespeare's late-sixteenth-century play, or whether the playwright knew it from oral tradition, either directly or indirectly. To suggest answers to these questions, we must attempt to determine the prototypic form of the wager in the folktales and then decide if Shakespeare's version could have given rise to it.

The elements of the wager which are most widely distributed and occur most frequently are easily picked out from section VI of Table II where the incidents from the tales are outlined.

Type 901: Historic-Geographic Study

The place of the testing of the wives is the father-in-law's house in a large majority of the versions, and *the occasion* for the testing in quite frequently after a dinner party given for all of the daughters and their husbands. The dinner party at the father-in-law's is distributed over the whole area where the wager is known. This location for the test seems surely more natural and logical than alternatives which sometimes appear—the son's house, a baptismal celebration, or at a smithy. (The smithy and several other details belong to a special German group of versions to be discussed later.) The place of testing is unspecified in only a few versions.

The reward for the husband who has the most obedient wife is the winning of a wager—for cash, or sometimes other stakes—in the largest group of widely distributed versions. Versions from a smaller group in generally the same area omit the wager and contain only a contest of wives. A small scattering of versions have some kind of prize from the girls' father as the reward, rather than winnings of a wager; in a few instances the dowry or the father's property or kingdom are mentioned. Such prizes would seem more likely to be chance generalizations of a wager rather than germs of the idea *for* the wager; otherwise we would expect to find the father-in-law's prize in more versions and more widely known. Very likely there is influence here from other folktales too, for a father's gifts of wealth and property to his son-in-law is a *Märchen* commonplace. In Denmark and near-lying parts of Germany and Sweden the prize has taken a specific form—a purse or canister full of money or simply a valuable silver cup or bowl. This detail seems to be a late local development of the idea of a prize from the father. The peripheral distribution of the wager suggests that it rather than the prize is the original form.

If a particular *action of the wives* is specified, it is in Ireland most frequently playing a game, usually cards, but occasionally dice or chess; this detail occurs once each in Sweden, Denmark, in GE Lit 3, and in three Canadian versions. In Scandinavia the wives are sometimes either working in the kitchen or looking over new clothes; the former detail also occurs once each in Ireland, Finland, and Estonia. More typical of northeastern Europe is the wives taking a steam bath; GG Lit 7 also has the improved shrew called from a bath. In seven versions from Sweden, Swedish-Finland, Ireland, and White Russia the wives are in bed when they are called. Since no one specific action of the wives appears both frequently and over a broad area, it would seem plausible to assume that the original form was simply that the wives had retired from the husbands' presence at the time of the wager and were busy with some occupation which would make it inconvenient or embarrassing to come in at once when called. The naturalness for wives of any of the details—looking at clothes, bathing, doing kitchen work, or sleeping—and the possible association of wagering with card playing are sufficient to explain the various specific forms of the trait.

The *husbands' commands* to their wives almost invariably begin with calling them to come at once. Depending on the previous actions of the wives, the obedient one throws down her hand of cards, drops a dish on the kitchen floor, or comes in her nightdress or even naked to reply to her husband's call. The disobedient wives refer to their actions when called—dealing or shuffling the cards, bathing, and so forth—as excuses for not coming. The wives are commanded to enter naked in the six eastern European versions which specify that they were in the steam bath, and in GG Lit 7. In one Irish version the wives are commanded to go to another room, disrobe, and return naked. The wives are simply commanded to disrobe on the spot in twenty-two Irish versions and four versions from Finland, Lithuania, and Russia. In one Finnish version the bad wife must disrobe and then embrace her husband; in another Finnish tale she must lift up her skirt. In four Celtic versions and one version from White Russia the wife must disrobe and then burn her clothes. Throwing down the cap only, as in Shakespeare, is found in two Irish versions, one of which specifies that it must be thrown into the fireplace. In one Canadian and two Irish versions the last wife takes off her shoes on command and in one of these Irish tales she then warms her feet by the fire when her husband tells her to do so. The peripheral distribution of all these traits which involve disrobing suggests that it is the original form. The general idea of disrobing has been localized in some versions from eastern Europe to tie it in with the local custom of steam bathing. In the center of the area where the wager is known—Scandinavia—there is no disrobing; indeed, there is usually no extra command to the wives at all. In five versions from Scandinavia the reformed shrew fills and lights her husband's pipe, and various other services or signs of affection are found in scattered versions.

This brief analysis of the variable traits which appear in the scenes of wife-testing suggest the following archetype: The husbands and wives meet at the father-in-law's house, where, probably after dinner, the woman retire to do something among themselves and the husbands compare their wives and lay a wager on which one is the most obedient. The wives are called in one at a time as a test; only the reformed shrew ceases her current activity at once and comes. She is in, or is forced to assume, some state of undress.

It is theoretically possible that the closing scene of Shakespeare's comedy is the original for the popular versions. There is no earlier printed source that so closely fits the same pattern. Furthermore, the archetypal form is not well preserved in Denmark, but seems more at home in Ireland where it could have come directly from England. In Scandinavia (probably Denmark) other distinctive traits have developed—the prize of coins in a cup, wives working in the kitchen, the reformed shrew waiting on her husband—and these forms have apparently replaced the wager, the card playing, and the undressing which are found distributed on the periphery of the area where the wager is known and are very strongly represented in Irish tradition.

It is difficult to imagine, however, Shakespeare's play giving rise to certain different details which are fairly regularly found over a wide area; at the same time one wonders, if the folktales derive the wager from the play, why certain specific elements in the last scene *The Shrew* are not in the tales also. For these problems a hypothesis that Shakespeare drew from and adapted traditional versions in England probably similar to the current Irish tales seems more satisfactory. The wives playing cards, for example, is a popular folktale trait which is not mentioned in Shakespeare. It is found, however, in GE Lit 3, where it must have come from some oral version. All of the various disrobing scenes in tales seem hardly to have been derived from the simple action in Shakespeare of Kate throwing down her cap. More likely Shakespeare either used a rather innocuous version to dramatize such as our version CI 2, which has throwing down the cap, or he simplified and made stageable a somewhat bawdy popular tale. There is certainly nothing further in CI 2 to suggest that it is a version based on Shakespeare's play, but rather it contains a fairly standard conglomerate of elements from the folktale tradition. The heroine's stamping on the cap in *A Shrew* is perhaps a step closer to the folktales, such as the two Irish tales in which she burns her cap. Several actions which Kate must perform in the last scenes of *The Shrew* and *A Shrew*, such as lecturing the other wives, seem to be literary embroidery and have no counterparts in folktales. The fact that the heroine must kiss her husband in GI 1 and SRW 3, as in *The Shrew*, does not necessarily imply direct contact between the versions. Kissing in public is probably just one more embarrassing action to be required on the wife. Since the evidence can tend to support either point of view, at this stage of the analysis, it is more prudent to withhold a final judgment on the origin of the wager incident until Shakespeare's relationship to the tale cycle as a whole has been examined.

The original form of the wager, at any rate, was attached to Type 901, from where, in the countries where Type 901 was popular, it has occasionally drifted to similar tales about bad wives. It does not belong in the *archetype* of the Taming of the Shrew, however, for the basic tale is much earlier attested in print and is known over a considerably wider area than is the wager. Thus, there is no necessity for the archetype of Type 901 to include sisters of the Shrew and their husbands; these characters are *essential* only if there is to be a comparison and testing of the wives. As we shall observe, the apparently older forms of the tale did not contain these extra characters, just as they did not have the wager incident itself.

Taming the Mother-in-law

Andrejev, in his translation into Russian of Aarne's index, added a number of types drawn from Russian folktales. He distinguished the form of the Taming of the Shrew in which the Shrew's mother is tamed by the hero after he has tamed the daughter, designating this as Type 901B.[2] Actually, Andrejev's one example of the type, version SRUk 3 here, is a combination of Types 901 and 901B; but Type 901B is found in other combinations in Russian tales, including some of those listed by Andrejev under different type numbers. The same tale is found in a number of other eastern European countries, nearly always in combinations with Types 901 or 1370. Andrejev's summary of Type 901B, however, holds true for most of these versions: "He punishes his mother-in-law for bad counsels, plows with her. He treats his father-in-law for good counsels." In some western European versions the mother-in-law may be tamed by some kind of bogus surgery, like cutting out her supposed "anger moles." (The bogus surgery device is also occasionally used to tame the wife.) These versions are here also put under the heading Type 901B, for there seems to be a definite relationship between them and the eastern European folktales about plowing with the mother-in-law.

Thirty-five examples of Type 901B (plowing form) were gathered for this study; only three of them are not in combination with other types and motifs. The following list shows the total numbers of each combination and indicates their distribution by countries.

Type	Number of Texts	Number of Countries	Total by Countries
1-901B	4	(2)	3 SY, 1 FH (1453*+901B)
2-901+901B	14	(5)	5 SY, 4 SR, 3 FE, 1 SRUk, 1FF
3-901+901B+wager	3	(2)	2 SR, 1 FE
4-901+1370+901B	1	(1)	1 SR
5-1370+901B	10	(4)	5 SY, 3 SRUk, 1 SR, 1 Gre
6-1370+W111.3.6.+901B	2	(2)	1 SY, 1 FE
7-W111.3.6.+901B	1	(1)	1 SY
	35		

Seven countries are represented here, and there are seven possible combinations of types. The countries may be ranked as follows according to the number of combinations which occur in each—Yugoslavia has five of the seven, Russia has four, Estonia has three, the Ukraine has two, and Hungary and Greece have one each. Ranking the countries by the total number of texts which contain Type 901B, we get this result: Yugoslavia has fifteen versions with 901B (out of a total of twenty Yugoslavian versions), Russia has eight (of twelve), Estonia has five (of twenty-eight), the Ukraine has four (of five), and Finland, Hungary, and Greece have one each (out of forty-five, four, and five, respectively). There are eighteen versions in the list which are combinations with Type 901 proper and the other seventeen versions are in combination only with other types. Clearly Type 901B is eastern European in origin and probably it was originally a separate type; at any rate, it has combined freely with various forms of the Taming of the Shrew Cycle. We would expect to find the place of origin of the type somewhere in the center of its area of distribution; the bare statistics alone might suggest Yugoslavia, the Ukraine or Russia. A closer examination of the various forms of the traits making up Type 901B throws more light on these questions.

Bad counsels by the mother-in-law to her daughter, which are overheard by the husband, occur in all eight of the Russian versions of Type 901B, in four Yugoslavian versions, three Estonian, two Ukrainian, and one Finnish. On the other hand, the father-in-law's good counsels occur more often in Yugoslavia (thirteen versions), but still in all eight Russian texts as well as in five Estonian versions and one version each from Hungary, Finland, and the Ukraine. The difference seems to be that the shrewishness of the mother-in-law is established differently in several Yugoslavian versions, though the father-in-law's part is about the same everywhere. Five versions from Yugoslavia without the mother-in-law's bad counsels begin with the suitor meeting the father of the Shrew who is being forced by his wife to work outside on a bad day (Table II, trait ID1). In eight Yugoslavian versions it is emphasized that the Shrew's mother must always be asked the opposite of what her husband wants, and in three of these versions she even makes her husband wear a bell around his neck in order to know if he is working hard (Table II, traits IIC2b and IIC2c). This "henpecked father opening" is also found in RF Lit 1 and in related Scottish versions which end with the anger-mole taming of the mother-in-law; this trait, however, is not known further in eastern Europe. Taken together, these data suggest the hypothesis that the mother-in-law's bad counsels and the father-in-law's corresponding good counsels belong to Type 901B in its original eastern European from and these traits are best preserved in the Russian texts.

Being tamed by having to pull a plow is the mother-in-law's most common fate. This trait occurs regularly in Russia and the Ukraine and in all of the other countries which have Type 901B except Greece. The Greek version, however, is like GE Lit 4, *Wife Lapped in Morrelles Skin*, for in both the mother-in-law is led to the cellar when she protests the treatment of her daughter, but no specific taming of her is described. The plowing occurs in Finland (as well as in two Estonian texts) in the form of both mother and daughter being hitched to a plow. In one Estonian tale and two Russian tales the mother is threatened with plowing, but manages to escape. In Yugoslavia various other animal-like punishments are administered to the bad mother in addition to, but more frequently in lieu of, making her plow. She is beaten, tied in a stable with hay to eat, tied to a tree or hitching post, or has a bell hung on her own neck.

In twenty of the thirty-five versions of Type 901B the father-in-law comes home from his own visit to the son-in-law's house in such a condition as to make his wife think that he had to pull the plow too. This trait is well known in all of the countries having the tale, but the reasons leading up to his condition at homecoming vary. In most of the Russian versions and also in some from the Ukraine, Finland, and Estonia, the son-in-law has managed to get the old man drunk. Sometimes in these same versions the son-in-law has given him some kind of a gift of food—a large cake (found also once each in Hungary and Yugoslavia) or bottles of wine—these he carries home around his neck so that he seems to be wearing a yoke or halter. In Yugoslavian versions, however, the gift is usually a red cloak (six versions) or in one instance an ox hide. The mother-in-law, seeing this, believes that his back is red from whipping and pulling at the traces. Possibly there is some connection to Type 1370 here with the animal hide or other object being beaten on the wife's back or wrapped around her when she has previously been beaten.

The simplest, most numerous and most widely distributed forms of the traits in Type 901B have proven to occur most regularly in Russia and the Ukraine. The archetype suggested by this analysis would seem to be exactly as Andrejev outlined the tale with the addition of the trait, "He rewards his father-in-law with drink, and the mother-in-law, seeing the old man coming home, thinks that he too has had to pull the plow." Seven of the eight Russian versions of Type 901B are in combinations also including Type 901 proper. This would suggest that the tale either was originally invented to supplement type 901—to show how the mother too was tamed—or that the separate tale of taming a mother-in-law was early combined with Type 901 because of their similar subject matter. It would seem that if the latter were true that we would also find more tales in which the Shrew herself were tamed by plowing. The Finnish and Estonian versions show some unique variations, but agree in general with Russia and the Ukraine rather than with Yugoslavia. The Hungarian version has no unique points except the combination with a separate tale type, but in Yugoslavia we find such individual developments as a different way of establishing the mother-in-law's basic shrewishness, different treatment of the mother-in-law, and different gifts to the father-in-law. Moreover, the traits from these versions which are known *outside* of eastern Europe are all characteristically Yugoslavian. This brings us back to the anger-moles form of the type.

Four western European versions of Type 901 end with the taming of the mother-in-law by means of some kind of bogus surgery. In RF Lit 1 the mother-in-law is sterilized by her son-in-law and she then becomes peaceful. In GG Lit 1 the son-in-law pretends to cut out his mother-in-law's anger moles— *Zornbraten*. Neither of these literary texts can be accurately dated, but they may be as old as the thirteenth century. In two German folktales (GG 2 and GG 13) the *Zornbraten* are likewise removed, and in CS 3 the son-in-law cures his mother-in-law by cutting her haunches and rubbing salt in the wounds. This sort of bogus surgery is used as the taming device for the wife herself in three English literary versions dating from the sixteenth to seventeenth centuries and in another German folktale (Table II, trait IVD1). Quite likely such brutality to shrewish women was a common theme in early cheap printed literature; the examples from print mentioned in this study were found quite fortuitously while searching for texts of the regular folktale types of the Taming of the Shrew Complex. No special effort was made to get them. The pertinent questions here are whether the anger-moles taming is an oral or a literary trait and whether any similarities can be pointed out between taming the mother-in-law by anger-mole cutting in the west, and by plowing in the east of Europe. At first glance there would seem to be little in common between the two forms of the incident. There are, however, some telling details which evidence a connection.

The opening of the tale in which the suitor comes upon his future father-in-law working in the fields on a bad day has already been pointed out as being found in five Yugoslavian versions which also contain Type 901B, but not found elsewhere in eastern Europe. Four western European versions are the only other ones which open in this manner, and two of these, RF Lit 1 and CS 3, end with the anger-mole taming of the mother-in-law. The other two versions with the same opening scene have links with the Yugoslavian tradition also. CS 1 has the mother-in-law tamed by being beaten, as in four Yugoslavian versions only, and GNe 1 has the suitor overhear bad counsels to his bride, in this instance from her sisters. (All of these particular western European versions, by virtue of other traits, as will be shown later, belong together as a special subtype of Type 901 which is closely allied to printed versions.) One of the other characteristic Yugoslavian features of Type 901B, the contrary mother who must be asked the opposite of what her husband wants, is also found in RF Lit 1, CS 1, 3, and 4. The shrewishness of the mother-in-law appears in the Taming of the Shrew Complex only in these versions of 901B and in five versions with the unsuccessful repetition of the taming device from Spanish literature, Portugal, Ireland, and the United States. Thus, the trait is uncommon enough and distinctive enough in this tradition so that borrowing would be suspected for an explanation rather than accidental independent invention. This is especially likely when the various other distinctive similar traits are considered.

The conclusion, then, which these data suggest is that the anger mole versions of western Europe are chiefly literary and are ultimately related to the Type 901B stories from eastern Europe and most probably migrated from east to west in Europe. Yugoslavia must have acted as an intermediary between the Slavic home of the type and the west of Europe. The anger mole device itself seems to be western in origin and possibly developed simply on the analogy of other such stories of bogus surgery on wives. The anger mole tale, always given as a sequel to Type 901, was known in medieval times in Europe, as GG Lit 1 and RF Lit 1 show. Possibly these very versions were based on some southeastern European versions and thus carried the tale westward. At any rate, these literary versions are clearly echoed in the few folktale versions of the anger mole story which survive. On the whole, this tale seems not to be very popular in western Europe and perhaps it never was widely told there.

TYPE 901

Preliminary

Like any large group of texts of a given folktale type, the 307 versions of Type 901 here assembled all have in common a basic narrative core, but each differs from the others in the exact selection and elaboration of other elements of the plot. That is, in every true "version" of this "type"—901—a husband metes out an apparently irrational death penalty or other severe punishment to an animal in order to frighten and improve his shrewish wife. Theoretically, there could be an almost limitless number of expansions and variations of this basic plot; but, actually, the variations that are found are fairly limited and tend to follow certain principles recognized in the study of other Indo-European folktales. Elements are added or dropped; general traits become specific or specific details are generalized; episodes from other types become attached, and so forth. For example, the "core plot" of the Taming of the Shrew may have added to it such incidents as another taming method, the taming of a second bad wife, an unsuccessful attempt to apply the taming device to another wife, or a final scene in which several husbands lay wagers on whether their wives will obey them. There are borrowed incidents from such other tales as *King Thrushbeard* (Type 900), *The Three Precepts* (Type 901A) and *The Slovenly Fiancée* (Type 1453*) which deal with situations similar to those in Type 901. These kinds of accretions are convenient to identify for the purpose of systematic classification of the versions, and such has been done in Chapter II.

Another kind of variation consists of internal elaboration in the basic plot of the type itself. In Type 901, almost always, an animal is either killed or severely punished, but the species of animal varies greatly from the most common dog and horse, to a cat, a cock, a falcon, a pig, a sheep, and even a fly in one version. Several animals are killed in many of the versions. The manner of killing the animals or the nature of the punishment, as well as the supposed reason for doing it, all vary widely. In many versions the wedding of the Shrew and her husband is not mentioned or is passed over lightly; in other versions there are quite detailed descriptions of the wedding serving to characterize the bridegroom, set the comic tone of the narrative, and create suspense about the motives for his strange behavior. Other common elaborations in the Taming of the Shrew are tests of the wife by making her agree to absurdities, visits of friends and relatives to the couple, more details about the wager and its outcome, and so forth. Most of these variations on the tale are traditional and have simply been combined and recombined by storytellers. Even fairly minute details in these 307 versions, plus the traits found in another 111 versions of related types, take only a relatively few pages to outline completely in Table II. Such elaborations are important to comparative study of the folktale because they contain specific details which are found in restricted geographical areas and which throw light on local developments of the tale and indicate the paths of dissemination. In general, when the variations are distinctive and occur regularly with other distinctive traits, their occurrences in different areas can be explained best by dissemination via automigration and print from a common original form (reconstructed as an archetype). When the variations are simple and general or could easily have been separately invented, oral dissemination may not be as fitting an explanation as polygenesis.

The different combinations of basic narrative elements in the texts, although useful in classifying the versions, are not of much help in plotting more than the general patterns of the life history of the tale. We can readily see, for example, that the wager is restricted to northern Europe and centered in

Scandinavia and Ireland; we may observe the combination of Type 901 with one form of Type 901B in eastern Europe and the occasional combination with another form of Type 901B in western Europe; we notice at once that Motif W111.3.6, though known as a separate tale or in combinations with other types in other countries, has seen linked with Type 901 only in Ireland; it is also interesting to note that Types 901 and 1370, though logically very similar, only have combined directly in a few versions from Finland, Norway, Denmark, White Russia, and Lithuania. Beyond such generalizations, the matrix of type, motif, and other general narrative elements in each version tells us little about the detailed history of the tradition.

We must turn to the smaller variations of details in the elaboration of the basic plot to work out a satisfactory hypothesis for a complete life history of the tale in its many forms. When the minutiae are compared and like patterns in versions grouped, "subtypes" of the tale emerge, usually within definite geographical boundaries and occasionally even in temporal limits; sometimes, the nature of the trait or its distribution may suggest a chronology. When such comparisons and groupings were made with the versions of the Taming of The Shrew, a number of obviously related subtypes was readily identified. These constitute, however, only a minority of the total number of texts. Furthermore, versions even with definite distinctive traits in them which clearly show their relationship to a given subtype also usually contain generalized traits which are common to a great many other versions *not* related to the same subtype. It is as if every informant has access to the complete outline of all versions and selects for himself elements to make up his own version. Most of those he selects are common and fairly standardized, at least in his area, but others may be quite unusual, and distinctive enough to equate with a distant or much older subtype. These overlappings in the tradition represent survivals of older subtypes and forms within newer forms of the tale—the process of change showing through even as it occurs. No one expects the folktale teller to be logical or to adhere to indexes and type outlines; these are merely abstractions made by those who analyze the material. Quite possibly few *pure* subtypes which are defined in comparative folktale studies exist in oral tradition; certainly, in this instance, few have been preserved.

The procedure in this section of the study of the Taming of the Shrew has been to assign versions to subtype groupings on the basis of the *dominant characteristics* of each text and then to point out other detached traits from the subtype elsewhere. Usually a *sequence of distinctive traits* has been required for the labeling of a version as an example of a specific subtype. The subtypes generally fit into geographical areas that can be explained in terms of likely paths and means of dissemination. For each subtype, however, there are also scatterings of traits in other versions from other areas surrounding or between the areas of its concentration; these show the influence of the distinctive local form on the contiguous tradition. The subtypes thus identified are discussed in what seems to be their possible order of development. In some instances, however, elements of the basic type are simply taken up where they seem to fit in logically. A list of the primary versions of each subtype is given with the "catchword" title of that genus of the folktale, but other versions may be referred to in the discussions. (Version references in parentheses are slightly non-standard.) When popular and widespread elements are taken up, only total figures are sometimes cited. When these general elements are discussed, all of the versions containing them are taken into consideration, without eliminating texts belonging to special subtypes. Charts and lists are frequently employed to help clarify the discussion.

The Cat Killed Subtype

Ind (1), 2, Per 1, Gre 2, 4, RS Lit 1, (3), (SY 8), SR 10, FE 2, 23, FF 7, 9, 10, 15, 16, 18, 25, 27, 28, 29, 31, 32, BLi 3, 4, GSF 5, CI 52, (81).

The simplest form in which the basic plot of Type 901 has been found is as proverbial sayings about a bridegroom killing a cat to frighten his wife. Such sayings from Burma ("For the newlywed, the cat has to die") and Turkey ("Tear off a cat's legs on the first night") are given at the end of Table II with data on sources. The informant's statements about the sayings clearly point to an understood narrative similar to Type 901. The list above contains references to all of the versions of tales in which a cat is killed except for four which seem to be obvious developments of Type 1370 and will be taken up later. Distinctive features in most of these versions indicate that they probably are genetically related, and the distribution of the subtype tells us something about its apparent age.

The cat is the only animal killed in the Persian and the two Greek texts. In Ind 2 a dog is also killed; in Ind 1 a dog and a parrot are killed (but the cat is not killed, since in this instance it obeys a command to catch a rat). In all of the other versions other animals are also killed, usually a horse, dog, cock, or other farm animal.

The reasons for which the cat is killed and the manner of the killing correspond in different areas. In Ind 2 the husband has just seated himself to eat a meal with his new bride when the cat mews. The man flies into a terrific rage at the thought of the cat's begging, and he wrings its neck off and throws the mutilated body away. In Gre 2, likewise, the cat, sitting under the dinner table, mews and is killed. The cat also dies for begging at the table in FF 10, 18, 25 and FE 2; the cat gets on the table and is killed in CI 52, FF 7, 15 and BLi 3; the cat simply mews and is killed in GSF 5, FF 9, FE 23, and SR 10. In RS Lit 1 the cat (as well as a dog and a horse) is killed for failing to bring water for hand-washing before a meal. (RS Lit 3 is a recent dramatization of RS Lit 1 and follows it in most traits.) Less widely distributed as a motive for killing the cat is his not leaving the house or not moving somewhere on command, known in Finland and Lithuania. In SY 8, similar to Ind 2, the cat is commanded to catch mice; in this instance, he disobeys and is killed.

The methods of killing the cat were unfortunately not included in Table II, but they appear to be significant. In Ind 2, it will be recalled, its neck was wrung in the husband's bare hands, and similarly the Turkish saying specifies "tear off a cat's legs." In FE 2 also the cat is torn apart in the bare hands of the husband. In RS Lit 1, FF 18, and GSF 5 the cat is picked up and thrown against a wall, and in BLi 4 it is cast down on the floor and killed. A stick is used to kill the cat in Gre 2, and it is decapitated with a weapon in Per 1, SR 10, FE 23, FF 9, 25, and 32.

It would seem reasonable to assume that a number of shrew-taming tales in which a cat is killed specifically for begging or mewing at mealtime and either with the bare hands or by decapitation must have been historically disseminated from a common source and not invented independently many times over. Versions with these traits in which a cat is the only animal killed are found in Persia and Greece; the saying from Turkey and Burma which mention only a cat seem to relate to the same narrative. Versions from India contain a dog, and in one instance, a parrot, but *not* the horse which is so common in Europe. Versions in which the cat story is combined with the killing of still other animals are found in India, Yugoslavia, Russia, Estonia, Finland, Swedish-Finland, and Ireland. All of the most easterly versions of Type 901 are included in this subtype, making it the most widely distributed of all subtypes. The distribution of the subtype is decidedly peripheral, suggesting that it is old and was probably once known in the center of the area (i.e., in Denmark, Germany, France, etc.) before it died out there, being replaced by more recent forms of the tale. The subtype is barely recognizable on its western border in two Irish versions, however, and it may possibly have reached Ireland by chance through direct transmission across northeastern Europe and not across the whole continent. Whether or not the Cat Killed Subtype was ever well known in the center of Europe, the preservation of traces of it in fourteenth-century Spanish literature, this being one of the oldest dated records of the type, and the concentration of the least elaborated versions in tales and sayings of the East where no other subtypes are known, suggests that this must be an old, possibly a near original form of the tale which had its beginning somewhere in the East.

None of the Eastern versions of the Cat Killed Subtype has more than one daughter in the Shrew's family; none has any description of a wedding or, of course, as we have seen earlier, a wager ending. The Greek, Spanish, Yugoslavian, and Russian versions of the Cat killed Subtype generally agree with the Eastern versions in these traits. In the Estonian, Finnish, and Irish versions, however, elaborations occur—more than one daughter and occasionally a wager.

In Ind 2, Per 1, and RS Lit 1 the fact that the Shrew's greater wealth and higher social standing give her a prerogative to rule her husband is emphasized in the story. The Persian storyteller especially mentioned the cultural significance of this kind of husband-wife relationship by prefacing his tale with remarks about a man "selling himself, as many do, to be the slave of those [passions] of an arrogant woman, who from superior birth or great wealth, considers herself as the ruler of him she has condescended to espouse." In Per 1 a poor but respectable gentleman retainer of a nabob marries his employer's daughter. In Ind 2 a man of humble origin marries a rich man's daughter who insists that her future husband promise to take five smacks of a shoe from her hand daily. In RS Lit 1 the son of a respectable Moor marries the proud daughter of a much richer Moor. The element of the wife's imperiousness by reason of her superior position is found in FE 23 only among the rest of the versions of the Cat Killed Subtype, but it is rather well known in other tales and is quite widely distributed.

Five versions of the Cat Killed Subtype contain an unsuccessful attempt by another husband to tame his wife by the same device. In Per 1 and Gre 2 and 4 a friend of the husband kills a cat in front of his wife. In RS Lit 1 the Shrew's father kills a horse and a cock; the cock is a variation found only in some manuscripts of the version. In CI 81 a friend of the husband begins to beat his dog. Such an "unsuccessful repetition" ending to the tale is known only in three other "non-cat" versions, all from southern Europe—RI Lit 1, RP 2, and Gre 1. The attempt is unsuccessful in these versions, as the bad wife explains, because the man and wife know each other too well and the husband has waited too long before asserting himself. (The informant for version GEAm 25 referred to an unsuccessful repetition episode as "an anticlimax" which he said he sometimes told with the story. This informant is well educated and most probably learned the ending from print, perhaps from a translation of Manuel's or Straparola's versions.) Thus we have here a distinctive element which is closely confined to the Mediterranean area—Persia to Portugal—and which is several times associated with the Cat Killed Subtype. It also reappears in Ireland in CI 81, one of the two examples of the same subtype there. The hypothesis is thus strengthened by this Irish tale that the Cat Killed Subtype was disseminated historically, probably from a center near southeastern Europe, and that it included an unsuccessful-repetition ending episode.

Although the largest number of tales in which a cat is killed comes from Finland, this area does not recommend itself as the home of the original form of the tale. Every Finnish version in which a cat is killed also has a horse; most also have one or two other animals, either a dog, cock, or pig. The characteristic development of the tale in Finland is that a series of animals is killed on the wedding trip and at home. The series progresses from small to large animals beginning with the cat or cock and ending with a horse. It is difficult to see how this strongly formularized pattern would give rise to a cat-only tale in southeastern Europe and the cat-dog-parrot form in India. The center of distribution suggests Persia or Greece, possibly India as the home of the subtype. Here the tale is found at its simplest state and from here it could have radiated northward though eastern Europe and westward to Spain.

The fact that the characters in the Spanish version of Manuel's are Moors seems to indicate that the story was not native to Spain, but came out of eastern tradition. Ticknor believed that the *Disciplina Clericalis*, an eastern-derived tale collection, was probably a prototype for *El Conde Lucanor*, "because the framework of both is similar, the stories of both being given as counsels; because a good many of the proverbs are the same in both; and because some of the stories in both resemble one another."[3] Ticknor singled out "The Moorish Marriage" as a tale of Manuel's which "points distinctly to an Arabic Origin."[4] York, in the introduction to his translation of *El Conde Lucanor*, pointed out, "From the Arabic phrases which we find scattered through the book, it may safely be assumed that Don Manuel had, during his long intercourse with the Moor, become tolerably proficient in that language. This inference lends probability to the idea that some of the Eastern collections of tales were not unknown to him, and that he may have drawn considerably from such sources in some of his narratives."[5] (But in his note to RS Lit 1, York shows that he regarded Don Juan Manuel as the originator of the Taming of the Shrew plot.)[6] From the Turkish and Burmese folk sayings we learn that the narrative was familiar enough there to be referred to proverbially. A folk saying collected from a Moroccan, given at the end of Table I—"When you beat the dog, the bride takes care"—may be analogous with the cat sayings in Turkey and Burma and, if so, demonstrates further familiarity with the simplest form of the type in Eastern-orientated countries.

At least in Persia, two beliefs pertaining to cats tend to show cultural significance in the tale. According to Henri Massé, In Persia, "shedding the blood of a dog or cat is fatal, and anyone who does so will die" and "a dead cat must be thrown out of the house in order to ward off imminent misfortune."[7] Thus, in Per 1, when the husband kills his wife's favorite cat, he is showing extreme bravado, and when he throws the corpse out a window, he is only properly attempting to ward off danger.

The number of versions which contain even traces of the Cat Killed Subtype is very small and the examples are scattered. The reconstruction of an archetype has weak foundations, but the following at least might be presumed to be sound: A man marries a girl of higher position than his own. To improve her imperious ways he pretends great anger when a cat begs for food or mews; he kills it with his bare hands. When a friend tries the same remedy on his own wife, he is unsuccessful because he waited too long and she is too used to his manner to change.

The Cock Killed for Crowing

In version Ind 1 a parrot is killed for chattering. Similarly in RS Lit 1, in the unsuccessful repetition ending, a cock crows and is killed by the father-in-law in an attempt to improve his wife. (The cock appears also in the dramatization of this versions—RS Lit 3.) In the following other versions of the Cat Killed Subtype a cock is also killed: SR 10, FE 2, 23, FF 9, 10, 18, 25, BLi 3 (a hen) and 4. A cock is found among the animals killed in two other versions from Yugoslavia, one from White Russia, three from Russia, three from Lithuania, four from Estonia, eight from Finland, seven from Ireland, and one from Spanish-America. In most of these versions the cock is killed for crowing.

The general trait—bird killed for making a noise—has its possible prototype in the East; it also has nearly identical distribution with the Cat Killed Subtype. The heaviest concentration of the trait is in northern Europe, where it appears regularly with a string of other domestic animals. There is only one cock-only version—SY 2. In two other Yugoslavian versions and two Russian versions a cock and other small farm animals are killed, but not a horse or dog. It is possible that the parrot trait spread from India to southeastern Europe, where it became a cock and was disseminated from there along the same paths as and often in combination with, the story about the cat. Perhaps it is safest to say only that the distributional pattern and the consistent motive for killing the cock suggest an origin and a pattern of dissemination of the trait roughly similar to that of the Cat Killed Subtype as a whole.

The Dog Killed for Begging or Barking

The dog is killed in version Ind 1 for barking, and in Ind 2 for coming to eat unbidden. In FF 25, a primary version of the Cat Killed Subtype, a dog is also killed for begging at the table; otherwise, this motive for killing the dog in Ind 2 has no parallels. One is inclined, therefore, to believe that the handling of the dog in FF 25 may have been invented simply on the analogy of the handling of the cat in the same story, and that this is not a direct survival of the eastern story. The dog being killed for barking, however, is also found in a scattering of tales from Yugoslavia, Estonia, Finland, Ireland, Denmark, and Swedish-Finland. None of these is a version of the Cat Killed Subtype or has any other apparent links with Indic or other eastern versions. It is at least theoretically possible for the barking dog to have been disseminated from India to the West, but without further distinctive similarities to be found between the versions, independent invention of the trait is as good an explanation for it. Certainly barking is the most natural of actions for a dog and could easily have been substituted for a forgotten motive several times over by different informants.

Possibly both the crowing cock and the barking dog that are killed deserve admission to the archetype of the Eastern original of the Taming of the Shrew. If they were original elements, then, as we have seen, the former remains limited to the same area as the Cat Killed Subtype, though often in different versions; the latter, as will be shown, has spread widely and has become part of several of the remaining Subtypes of the tale.

The Development of the Horse Killed Trait from the Cat Killed Subtype

If, as it is argued in the foregoing section, a story in which a cat is killed (possibly a dog and bird also) originated somewhere in the East and was disseminated to Europe, giving rise to the forms of Type 901 found there, then it is necessary to explain the characteristic developments in European subtypes from this supposed prototype. The chief addition to the basic plot in Europe that must be accounted for is the killing of a horse—the most common single taming device in all of the remaining versions.

The genetic relationship of the various Cat Killed versions has been supported on the grounds of the other distinctive traits in them—the cat begging for food or mewing, the killing with the bare hands, the unsuccessful repetition ending, and the general lack of such elaborations as the marriage and the wager episodes. The antiquity of the Cat Killed Subtype has been shown by such evidence as peripheral distribution, appearance in an old printed source, its exclusive occurrence in pure form in the eastern area, and its simple form there as opposed to more complex plots elsewhere. The eastern origin of the subtype is suggested by several of the above details as well as by the appearance there in the form of sayings, the evidence of oriental influences on the old Spanish text, and the cultural significance of certain traits of the subtype in Persia. The crowing cock and the barking dog share some of the same features accorded the mewing cat and possibly also belong to the archetype of the subtype.

The horse trait in the known versions lacks many of the most important features which might tend to place it in the oldest form of Type 901, though excluding the horse solely on the grounds of absence of data would be risky. However, there is other evidence that the horse is a later development. The horse is found evenly spread over Europe, but not in tales further east than Yugoslavia. It is killed with a sword or a gun rather than with the bare hands alone. In the cat, cock and dog stories of this subtype these small animals are killed *in the home* of the married couple, usually for begging at the table, but the horse is almost always killed *on a trip,* either going home from the wedding or going back to the in-laws for a visit. In Spain alone, in Manuel's version, the horse is killed inside the house when it fails to obey the husband's command. A horse is out of place in a house, of course, and so here it seems to be only the third member of a sequence which progresses from smaller to larger animals or from the least valuable to the most valuable. In Finland a similar series occurs, but the last member—the horse—has been provided with a plausible function in the tale. Here the characters are taking a trip back to the wife's home with the horse and the husband punishes it for disobeying. The development of a sequence of increasing size and value is in accordance with normal folktale variation. Examples of this tendency are numerous—the copper, silver, and gold weapons or armor; the progressively more difficult tasks or more beautiful maidens; the series of giants, each stronger than the last; and so forth. It seems a completely natural development for the most important and valuable member of the series—the horse—to persist in tradition when other possibilities disappear. This emphasis on the top trait in the ascending sequence gives the taming device its maximum effect, both on the wife and to the listener.

The most common setting for the killing of the horse is on the trip home from the wedding. In a medieval French version there is no particularized description of the wedding itself, but simply on the trip home the husband shoots his horse for disobedience. In a contemporary German version the groom's arrival at the wedding is more fully described. (See the following subtype for these examples.) In folktales from northern Europe the wedding description reaches its greatest degree of elaboration. The development of this point also seems natural and in keeping with folktale changes. A logical place for extra details to be attached in the tale is the opening where the shrewish girl and her suitor are introduced. Since they must wed, the couple's marriage is a perfectly natural setting for the introduction of appropriate details for the characterization—the groom's outlandish arrival, his miserable horse, the bride having to be forced to leave the celebration early and so forth. The wedding trip provides the natural place then for the horse to fit into the newly-elaborated tale and for the taming to take place, and the dog's function is easily adapted to the same setting; the cat or cock belong at home and so tend to drop out.

The stock characterizations of the groom, as will be seen in detail in a later subtype, also tend to furnish support to the horse trait. In the eastern tales he is some kind of a lowly character marrying high, and in medieval versions he is a knight. The first type, as we shall observe, has been particularized to "farmer" or "peasant," and the latter type has become simply "gentleman." In either case the horse is appropriate transportation for the bridegroom. The dog in one instance becomes a hunter or a favorite pet and in the other instance is a farm dog.

The discovery of a version of the Cat Killed Subtype in ancient Indic literature would strongly support the hypothesis of its having originated there and would help to validate the course of later development of the tale here suggested. Lacking this evidence, we can only submit that the present hypothesis best explains the present evidence.

Medieval Literary Versions in France and Germany and a Corresponding Subtype in Northern Europe

GG Lit 1, 2, RF Lit 1, GG 2, (13), (GNe 1), CS (1), 3, CI 6, 7, 16, 17.

GG Lit 1 and RF Lit 1 are the oldest versions of Type 901 in German and French literary sources; both date from at least the thirteenth century. *Der vrouwen zuht* is a Middle High German poem by a writer known only as "Sibot." It has been preserved in at least five manuscripts, giving some indication of its popularity.[8] The saddling and riding of the wife in it, according to one editor of the text, is a trait belonging to a fairly late expansion of the story in one version.[9] The fabliau *De la Dame Escolliée*, often called *La Male Dame*, is another versified text of the story from about the same period. It too seems to have been fairly popular, judging from the manuscripts which remain. Per Nykrog, in his study of the history of fabliaux, has found *La Male Dame* preserved in six

Type 901: Historic-Geographic Study

manuscripts. Only four other fabliaux are known in more versions—two is seven manuscripts each and two others in eight manuscripts.[10] Both of these medieval European versions share many traits in common, and they clearly derive from the same basic strain of the Taming of the Shrew tradition. Thus, they give us a definite image of at least one phase of this folktale complex in western Europe during the Middle Ages. Neither version has strayed very far from what sounds like authentic folk material, and several modern folktales from northern Europe contain enough corresponding traits to establish a subtype which is closely related to the medieval texts and which must derive either directly from them or from their oral prototypes. The following list of traits, drawn from Table II, contains the distinctive elements of this subtype. The traits are contained in both GG Lit 1 and RF Lit 1 unless otherwise noted.

I	D1	Henpecked father opening (RF only)
II	A1g	Shrew is an only child
	B3	Suitor is a knight
	C1f	Father of Shrew is a knight or other nobleman
	C2a	Mother counsels her daughter to be shrewish
III	E1ci	Man rides a nag to the wedding (GG only)
	E1e	Man is followed by a dog
	E1g	Man has a falcon with him (GG only)
	E2b	Husband refuses to stay after the wedding (RF only)
	E3b	Bride and Groom leave wedding riding one horse
IV	A4	Bride tamed on the wedding trip
	B1a	Horse killed for ignoring a command
	B1dii	Wife must carry the saddle *and* husband (GG only)
		Dog killed:
	B2ai	Does not follow closely (GG only)
	B2axi	Fails to catch a hare (RF only)
		(Cf. another reason involving a hare, IVB2bii—Dog chases a hare against master's command)
	B4b	Falcon killed (GG only)
	[No traits from sections V or VI]	
VII	A4e	Mother-in-law tamed by bogus surgery

It can be seen here that the two medieval literary versions correspond generally with each other in having one daughter and a shrewish mother, some details about the Shrew's wedding, both a horse and dog killed, no wager and a "bogus surgery" taming of the mother-in-law. A few quite specific traits serve to make each version distinctive—the falcon, and the wife having to carry her husband on her back in the German text; the special opening and the dog chasing a hare in the French text. The knightly characters, the falcon and the bloody taming of the mother-in-law all tend to give both versions a definite medieval tone.

One seventeenth-century German printed version and nine northern European folktales contain several traits of the medieval tradition and make up the subtype which corresponds to it. GG Lit 2, from a jestbook of 1667, has only a few clear traces of the older tradition represented by *Der vrouwen zuht*; the chief connections are in the knightly suitor, the dog killed for failing to follow closely and, especially, the falcon. The father here is a rich merchant, rather than a nobleman. GG Lit 2 has no details about the wedding, and the taming takes place on a hunting trip rather than on the honeymoon. There is no mention of a bad mother-in-law. GG 2, a folktale collected in Schleswig-Holstein, corresponds more closely to the German medieval version. Here we find the father still a knight, though the suitor is not; the Shrew has a bad mother. The dog is brought to the wedding, but instead of a falcon, the groom carries a raven. Bride and groom ride off on one horse, and when the husband kills his horse he commands his wife to carry him on her back. She cannot bear the weight, however, and is spared that task. The dog is killed for failing to retrieve game, a trait reminiscent of the French medieval text; the raven dies for failing to sing on command. The tale ends with the anger mole taming of the mother-in-law. GG 13, preserved in Pomerania, contains only the dog chasing a hare and the anger mole taming of the mother-in-law to recall the medieval texts.

The single version of Type 901 collected in The Netherlands has some distinctive traits of this subtype. Like RF Lit 1, the tale opens with the suitor meeting the Shrew's henpecked father working outside on a bad day; the mother is a bad wife who counsels her daughter to treat her future husband badly. An old nag and an old dog appear in the tale when the couple make a trip back to visit the parents. The wife is forced to pull a buggy after the horse is shot; the dog is killed, as in GG Lit 1, for failing to follow closely behind. The bad mother-in-law is apparently subdued by her daughter's report of her own taming, for there is no action against her by the son-in-law.

Two Scottish versions relate to the subtype. CS 1 has the by now familiar pattern of the henpecked father opening and a taming of her mother-in-law, in this instance simply by a beating. The rest of the tale is fairly unique and does not pertain to the subtype; wedding details are lacking and no animals are killed, but instead the daughter is beaten until she improves. CS 3 is much more closely allied to the medieval tradition. We find the henpecked father opening complemented by the standard anger mole taming of the mother-in-law. The bad mother-in-law, in this instance, shows her true colors when she supplies her daughter with a bundle of sticks for beating her husband. The bridegroom arrives to fetch his wife on a horse and with his dog; the couple rides off together on the single horse. The wife must carry the saddle after the horse is destroyed, and the dog is killed when he persists in chasing a hare. There is a wager in this version, but, according to the folklorist who collected it, the informant did not always include this episode in his telling of the tale. Both of the Scottish versions have been collected since 1958.

In Ireland four versions survive, all collected from County Donegal in the 1930's, that have clear connections to our medieval literary subtype. These versions, however, also include the apparently more modern traits of having two sisters for the Shrew and a wager ending. In CI 6 a nobleman marries the daughter of a king; the distinctive traits of her taming are that she must carry her husband on her back and that the dog fails to catch a hare on command. Version CI 7, 16 and 17 are the only folktales anywhere which retain the killing of a falcon, although in GG 2, as we have seen, a raven has been substituted for it. None of the three, however, has knightly characters or a bad mother-in-law. CI 7 and 17 lack details about the wedding, but it is clear from the description of the wedding trip that the husband must have arrived with his horse, dog and falcon. In all three versions the dog has either chased a hare against its master's command or has failed to catch a hare when commanded to. The wife carries the saddle in CI 7 and 17, and in CI 16 she carries home a large bag of gold, part of the dowry. In CI 7 and 17 the stumbling horse gets stuck in a bog, in the former tale depositing the two riders directly into it.

The ten versions of Type 901 which we have just examined all correspond in several traits rather closely to the German and French medieval literary versions; however, in all four countries represented and in most of the individual tales, this agreement is with the combined outline of both GG Lit 1 and RF Lit 1 and not with one specific text or the other. This shows that the literary versions have probably not simply been retold in folktales, but rather that there is still some continuity of the form of the subtype dating from the same European popular tradition which lay behind the medieval texts. GG Lit 1 and RF Lit 1 are only accidental records of some elements of contemporary forms of Type 901; similarly, the folktale texts resulted from a process of selection, by means of oral tradition, from many available elements of the story. The subtype designations of versions are mainly a matter of the choice or sequence of the tale's traits. Medieval storytellers seemed to favor a particular combination of elements in their versions, and we can still detect survivals of the same sequence of traits in these few modern tales.

Apart from the structurally recognizable, whole-tale survivals of the medieval form of the Taming of the Shrew, the separate traits themselves have persisted individually in otherwise undistinctive versions. A review of some of the most specific of these traits further demonstrates that a folk tradition in this particular form existed apart from the literary versions; also this review aids in postulating an archetype for the subtype and in giving some idea of the area of its genesis.

We have already seen that the henpecked father opening and the taming of the mother-in-law conclusion must have migrated, via southeastern Europe, to the west, the plowing being replaced with the cutting of anger moles. This development apparently appealed to the medieval audience, but it has not stood up well in more recent tradition. Only the introductory trait, for example, remains in the version from the Netherlands. One Scottish tale has kept the beating of the mother-in-law rather than the bogus surgery episode, which is now found only in a second Scottish and two German tales. The

Type 901: Historic-Geographic Study

whole idea of taming the mother-in-law, judging from the available texts at least, has not gained anything like the popularity Type 901B has in eastern Europe. The knightly characters in the medieval versions and the falcon have quite naturally also dropped out of most of the folktale tradition. Even when the former trait does appear in a version of Type 901, this alone does not show a medieval survival. More likely, the idea has simply come in from the influence of many other fairy tales with royalty in them.

The general idea of the bridegroom's slovenly appearance and accompanying animals at his wedding has been strongly preserved, along with some other elaborations, in Denmark. A northern European subtype which centers on these Danish versions and extends somewhat into the rest of Scandinavia, as well as Northern Germany, England, and Ireland will be taken up in detail later. Shakespeare, of course, used such a scene in *The Taming of the Shrew*, but he did not originate the idea, as is clearly shown by the Old French and Middle High German predecessors.

The bride is tamed on the wedding trip by the killing of a horse and a dog in the majority of the texts of Type 901. These in themselves, however, are not distinctive enough traits to concern us here. The reason for killing the horse varies widely and can best be discussed when the main group of horse-dog versions is analyzed. Especially striking in the German medieval literary version, however, is that the wife must carry the saddle on her back *with her husband mounted in it* after the horse has been killed. As we have seen, this exact form of the trait occurs only in two versions of the related subtype, GG 2 and CI 6. Outside of the subtype, the trait is preserved in two other versions. GE Lit 9, a comic poem printed in the eighteenth century, has the trait set in a spare framework of the taming tale. The narrative here is told as an account of a successful taming by a husband who forced his wife to wear a saddle and bridle and to carry him; another man then uses the same method on his own wife. The poem is titled "The Taming of the Shrew" and obviously reflects Shakespearean tradition also in the heroine's name—Kate. A Yugoslavian tale provides the final example of the riding on the wife's back and, thus, further supports the hypothesis of a southeastern European origin for that phase of the Taming of the Shrew tradition which the medieval texts reflects. In SY 15 we have, in fact, evidence that a sequence of elements analogous to RF Lit 1 and GG Lit 1 did exist in this area. The version has the bad mother who has bought up a bad daughter, killing of horses and dogs (in this instance, three of each) on the wedding trip, riding his wife, and taming the mother-in-law by plowing. Such a version would need only knightly characters, elaboration about the wedding and bogus surgery to match the western European versions of the subtype; these very traits are the ones which seem to be western in origin. A simplified form of the wife-riding trait—carrying the saddle only—has achieved fair popularity, mainly in northern Europe. This trait will be taken up more directly later.

The killing of the dog for failing to follow closely, as in GG Lit 1, is probably too general a trait to concern us here. The form of the trait in RF Lit 1—the dog failing to catch a hare on command-and a comparable trait—the dog chasing hares when forbidden—are perhaps specific enough to bear more notice. Both of these hare traits are most common in Irish versions, where they occur widely even apart from the medieval subtype. Otherwise the element has turned up only once each in Scotland and Germany and has penetrated only once each beyond the subtype area into Denmark and Finland; it also appears, significantly, in one Yugoslavian version—SY 3.

It would not seem necessary to construct a special archetype for this subtype. The combined outline of RF Lit 1 and GG Lit 1 clearly enough shows the traits which would seem to typify the development by medieval times of the tale in western Europe. The basic plot of the subtype appears ultimately to have been disseminated through southeastern Europe, as Yugoslavian data supports, except for a few distinctly western elements like the knightly characters, the elaboration about the wedding and the falcon. The subtype may owe some of its more recent survival to literary means via the circulation of manuscripts of the medieval texts, but, on the whole, the evidence suggests rather that some individual elements of it have simply persisted in oral tradition. Two of these traits are fairly securely lodged in folktales even up to quite recently, but in restricted areas; the wedding elaboration clusters around Denmark, and the hare traits center on Ireland.

Spanish-French-Danish Connections

The relationship between the Spanish and the northern European versions of Type 901 has been a matter of considerable interest to previous scholars concerned with the tale. Knowing, as these scholars have, usually only *El Conde Lucanor*, Shakespeare's play, and the Danish text of Grundtvig's which Köhler translated, various guesses have been made as to whether Shakespeare knew the Spanish collection or the folktale tradition and whether the northern European and the Spanish versions are truly comparable enough to be related. The possibility of much north-south connection in the tradition has not been well supported, and even the most striking trait, the bridegroom's absurd statements to which his wife must agree (found in all three of the above sources) has not been satisfactorily explained. The discussion of the absurd statements and the other elaborations, best known though Shakespeare's comedy, appears later under the appropriate subtype heading. First, however, it is possible to point out other definite Spanish-French-Danish and other north-south interrelationships in a group of separate folktale versions. The following chart shows distinctive traits of this group and the versions which contain them.

	RS 3	RS 4	RS 5	RF 1	GD 1	GD 8	GD 12
Shrew is a widow	X	X	X	X	X	X	X
Friends warn suitor	X	X	X		X		X
Early wedding, widow's home		X			X	(X)	
Carrying the saddle		X		X	X	X	X
Pulling off boots				X	X	X	X

The Shrew is a widow in the above three Spanish, one French, and three Danish versions and in eleven other versions only. The above seven widow-versions belong to a definite subtype distinguished also by the presence of the other traits listed. (Three other northern German versions with a widow, and one other Danish version belong to a special local subtype which is discussed in Chapter VII.) RF Lit 3 from the eighteenth century has a widow, but the text is too brief to indicate what subtype it belongs to. The remaining one German and four Estonian versions which have a widow in them are not distinctive in any other way. The element of friends of the suitor warning the suitor about the widow's temper occurs in several other versions from northern Europe and in one Greek text and one other Spanish tale.

In RS 3 and GD 1 the wedding takes place early in the morning at the home of the shrewish widow; surely this is so specific a trait that, even not knowing the sequence of other traits, we would believe it to be the result of some kind of direct borrowing between one area and the other. In GD 8 the couple is wed in a normal church ceremony; but upon coming out afterwards, the bride is surprised to see two horses there ready to be used on the trip. The Spanish version, RS 3, has a similar scene of the bride's surprise at finding a burro saddled for the trip.

Carrying the saddle is a common trait in the north of Europe, but apart from the one French and one Spanish version listed above, it occurs only in RP 2 in southern Europe. In the one French and three Danish folktales only does the pulling off of boots occur as a conclusion of Type 901; here the wife is forced to pull off her husband's boots and, to her surprise, *he* then pulls off *her* boots and declares that henceforth he will continue to return whatever treatment he gets at her hands. In RS 3 the husband performs in the spirit of this boot-pulling scene when he gives his wife money from a trunk and says, "I earn and you'll spend with me." Only in two Irish tales does the husband also reward his wife with money.

GD 1 alone contains all five of the traits in the chart, but the other versions contain two, three, or four of them each and are not otherwise connected to separate subtypes. The same series of elements is not found in other versions of Type 901; both the early morning wedding at the widow's home and the boot-pulling scene are restricted to this subtype. These versions from the extreme north and south of the European continent, thus, stand apart clearly from other forms of Type 901 and undeniably must be related in origin. There are other evidences also of Spanish-French-Danish links, both in further details of these texts and in separate elements of other versions.

GD 1 is a version which was printed in a popular periodical in Copenhagen in 1818. It is one of two known versions in which the tale's setting is France; in this instance the northeastern province of Champagne is mentioned. According to Levinson the same text was reprinted in a chapbook in 1857, but here the setting was changed to Sweden.[11] The other text mentioning France as the setting is GS 2, collected in Bohuslän, central Sweden, in 1919. Here the suitor is a Spaniard whose bride comes from Paris. GS 2 is also one of only two Swedish versions which has the wife carrying the saddle, a trait often found in our present subtype. (The only other Swedish tale with carrying the saddle is GS 4, in which Type 900 and 901 are combined, taken from an early nineteenth-century manuscript copy book.) The other two Danish texts of this subtype are from north-central Jutland and were collected by E. T. Kristensen in 1871 and 1875. Conceivably these two Danish folktales and GS 2 could have been influenced by either of the printings of GD 1 or by other printed versions that are now lost.

RF 1, the sole French folktale version of Type 901, is from the former province of Gascogne in extreme southern France, near the Spanish border. The elements of this tale match Danish or Spanish versions of the subtype equally well, with the exception of one possibly accidental trait. In RF 1 the husband, upon arriving home, requests a basin of water from a servant, in this instance to wash his feet. In Don Juan Manuel's version of Type 901—RS Lit 1—the husband gives the same order for washing water, but here for his hands. The cat, dog, and a horse do not bring water, and they are killed; the wife must bring it. Also in GSF 5, during the wager scene, the husband commands his wife to bring him some water to wash with. Possibly there is a north-south link evidenced in these various analogous requests for washing water.

RS 4, RF 1, and RP 2 are the only southern European versions which have the wife carrying the saddle. RS 4 otherwise has no particularly distinctive traits. RS 3 and 5, however, are the only Spanish folktales which have the husband's absurd statements to which the wife must agree. This very interesting element is in a different chapter than is Type 901 in *El Conde*

Lucanor, but otherwise belongs to a distinct northern European subtype. The possible relationships of these versions will be discussed further in Chapter IV.

A number of other examples in miscellaneous versions show further evidence of isolated Spanish and sometimes French and Portuguese counterparts to traits known otherwise just in northern Europe. These traits will be mentioned only briefly here in the order in which they appear in Table II. (1) The father posts a sign warning possible suitors against his shrewish daughter (IIIAl) in one Danish and one Spanish-American tale only. (2) Quite commonly in northern Europe the couple rides home from the wedding both on one horse (IIIE3b), and this trait is also found in one Spanish and one Spanish-American folktale. (3) In only six versions the Shrew is tamed while she and her husband are riding out to look over his lands (IVA5a); one of these tales is German, three are Irish and two are Spanish. (4) In a group of twenty-six northern European tales, most of them Irish, and in two American versions, the horse is specifically killed for refusing to cross a marsh, stream, river, or bridge (IVA1avi); this trait occurs also in the French and one Portuguese folktale. (5) Two other reasons for killing the horse, its refusing to stand still (axi) and its eating when commanded not to eat (axiv) have similar "split" distribution between Spain and the north. (6) Visitors to the couple are warned by the wife not to talk loudly and disturb her husband or not to complain (VCld, di) in RS Lit 1, a Spanish-American tale, and one German tale. Any of these traits, if discovered singly, might be discounted as a mere chance similarity. But when considered as a group and judged in view of the subtype just outlined, they suggest with some force that real connections must have existed at some time in the development of Type 901 between Spain and near-by Romance language countries on the one hand, and northern Europe on the other.

What, if anything, can these elements and the subtype represented by three Spanish, one French, and three Danish versions tell about the direction of borrowing between northern and southern Europe, whether it was by oral or written means and whether it took place in the distant past or more recently? The data give no clear-cut answers at once to these questions, but only suggest possible explanations, some of them in apparent contradiction to each other.

The distribution of the traits in the subtype might indicate that a northern development of Type 901 somehow reached Spain. The shrewish widow, the warning of friends, and carrying the saddle—even the idea of shooting a horse—are all more frequently found in the countries around Denmark than in the south of Europe. It would appear, perhaps, that several typical northern elements had coalesced in a special subtype in Denmark and then had been carried south. Such an explanation, however, would ignore the important consideration of the relative amounts of folktale collecting in different areas. In Denmark and in northern Europe in general there has been a great deal more collecting of folktales than in Spain or elsewhere in southern Europe. The Danish collector E. T. Kristensen alone was responsible for recording no less than fourteen of the twenty versions of Type 901 from Denmark, including two of the present subtype. Without these texts we would have a much different conception of the whole Danish and even the northern European tradition. Until France, Spain, Portugal, Switzerland, Italy, and other countries find their E. T. Kristensens, we can not safely judge any of our decisions as final.

The degree of representativeness of the subtype within countries must also be taken into account. The present widow tale occurs only three times out of twenty in Denmark; it is far overshadowed by other forms in popularity. In Spain, on the other hand, the subtype represents one hundred percent of the versions of Type 901 collected, for the other three texts listed in Table I are examples of Type 1370 and another related story. The French versions is also the only evidence of Type 901 in that country's present folklore. The early printing date of 1818 for GD 1, as compared to RS 3–5 being published between 1942 and 1947 and RF 1 in 1886, is of very little, if any, significance to this discussion. As we have seen, RS 3 and 5 preserve a trait known in Spanish literature from the fourteenth century, namely the absurd statements; the versions could, thus, possibly date back through oral transmission several centuries. RF 1 also possibly preserved an old trait in the washing-water request, but this interpretation of an only roughly analogous element could be questioned seriously.

The general conclusion of the examination of the currently available texts of this subtype would seem to be that the typical Spanish development of Type 901 was transmitted, by way of France, to Denmark. One trait only, the pulling-off of boots scene, is not known in Spain and may have been added en route through France. The subtype survived more or less as a whole in Denmark, owing possibly to being frozen in print in the first half of the nineteenth century, but only isolated traits of it have been collected in countries surrounding Denmark. Both the French setting for GD 1 and the French and Spanish references in GS 2 would appear to bear witness not only to the direction of borrowing, but possibly also of transmission through printed sources which somehow indicated to Danes the origins of the tale. The straight-line course of the borrowing and the lack of evidence of intermediary versions in Germany further suggests printed transmission, at least in the move from France to Scandinavia. No earlier date than 1818 can positively be attributed to the subtype, but the appearance of at least one trait, the widow in an eighteenth-century French printed source, the appearance of medieval traits in the Spanish folktales, and the strong replacement of this subtype by more typically northern elaborations in Denmark all tend to suggest a fairly early borrowing.

The miscellaneous traits which are split in their distribution between Spain or near-lying other countries (or Spanish-America) and Denmark or elsewhere in northern Europe admit of no simple explanation. In general these are fairly uncommon traits; in several instances they are nearly unique. Probably the only generalization it is possible to make is that these traits show further that definite interplay between northern and southern Europe did take place in the transmission of Type 901. If we judge on the basis of our conclusions about the subtype, we would expect that most probably Spain was the place of origin of most of these elements. The Spanish-American examples of some of these traits tends to support this estimate, since colonial versions of folktales frequently preserve older elements than do contemporary versions from the homeland.

Relationship of French-Canadian and European Versions

Three versions from French-Canadian tradition—RFAm 1, 2, and 3—are the longest and most detailed texts of Type 901 in the New World. One might think that these would simply represent the survival of continental French folktales in Canada, but, since only one French folktale text is known, and this one comes from the south of France and is closely allied to Spanish tradition, a better explanation must be considered. A comparison with Old World versions of five of the most striking traits from French-Canadian versions is revealing. As the following chart shows, these traits appear most frequently in versions from Ireland, England and, to a lesser degree, Denmark. Only a few very scattered individual versions from elsewhere in northern Europe have any of these elements in them.

	RFAm	CI	GE	Lit	GD	Other
Father's rule on marriage	3			2	(2)	
Horse-training test of suitor	2	25			1	3
Bridegroom wears old clothes	2	(1)		2	(2)	(1)
Horse killed for not jumping fence	4	59				1
Wives play cards	3	93		1	1	2

Two of these traits are closely paralleled only in Shakespeare's play and in the related quarto, *A Shrew*. In the three French-Canadian texts, as in *A Shrew*, there are three daughters (in Shakespeare two), one of whom is a shrew; in all of these versions the father rules that his shrewish daughter must be married before the others. (In versions GD 10 and 11 the same effect is accomplished by the storyteller's saying that it was a *custom* for the eldest, who is the shrew here, to be married first.) The suitor's wearing of old clothes to his wedding is also given in the same form in the Canadian folktales as in *A Shrew* and *The Shrew*. Four other northern European versions have traces of the same element. In GD 3 the bridegroom arrives in "traveling dress," and in GD 7 and GG 6 he is wearing a pair of thick woolen gloves. In CI 32 the husband arrives in old clothes a few days after the wedding to fetch his new wife home. (RFAm 1–3 also have a variation of an element peculiar to *A Shrew*— the confining and simultaneous starving of the wife at home.)

The other three traits from French-Canada are found frequently in Ireland, but only occasionally elsewhere. In two of the Canadian tales and twenty-five of the Irish ones the suitor is selected by the father of the Shrew on the basis of his demonstrated skill in taming horses or other farm animals; in RFAm 2 and 3, as in one White Russian version and twenty of the Irish versions, the suitor's technique is to lead the stubborn animal with a wisp of hay tied to the tail of a lead animal. (Leading a stubborn horse with hay occurs as an *ending* episode in GG Lit 3, CI 1, and FE 3.) Other animal-training devices figure in one Danish, one Ukrainian, and one Greek tale. The specific reason for which the horse is killed in RFAm 1, 2, and 3 is refusing to jump a fence or other obstacle; this trait is also in the fourth French-Canadian version of Type 901, an otherwise highly individual text in a somewhat literary style. The same reason for killing the horse is found only in fifty-nine Irish versions and in one Estonian version. The wager episode concludes all four French-Canadian versions of Type 901 and even appears in RFAm 5—a versions of Type 1370. In RFAm 1, 2, and 5 the wives are specifically playing cards when the husbands lay their wager on which wife is most obedient. The card-playing, as we have already noted, occurs very frequently in Ireland, but also in two Danish versions, one version each from Scotland and Sweden, and in GE Lit 3.

Judging from the point of view of the distribution of these traits alone, it would seem obvious that the French-Canadian versions must somehow have been derived from a strain of Type 901 in Irish tradition which was also at one time felt in England and more weakly in Denmark and in a few points further east in northern Europe. (RFAm 3 also has one nearly unique trait which is known otherwise only in Finland—the wife must carry home the skin of the dead horse.) Not only are the totals for three of the French-Canadian traits very high in Ireland, but ten versions from that country contain all three of these traits and in other respects are very similar to the New World versions. These Irish versions are CI 25, 32, 29, 50, 74, 91, 98, 107, 121, and 132. The presence of two distinctive traits in the French-Canadian versions which are paralleled in Shakespearean versions but known only incompletely or in another form in Ireland and Denmark today, suggests that the Canadian versions do indeed preserve older forms of the tale, not from France, but from the British Isles. The card playing in GE Lit 3 links that text, at least as regards the wager episode, clearly with the folktale tradition, rather than with Shakespeare.

There is good external evidence from other folktales and from the field that Celtic tales were absorbed by the French in Canada. Paul Delarue pointed out a group of Canadian tales, some of which are not found in France at all, which must have been learned from Scotch and Irish people in the New World. These particular tales are quite common in Ireland, and some are even among those usually considered to be "typically Irish."[12] It appears very likely that Delarue's list should also include Type 901. Luc Lacourcière, Director of Les Archives de Folklore in Quebec and himself the collector of RFAm 2 and 3, sent me these texts; he commented further on Scotch-Irish borrowings in Canada in a paper delivered at the Kiel Folktale Congress in 1959, "Le conte populaire français en Amérique du Nord."[13] Lacourcière admitted here that the assimilation of Celtic material by the French in America ought to be more carefully studied, but he said that probably it could best be explained by intermarriage and the common work of both groups in lumber camps. Surprisingly, Lacourcière has noted no corresponding assimilation among the Scotch-Irish of folktales from French tradition.[14] (Reidar Th. Christiansen, however, has pointed out various "displaced folktales" that have resulted either from unexpected borrowing or the influence of print.)[15] I have not been successful in trying to find Scotch or Irish versions of Type 901 collected in Canada,[16] but M. Lacourcière has very kindly sent me the following notes on the informants of RFAm 1, 2, and 3 which further substantiate the theory that these are in reality versions which go back to Celtic sources:

> Au sujet des 3 informateurs, Benoit Benoit, Léandre
> Savoie et Fidele *McGraw* [my italics, ils sont tous de langue
> française et parlent trés peu l'anglais. Cependant ils ont
> fréquenté les chantiers (lumber camps) de la région de
> Miramichi où il y avait beaucoup de bûcherons de langue
> anglaise. Personne ne parle le gaélique dans cette région.
> Le conteur du nom de McGraw était cependant d'origine
> gaélique. Mais élevé dans un milieu acadien, comme son
> père, il était considéré comme acadien de langue française.
> L'assimilation remontait surement à 2 ou 3 générations. Je
> n'ai pas pu interroger longuement ce conteur, quand je l'ai
> connu, il était déja malade et il est mort peu de temps
> après. Monsieur Benoit lui aussi vient de mourir le 6
> décembre dernier. Il était parmi les meilleurs informateurs
> que j'ai jamais recontrés. Il nous a chanté environ 160
> chansons et conté une vingtaine de contes. Il ne parlait
> pas bien l'anglais, mais, par un phénomène curieux, il avait
> retenu quelques trés longues ballades en anglais, aussi il
> nous a chanté quelques berceuses en micmac. Ces details
> me paraissent significatifs pour expliquer les phénomènes
> d'acculturation par le folklore.[17]

Judging from the three French-Canadian versions and the ten best preserved counterparts from Ireland, then, we can roughly postulate the following archetype for this older English-Irish form of our tale. One of three sisters is a shrew, and her father rules that she must be married before the good daughters. A farmer who is observed cleverly enticing a stubborn horse to work is given the girl in marriage. The groom arrives to be wed dressed in old clothes and otherwise ill appearing (various details occur). On the trip home, which is either on horseback or in a horse-drawn vehicle, he shoots the horse for refusing to jump a fence or another obstacle. Later, while the wives play cards, the husbands wager on which has the most obedient wife, and the former shrew's husband wins when his wife comes at once on command. (The full or partial disrobing occasionally appears.)

A more specific form of the archetype cannot be hypothesized when so few versions are available and when so many of the other traits in them appear widely elsewhere. Neither can a date be given to the archetype other than that two elements at least were known, "by Shakespeare's time." The scattered distribution of a few distinctive traits shows only that the influence of this strain of the development of Type 901 was felt, however weakly, across northern Europe in Scandinavia, Finland, Estonia, and parts of Russia.

Deferment of the Shakespearean Subtype

No subtypes of the tale can be very accurately dated beyond making guesses on the basis of their form or distribution, or stating the time by which they were printed. Logically the subtype to which Shakespeare's plot corresponds belongs here, just after the old subtype which in several traits echoes the same tradition, and just before the generalized modern subtype. Shakespeare's plot and the enclosing tradition from northern Europe, however, are being deferred for a separate chapter. By this arrangement it is possible to examine the subtype closely apart from the tradition and then to fit it into the most appropriate niche. The sequence of these subtypes can in no way be surely proven, but the general pattern already suggested by the data is that a simple original tale was eventually elaborated quite broadly in one limited area, but in most other areas it either never reached full fruition or dwindled to a simplified form. These less complex general versions, whatever their backgrounds, are taken up next.

General European Versions

Only about twenty percent of the versions of Type 901 have been placed in the subtypes already treated, though some reference has been made to the whole body of material. Roughly another twenty percent will be taken up in the following two chapters on the subtype to which Shakespeare's version belongs and the currently circulating American subtype. Thus, about sixty percent of the texts remain to be considered as a unit. This large group represents the fairly standardized, relatively modern, general European folktale that has most often been collected and archived as Type 901. Throughout this body of material various elements of more definite subtypes can be identified, but, on the whole, no important further groupings of versions can be made. Local variations of specific traits can be pointed out, but no very significant sequences of distinctive elements occur.

Grouping these versions by the animal that is killed (discounting miscellaneous animals infrequently encountered) shows seven dog-only tales, sixty horse-only tales (plus the thirty-one in the American subtype), and ninety-nine horse-and-dog tales (plus the thirty-seven in the Shakespearean or "elaborated" subtype). Closer examination of the texts in these groups, however, reveals no other significant basis for setting them up as subtypes; the animals killed in these versions seem to be purely a matter of forgetting or adding traits on the parts of individual informants. The percentage of tales in each country remains about the same in all groups, except that only Ireland and the United States have dog-only tales. RF Lit 2, from an eighteenth-century Parisian newspaper, has only the bare mention of a dog killed as an example to an unruly son; the taming technique but not the narrative frame-work of Type 901 is present here. Vance Randolph's Ozark version—GEAm 23— has only a dog killed, but his seems only to be a local development of the usual American subtype. Straparola's tale— RI Lit 1—is the earliest horse-only version. This literary tale seems to have had remarkably little influence on either written or oral versions of the tale, at least judging by available texts. (No Italian folktale versions, however, have been collected to date.) There are no distinctive traits in Straparola which can clearly be traced in oral tradition. There *is* an unsuccessful-repetition ending here, in keeping with general early southern European tradition. The fight over the breeches in Straparola is a literary element which is briefly treated in note 7 to Table I.

Distributing these general versions by countries, we find that by far the largest number are from Ireland with only Finland and Estonia, Lithuania, and Russia being represented by more than a few versions each. A bare scattering of versions are Icelandic, Danish, Swedish, Swedish-Finnish, German, Yugoslavian, and Spanish-American. The presumably earlier subtypes have accounted for most of the versions of southern Europe while the two subtypes yet to be treated contain most of the versions from Scandinavia and the United States. Thus, one may say, in general, that more specifically distinct forms of Type 901 existed in its earlier history throughout southern

Type 901: Historic-Geographic Study

Europe, in eastern Europe, and in old literary versions until a widespread generalizing of the tradition replaced them. In two limited areas (i.e., the United States and around Denmark) strong special subtypes developed which either replaced the general forms or prevented their gaining wide popular acceptance. A so-called "generalized" version could develop anywhere by the mere forgetting of specific traits or by traits individually losing their specific qualities. There is no necessity to assume that all of these general versions developed from a single "general archetype" which was distinct from the archetypes for the subtypes. A discussion along historic-geographic lines, however, of the traits in the general versions is useful both in studying the typical developments of traits in different areas and for the construction of "normal forms" for eastern and western Europe.

This analysis is based on 158 general European versions. Tales made up of combinations with Type 1370 or other miscellaneous taming stories have been left out and are related to their proper subtypes in subsequent chapters. The following versions make up the present group: GI 1, 2, GS 4, GSF 1, 2, GD 21, GG 11, CI 2, 3, 8, 10, 13, 15, 18, 19, 21, 22, 24, 26, 27, 29, 30, 34–38, 40–49, 51, 54–57, 60–68, 71–73, 75–77, 80, 82–90, 92–97, 99–106, 108–116, 119, 120, 122, 123, 125–131, 133–139, FF 3–5, 8, 11–13, 17, 19, 21, 22, 26, 30, 34, 39, 41, 44, 45, FE 1, 3, 5–7, 9–14, 17, 20–22, BLi 1, 2, 5, 8, SRW 3, SRUk 3, SR 1–3, 7, 8, 12, SY 3, 15, 16, RSAm 1.

No special introductions, save a very occasional combination with a different tale type, occur in the general versions of the Taming of the Shrew. The tale normally begins simply with a description of the Shrew, the suitor, and sometimes extra characters. Except in a few versions, mostly Irish, where from four to seven daughters appear, the Shrew is always one of three daughters. Although the total number of *all versions* which specify three daughters is distributed almost exactly evenly between the oldest (fifty-five), the youngest (fifty-five), and unstated (sixty), the *general versions* state either no particular position (thirty-seven) or eldest daughter (thirty-seven) more than three times as frequently as they specify the youngest (twenty-one). Since the wager ending does not seem original to the whole tradition, but has spilled over from a more elaborated subtype centering on Scandinavia, more than one sister is not essential to the tale as a whole; indeed, it is an unnecessary and even confusing detail. One concludes, then, that the presence of three sisters is found in general versions partly as a carry-over with the wager episode, and partly from the formularizing of elements which is typical of verbal folklore.

The status of the suitor is left unspecified in sixty-two percent of the general versions, though "farmer" or "peasant" is often implied and is directly mentioned in twenty-seven texts. The only other designation which appears frequently is "gentleman" or something similar, which occurs fourteen times. Recalling that in early literary versions and other subtypes the suitor was specified either as a knight or other minor nobleman on the one hand, or a lowly hero marrying high on the other, we can postulate various possible changes that could have worked on this element. The knightly hero may have been generalized to "gentleman" while the lowly suitor was made specifically "farmer." Or, quite as possibly, the need to have a character associated with horses could have given rise to either the high or low-status designations which we have today. Either kind of change could explain the presence of a soldier as suitor in several Finnish versions. The knight himself lives on in four versions. Probably the influence of other folktales is responsible for such specifications as the occasional "widow's son" or "prince." The miscellaneous animals that are sometimes killed nearly always relate to a farmer or peasant suitor rather than a gentleman type.

The parents of the Shrew are seldom given any specific stations in life. In the few general versions which give details about the father, he is either a wealthy man, a king, or a minor nobleman. The mother of the Shrew even less commonly figures in the story. In about one-third of the versions someone warns the suitor about the shrewishness of the girl; usually it is the prospective father-in-law, but sometimes it is the mother or the suitor's father and/or friends. Avarice is implied as the suitor's motive for marrying the Shrew in about twenty percent of the versions where the father offers a large or valuable dowry. Occasionally the dowry is something which figures in the rest of the tale, like a prize for taming the Shrew (two versions), a horse, hound, and gun (two versions), or a horse and carriage (one version).

Type 901: Historic-Geographic Study

Except where the influence of the more elaborated subtype of Scandinavia has been felt, usually no significant details are given about the wedding. Since the taming almost always takes place, at least in part, on the trip home after the wedding, it is sometimes specifically stated that the bride and groom departed riding horses, but usually even this detail is simply implied. Whether it is stated or implied, the couple most frequently are riding on one horse, except for the versions from Finland, Estonia, and Russia, where most often they are in a buggy or sleigh pulled by one or more horses. The original form of the trait would seem to be horseback, with the buggy or sleigh a local invention (which also occurs in American versions). The only significant variation in the place of taming is in eastern Europe, where in about half of the versions from Finland and some from other countries it has become a trip to visit the parents of the Shrew, some time after the wedding. The distribution of this form of the trait suggests that it stems from Finland, where a cat and cock are often killed at home and a dog and/or a horse on the trip to the in-laws. In western Europe the order is usually horse or dog first and if other animals are killed (which is infrequent), these at home. In one group of eleven general versions from Ireland, the occasion for the taming is a hunting trip, a detail perhaps related to version GG Lit 2, but more likely just invented for the sake of giving a logical modern setting. A number of versions scattered over the whole area of distribution have only the designation "on a trip" or the like for the place of the taming; these, surely, represent instances of individual forgetting or simplification.

There are so many possible reasons for killing the horse that it is quite unexpected to find a rather high degree of homogeneity in the general versions. Yet in about seventy percent of these texts the horse is killed for failing to obey a command. In eastern Europe the command most frequently is to start moving, speed up, stop, or go where required, but in Ireland the command is most frequently to jump over something or cross through water, less frequently to remain in one spot. In seven Irish versions the horse is ordered either to drink or not drink some water; in either case the horse disobeys. In the general versions in which the horse does something on its own which irritates the husband, this is usually merely stopping without a command.

Carrying the saddle survives as a task for the wife in only thirty general versions, mostly western, but her substituting for the horse in having to pull the buggy or sleigh is nearly universal in eastern Europe. Probably the difference can best be explained by saying that when a riding horse is shot in a folktale, a storyteller might not readily remember that the saddle should be disposed of; the trait would tend to be forgotten and eventually be dropped out. The presence of a horse-drawn vehicle in the tale, on the other hand, is less likely to be forgotten; the vehicle is an item quite separate from the horse and it can hardly be left standing on the open road. When the horse is killed, the logical conclusion is for the wife to take over. There would seem to be no necessity to connect the buggy-pulling in eastern Europe with saddle-carrying in the west; assuming that the trip in a vehicle rather than on horseback could easily develop locally, the wife's task to pull in the horse's place is a logical following development. The same trait did not develop in the American versions which have buggies because the new "punchline" addition tends to make the tale end as soon as the wife has reacted to the killing of the horse and has been rebuked herself.

A dog is killed in about sixty-four percent of the general versions. The presence of a dog in the entire area of distribution of the type and in most of the old literary versions suggests that this is an original trait, even older than the idea of killing a horse. The nearly universal presence of the horse in recently collected versions shows that this animal must gradually be replacing the dog in tradition. In the United States the dog seldom appears at all. The reasons for killing the dog are less consistent than those pertaining to the horse, but hunting and general obedience are the most common themes. In a few versions an attempt has been made to relate the killing of the dog to the horse's death, by having it be commanded to pull the horse's load, drag off the horse's head, eat the corpse, and so on. Five Irish versions are more agricultural—the dog is commanded to herd cattle. The command may be quite arbitrary, as in one Estonian versions where the dog is commanded to leap over a grave, or an Irish version where the dog is commanded to jump up on horseback. In versions where no command is given the dog may irritate its master by jumping up on him, getting in the way, or barking. The pattern we find in RS Lit 1, in which a series of animals is given the same command (to bring water) and each fails to obey it, does not seem to occur in folktales. In the folktale, therefore, there seems to be a tendency for the husband to complain about some natural ignorance or reluctance of the animal rather than for him to demand, as in Manuel's story, absurd obedience to a command which is beyond the capabilities of the animal.

The other miscellaneous animals that may be killed have already been discussed with the Cat Killed Subtype; as shown there, the cock is the only miscellaneous animal which survives well in general versions. Pig, cow, bull, ox, and sheep appear only sporadically. A special development is a unique Portuguese text—RP 2—which has the husband punish inanimate objects which disobey him; he splits the door with an ax for not closing on command, and he shoots out a light that stays lit when he orders it to extinguish itself. In CI 58 there is a unique generalizing of Type 901 in which the husband simply keeps a gun on hand "to shoot disobedient people," but he never has an occasion to use it. As shown in Chapter II and in the accompanying chart, there are forty-four Irish versions which continue the taming at home with Motif W111.3.6., "Who will not work, shall not eat"; twenty-eight of these are general versions of the tale. This combination of Motif W111.3.6. and Type 901 is unknown outside of Ireland, though the motif appears elsewhere as a separate tale, or in other combined forms. It will be discussed separately in a later section. Direct physical attacks on the wife are found in only a few eastern European versions. Generally speaking, such rough treatment occurs in separate tales rather than in Type 901, where the wife is directly punished only in having to carry a saddle or pull a buggy.

The wager concludes about two-thirds of the general versions and probably belonged to the original form which gave rise to them. Eight versions from eastern Europe end with Type 901B.

On the basis of this examination of the general versions, the following *normal form for western Europe*, mainly Ireland, may be sketched: One of three sisters is a shrew. A man, often a farmer, but sometimes a gentleman, marries her, in spite of warnings. They go home from the wedding riding double on one horse. The husband kills the horse when it fails to obey his command either to jump a fence or hedge or to cross a stream. (The wife sometimes has to carry the saddle then.) A dog is likewise killed for disobeying a command. At home the husband does not allow his wife to eat, or to eat *well*, unless she works. Later he wins a wager on his wife's obedience.

The *normal form of the eastern European general tradition* is as follows: One of three sisters is a shrew. A man, often a farmer or peasant, but sometimes a gentleman, marries her, in spite of warnings. They go home from the wedding in a horse-drawn buggy or sleigh; sometimes they go later to visit the bride's parents instead. The husband kills the horse when it fails to obey his driving command. The wife must pull in the horse's place. A dog is likewise killed for disobeying some command. Later the husband wins a wager on his wife's obedience. Sometimes he also tames his mother-in-law.

It is understandable that the general tales in each area reflect the more distinctive subtypes best known in them. Probably, therefore, the degeneration of complex versions into simpler tales best explains these examples and no overall archetype for them is appropriate.

NOTES TO CHAPTER III

1. John W. Shroeder, "A New Analogue and Possible Source for *The Taming of the Shrew*," *SQ*, X (1959), 251–255.
2. N. P. Andrejev, *Ukazatel' Skazochnykh siuzhetov po systeme Aarne* (Leningrad, 1929).
3. George Ticknor, *History of Spanish Literature*, 6th American ed., I (Boston, 1888), 75–76, no. 31.
4. Ticknor, I: 77.
5. James York, tr., *Count Lucanor: or the Fifty Pleasant Stories of Patronio* (London, 1888), p. ix.
6. York, p. 207.

7. Henri Massé, *Persian Beliefs and Customs* (Behavior Science Translations: New Haven, Conn., 1954), pp. 189, 196.
8. Friedrich Heinrich von der Hagen, *Gesammtabenteur*, I (Stuttgart and Tübingen, 1850), Introd., lxxxii–xc.
9. Hans Lambel, *Erzählungen und Schwänke* (Leipzig, 1883), pp. 325–329.
10. Per Nykrog, *Les Fabliaux: Estude D'Histoire Litteraire et de Stylistique Medievale* (Copenhague, 1957), pp. 324–325.
11. Niels Levinsen, *Folkeeventyr fra Vendsyssel*, Udgivet af Laurits Bødker (*Danmarks Folkeminder*, No. 68: København, 1958), p. 240.
12. Paul Delarue, "Collections de contes canadiens," *Arts et Traditions populaire*, I (1953), 278.
13. Distributed by the author in mimeographed form (Les Archives de Folklore: Université Laval, Québec, 1959), 12 pp.
14. *Ibid.*, p. 9.
15. In "Et Eventyrs Krokveier," *Studia Septentrionalia*, II (1945), 69–83, Christiansen show that a version of Type 328 collected from Indians in Wisconsin is closer to Scotch-Irish versions than to its supposed French origins. There is a possibility, of course, that this tale is another example of New World French borrowing from Scotch-Irish tradition, but the other French-Canadian versions which Christiansen mentions are French in background. Christiansen takes up similar cases as well as obvious borrowings from print in *Studies in Irish and Scandinavian Folktales* (Copenhagen, 1959), and in "'Displaced' Folktales," which appeared in *Humaniora*, ed. by Wayland Hand and Gustav Arlt (Locust Valley, New York, 1960), pp. 161–171.
16. I queried by mail Dr. MacEdward Leach, Dr. Helen Creighton and Rev. P. J. Nicholson, all of whom have collected Celtic folktales in the Maritime Provinces. Only the latter reported "a vague recollection" of having heard Type 901.
17. From a letter dated December 28, 1960.

CHAPTER IV

Type 901: The Northern-European Elaborated Subtype and Shakespeare's *The Taming of the Shrew*

Type 901 is found in folk tradition in its fullest stage of elaboration in Danish versions. In Denmark alone the majority of collected texts contain at least two of three distinctive elements in Shakespeare's shrew-plot—description of the groom's arrival at the wedding, absurd statements to which the wife must agree, and a wager on the wives' obedience. Several folktales also contain an elaboration not in Shakespeare, a demonstration by bending a green branch of the right way to tame a shrewish wife. The area in which a subtype made up of these elaborated versions is known centers strongly on Denmark, but also extends outwards in a few versions from Sweden, Swedish-Finland, and Germany. Distinctive individual traits are found further afield also in Norway, Finland, Estonia, Ireland, French-Canada, and Spain. Because Shakespeare's comedy belongs to it, this subtype has received more attention than any other part of the complex, though the nature of the larger tradition has never been specifically spelled out. One Danish version has received almost all of the attention accorded to oral tradition, because this text happened to have been published in a German translation in a literary journal. Our first tasks, therefore, in studying this Northern-European Elaborated Subtype are to review the studies that have already been made and to show the relationship of the subtype to the whole tradition.

Previous Studies and the State of Present Knowledge

Students of English literature have always been more interested in the relationship of *The Taming of the Shrew* and the anonymous quarto *The Taming of A Shrew* (1594) than in any other aspects of this comedy of Shakespeare's. With detailed and ingenious arguments, different scholars have worked out the following theories concerning the two plays: (1) *A Shrew* was written by another author and later revised by Shakespeare; (2) *A Shrew* was written by Shakespeare himself but he later revised it; (3) *A Shrew* is a "bad quarto" of *The Shrew*; or, (4) *A Shrew* is a "bad quarto" of a lost original of Shakespeare's *The Shrew*. All of the theorists have also considered the possibility of joint authorship of the plays.[1] The fact that, as we have seen, the main plot of the comedy was widely popular in subliterary sources and is well known in oral tradition has never been investigated deeply. Those who have been aware of the extent of this tradition have not usually been equipped to explore it.

For our purposes—tracing the life history of this tale complex and establishing the primary relations of oral and literary versions—the controversy about *A Shrew* is of little interest. There is value, however, in examining the earlier studies which have attempted to deal with sources beyond *A Shrew*. After a perusal of such studies we can better judge which principles in the comparative methods of folktale scholarship might best be applied to our subject. Most of the attention in these studies has been devoted to a possible connection of *The Taming of the Shrew* and *El Conde Lucanor*.

Apparently the earliest mention of the parallel for Shakespeare's comedy in Manuel's book was a cryptic note published by Francis Douce in 1807.[2] Douce commented only that "the outline of *The Taming of the Shrew* may be found in a Spanish work entitled *El Conde Lucanor* . . . composed by Don Juan Manuel, nephew to Ferdinand the fourth king of Castile." *El Conde Lucanor*, despite its considerable literary significance, was, and is, a relatively obscure book. The first edition of 1575,

Ticknor commented, is "one of the rarest books in the world."[3] Translations into French and German appeared only in the middle-nineteenth century, and the standard edition of the text was published in 1900.[4] An English translation of the thirty-fifth chapter (our RS Lit 1), the tale belonging to Type 901, appeared in *The Athenaeum* in 1867, but the whole collection was not published in English until 1888.[5] It is not surprising, then, that Douce's remarks caused some confusion at first.

Karl Simrock, when discussing *The Shrew*'s sources in 1831, managed to turn up an eighteenth-century reprint of *El Conde Lucanor* and fixed on the twenty-seventh chapter (our RS Lit 2) as that to which Douce had referred.[6] However, this is the tale which contains only the test of the wife by making her agree to absurd statements. Friedrich von der Hagen in 1850 correctly identified the taming story in Manuel's collection as Douce's alleged parallel.[7] Simrock then took note of this in the second edition of his commentaries on Shakespeare.[8] Both of these scholars, in common with others in the nineteenth century, regarded Straparola as an intermediary between Manuel and Shakespeare. A third early commentator, George Ticknor, regarded *A Shrew* as the only immediate source for Shakespeare, but he believed that *El Conde Lucanor* contained the earliest European version of the story, recognizing that it had been instrumental in transmitting it from the East.[9]

A milestone in publicizing the larger tradition of the shrew-taming tale, as previously noted, was provided by the notes of Reinhold Köhler.[10] This pioneer annotator of folktales in 1868 not only listed in a Shakespeare journal the relevant early literary parallels of The Shrew, but also gave a German translation of a close Danish folktale analogue. In Köhler's collected writings, published from 1898 to 1900, further folktale references were gathered. Köhler sensibly believed, on the basis of the texts he knew, that the tale must be an old and a widespread one.

However, Reinhold Köhler's valuable data and his insight did not lead to the broader comparative studies which the material deserved. Richard Urbach, for example, wrote his dissertation on the sources of *The Shrew* in 1887, and he knew Köhler's 1868 article; still he relegated all parallels except *A Shrew* to a minor section of "Other Possible Influences."

Urbach discussed Shakespeare's creative revisions of the "crude and ridiculous distortions of his models" (without making it clear which works he thought were the models) and he commented, "This is surely the best proof of the great popularity of the work, that it was taken over so diversely in other languages, even other forms, as in shown in the major references in Part IV of this work."[11] A dissertation on *The Shrew* published three years later by Albert H. Tolman likewise dispatched popular versions to a section of "Remoter Sources."[12] Tolman, though impressed with the similarity of the Danish tale to Shakespeare's play, failed to recognize any great significance in such parallels. He merely listed a number of other analogues by way of example, and then he confused the point by referring in the same section of his paper to other early English works about shrewish wives in general, and to works *based on* Shakespeare. When reprinting his study sixteen years later, Tolman chose to delete the section on remoter sources in order to concentrate on identifying true Shakespearean lines in the play.[13]

In a study done in Swedish, a new Finnish parallel of Type 901 was given, but the interpretation of popular versions was badly garbled by the author, Hanna Lindberg.[14] This writer erred mainly in concentrating on "the Shrew Type" as a typical character in literature instead of examining specific plot parallels in different versions. As a result, all kinds of unrelated stories about bad wives, both English and foreign, were cited as supposed parallels. Lindberg also made the mistake of equating the killing of the horse in *The Wyfe Lapped in Morrelles Skin* with versions that are of Type 901, rather than, properly, with other versions of Type 1370. Lindberg seemed incapable of giving weight to any but English sources in studying forerunners of *The Taming of the Shrew*; as a consequence, she put undue stress on *Morrelles Skin* but dismissed the real plot parallels from other countries. What was true of Hanna Lindberg in this respect still is true of most other Shakespeareans as well.

The first publication of a Spanish folktale version of Type 901 in 1923 prompted Ralph S. Boggs to reappraise the Don Juan Manuel-Shakespeare question.[15] Boggs found that there were enough significant similarities in these three versions to justify saying that they must be ultimately related to each other.

He based his judgment on the elements of the groom's low and the Shrew's high status, the warnings to the suitor, the taming method, the absurd statements, and the wager. A Mexican scholar, Manuel Alcalá, took note of Boggs's assertions and tried to reach a more specific conclusion about possible relationships of Shakespeare's and Manuel's two works by a close comparison of their contents. Alcalá's conclusion is announced in the title of his article—"Don Juan Manuel y Shakespeare: Una Influencia Imposible."[16] The fallacy of his method was shown in Boggs's own bibliographical description of it in *Southern Folklore Quarterly*:

> —Compare once more these two well-known literary variants of the international folktale theme of The Taming of the Shrew, and concludes that they are *independent germinations of a universal theme*. [My italics.] However, author's conclusions are based chiefly on comparison of just these two texts and not on a detailed study of all variants, literary and oral, which might reveal links between them and would be the only way to solve the problem definitively.[17]

It should be noted that Alcalá acknowledged his debt to Bédier for the theory of polygenesis.

Conclusions from specialized studies of *The Shrew* are reflected in a variety of forms in more general comments on the play. Alcalá quoted a number of general statements taken from Spanish literary histories and editions of *El Conde Lucanor*.[18] The opinions he found ranged from simple affirmation of connections between Shakespeare and Spain to flat denial of any possible link; most of the statements, however, were guarded generalizations about the apparent similarity of theme in various sources. The same range of opinions prevails among scholars writing in other languages.

Most writers who have had occasion to make general remarks concerning Shakespeare's source for *The Shrew* had at least a fundamental idea that a larger tradition of the tale existed. Two commentators, however, seem to have lacked this information, and their remarks represent an extreme of bad judgment. Martin Hume in his *Spanish Influence on English Literature* considered *El Conde Lucanor* alone to have transmitted the shrew-tale from the Orient to Europe. Literary adaptations and translations of *El Conde Lucanor* he believed were the sources of the early French, German and Italian texts. Hume concluded, "There is no difficulty whatever in believing that the following story from *Count Lucanor* [chap. XXXV] is the origin, indirectly at least, of *The Taming of the Shrew*."[19] an article in *Folk-Lore* by H. Coote Lake provides a glaring example of unconcern about the wider tradition of the tale.[20] Lake listed *The Shrew* among works of Shakespeare which are "based upon or contain incidents from types in what we may call the official list of folktales." (He was referring to the type-list issued in *The Handbook of Folk-Lore*, and not to the *Type-Index*.) But this play was summarily dismissed by Lake as one which "need not detain us" while attention was turned to *Lear*, *Cymbeline*, and *Winter's Tale*. Yet, as we shall show, *The Shrew* is probably closer to being a pure dramatized folktale than is any other of Shakespeare's plays.

H. Thomas, who took Hume to task for saying that *The Shrew* was derived from *El Conde Lucanor*, went to the opposite extreme and declared that since "the theme of both [is] a widespread folk-lore motive," one should "simply regard the Spanish story as an interesting Shakespeare parallel."[21] On the whole, Thomas found very little support for any Spanish influences at all on Shakespeare. Felix E. Schelling and E. K. Chambers are representative of those who believe that, despite the complex of traditional folktales, reference to *A Shrew* as a predecessor to *The Shrew* settles the question of sources. Schelling wrote, "*The Taming of the Shrew* is a world story traceable in many tongues and versions; there is an older play extant which Shakespeare merely heightened and corrected"; he felt that this explanation would stand "without the peradventure of a doubt."[22] Chambers expressed a similar opinion: "Shakespeare himself probably used no other literary source than *A Shrew*, which had already incorporated widespread story-motives."[23]

Two scholars, Wilhelm Creiznach and G. I. Duthie, who were not satisfied that *A Shrew* had all of the requirements of a source for *The Shrew*, postulated further lost versions in England. Creiznach recognized the shrew-taming device as an old and a widely known narrative motif, but he was troubled by the lack of an English version from Shakespeare's time. He felt that *Morrelles Skin* was related to Shakespeare's play because in both plots there is the character of a mild younger sister who has suitors of her own. Creiznach concluded, "Shakespeare also certainly must have used a lost version in which the motifs only known separately are combined."[24] Duthie, one of the scholars who believes *A Shrew* to be a "bad quarto" of an earlier version of *The Shrew*, wrote, " . . . it is interesting to note that in Svend Grundtvig's collection of Danish folk-tales there is a story on the subject of the taming of a shrewish wife which in certain respects closely resembles Shakespeare's (it is indeed the closest to it of all the extant folk-tale analogues) and in which the character corresponding to Kate has two sisters. It is quite possible that a similar story was current in England in the sixteenth century, and that the hypothesized early play was based upon it."[25]

Editors of Shakespeare's works have reflected a range of opinions about the sources of *The Shrew*. A few examples quoted from their headnotes suffice to show general tendencies. R. Warwick Bond cited Köhler's note and all of the data in it, concluding, "In spite of the close resemblances here between tale [i.e., the Danish version] and play, Köhler declined to recognize any direct connection, but assigned them a common origin in far more ancient tradition."[26] George Lyman Kittredge's headnote had much of the same information, but Kittredge also ventured the guess that perhaps a tale similar to the Danish one was known in Elizabethan England.[27] More recent editors seem to have become less daring, or perhaps they are simply not well informed. Charles Jasper Sisson's headnote, for example, says only, "The Shrew-taming story is ancient, re-told many times in different settings, and Shakespeare told it again after his fashion."[28] As recently as 1957 an editor of Shakespeare, John Munroe, referred only to Tolman and to the 1908 Boas edition of *A Shrew* for information on popular analogues. Munroe learned here that the plot was widespread in folklore and literature, but he only mentioned one example—*Morrelles Skin*—and said, "The story of the wager on the wives exists separately and a variant occurs in *The Book of the Knight of La Tour-Landry*."[29] He made no mention at all of the Danish tale which also has a wager. The nadir of headnote information about sources seems to have been reached in the edition of *The Shrew* prepared by Sir Arthur Quiller-Couch and John Dover Wilson.[30] The former wrote in his introduction:

> [as to] the Induction and all the Petruchio-Katharine business ... The 'sources' or 'derivation' of both of these can be dismissed by sensible men at once; the Induction theme—of the drunken sleeper awakened—being at least as old as the ... *Arabian Nights*, the shrew-taming scenes as old as the hills. Whoever possessed a grandfather that could not be roused from the chimney corner as by the sound of a trumpet to cap either of them with an analogous local tradition? The affair of the wife's wager at the end, too, is pure folk-lore.[31]

A glance at some survey works on sources shows probably the most conservative and noncommital stands on the question that are current. Geoffrey Bullough in his *Narrative and Dramatic Sources of Shakespeare* says only "This is a variant of the Shrew theme common in fabliaux from classical times."[32] He then cites a list of supposed analogues—like the Wife of Bath and jest-book versions of other tale types—most of which have no relation to Type 901 at all. In Werner P. Friederich's *Outline of Comparative Literature*, under a discussion of Oriental influence in medieval literature, we learn only that *El Conde Lucanor* "may have influenced both Chaucer and Shakespeare."[33] Kenneth Muir in *Shakespeare's Sources* reviews only the *A Shrew* question and then writes, "The state of our knowledge is such that it would be unprofitable to discuss the question of sources."[34] Finally, Selma Guttman's bibliography *The Foreign Sources of Shakespeare's Works*, though it contains a section on "influence of Spanish Literature," makes no mention whatsoever of the scholars who have linked *The Shrew* with *El Conde Lucanor*.[35]

Commentary on Previous Studies

The purpose of this rather lengthy summary of learned opinions on the relationship of *The Shrew* to oral and literary analogues was not merely to set up straw men that can be knocked down, but to point out shortcomings in previous studies, in order to pave the way for a fuller investigation of the problem. After surveying these studies, we can realize why it is desirable for literary scholars dealing with works that are derived from folk narratives to be familiar with the ways of tradition and the means of its study.

The major shortcoming in studies of analogues of *The Shrew* made by Shakespeareans has been too strict adherence to the methods of investigating purely literary influence and the attempt to apply these methods to folklore. For instance, in literary studies one work cannot be considered a possible source of another unless it is an earlier published text from the same country or one which had been translated or could have been read in the original by the author in question. Such criteria are almost meaningless in terms of folktales. The date of collection of folktale texts from oral tradition tells us nothing about the actual age of the tales. The places where a given tale is known indicate generally the area of its traditional life, but the absence of collected versions from an area never proves the tale in unknown there. On the contrary, a broad scattering of versions in Europe is good evidence that the tale *is* known in much of the Indo-European area, though it may not yet have been collected everywhere. Different languages seem to constitute no serious barriers for oral transmission of tales.

Partly as a result of demanding the early-dated-printed text as a source, literary investigators have found themselves bound to treat such unlikely candidates as Don Juan Manuel's Spanish tales, Straparola's *novella*, and *The Wyfe Lapped in Morrelles Skin* as possible sources for *The Taming of the Shrew*. Their task has not been easy, for none of these versions is very close to Shakespeare's plot. Only *Morrelles Skin* of the three stands a very good chance of having been known to Shakespeare, and this is the least similar to his play, being a version of Type 1370 in the "hide form" (see Chapter VI below). Whether or not Shakespeare knew Spanish seems a very idle topic to pursue, but it has loomed importantly in the arguments of those who would prove or disprove his dependence on *El Conde Lucanor*. Straparola's influence on any part of this tale complex, as we have seen, was apparently negligible. Strangely, two early printed versions that *are* more closely related to Shakespeare's plot, the medieval German and French texts, have been left out of most discussions.

A Shrew has led the field as the chief candidate for Shakespeare's source, but few scholars have asked the logical question, "From where then did *A Shrew* derive?" Interesting as the question of the immediate origin of this quarto is, it is surprising that so many scholars have been willing to narrow their view to the two English plays exclusively and never to inquire about the whole ancient and widespread tradition of the story. Had they done so, the scholars would have found that both *A Shrew* and *The Shrew* contain elements not in the other play, but paralleled in the folktale tradition. For some reason the point of view which inspired wide-ranging studies of some of Chaucer's tales has not apparently affected those who speculated about *The Taming of the Shrew*.

The handling of the one folktale version well known to Shakespeare scholars, Grundtvig's Danish text, illustrates a second major shortcoming in these studies—too little knowledge of or understanding of oral traditions. This version (GD 7 in this study) has almost invariably been treated as a unique survival of an old Danish story rather than as a chance recording from a continuum generally known all over Europe and found eastward as far as India. Lack of much information about analogous folktales in other countries contributed to this attitude; still it is surprising that few scholars made some simple deductions from these data that might have redirected the studies. To wit: since two distinct elements of the plot—the taming device and the absurd statements—occur separately in *El Conde Lucanor* but occur together both in Shakespeare and the Danish tale, then if Shakespeare based his play on the old Spanish story one of the following corollaries must be true: either the Danish storytellers developed the same conglomerate independently, or the tale in Denmark was derived from Shakespeare's play. Neither of these possibilities would stand up under scrutiny. Therefore, since the Danish tale *also* has the

Type 901: The Northern-Elaborated Subtype

wager, it clearly represents the kind of primary link which must have existed between Shakespeare and the popular tradition; the other literary versions, are separate offshoots of the tradition, but none could be the single source for Shakespeare's play. Reinhold Köhler made these basic steps in reasoning in his 1868 article, and R. S. Boggs made essentially the same deductions on the basis of a Spanish folktale and the two literary texts. Alcalá, however, "proved" that the stories Boggs considered must have arisen independently since Shakespeare knew no Spanish!

Some scholars, either by intuition or because they knew something about other forms of folklore, guessed that a broad traditional background of the tale might have extended at one time to England. Creiznach, Duthie, and Kittredge have been quoted in this vein. Unfortunately these particular scholars were preoccupied with other problems about the play and did not follow up their hunches. It is intriguing to think that Kittredge and Duthie (along with five others quoted from before 1928) might have found additional analogues in the *Type-Index*; five others mentioned wrote recently enough to have used *The Folktale* as well. Such reference works, however, are not well known outside of the field of Folklore, and folklorists themselves are just as culpable for not using their resources for literary studies as Shakespeare scholars are for not branching out into Folklore when the subject matter demands it. The only really shocking lapse by a literary scholar is Munroe's failure to mention that the wager episode is combined with the shrew-taming tale in versions other than Shakespeare's.

The kinds of shortcomings in dealing with oral tradition which have been pointed out lead particularly to misunderstandings when special interpretations are developed from them. Such an example for our play is a recent article by Muriel C. Bradbrook, "Dramatic Rôle as Social Image; a Study of *The Taming of the Shrew*."[36] Bradbrook begins with the truism that "in comedy, characters tend to be presented socially, in terms of rôles, which. . . are fairly stereotyped."[37] Shakespeare's characters in *The Shrew* are examined to see how their typical popular roles have been remade by the artist, and to find what different social images emerge. Much reference is made to the traditional social image of shrewish wives, and Shakespeare is said to have used "a main plot based on the popular dramatic rôle of the Shrew."[38] Although Bradbrook lists "folk tales" among the sources of her conception of this traditional role, *not a single oral analogue* of Shakespeare's plot is cited. Instead, such examples as the Wife of Bath, Noah's wife, *Tom Tyler and his Wife* and other plays, Childe (sic) 277 (*Wife Wrapt in Wether's Skin*), and *Morrelles Skin* are listed. Bradbrook concludes that "traditionally the Shrew triumphed" (though not in all of her examples) and that the great novelty of Shakespeare's plot is that Petruchio, the tamer, takes over the role of the tamed. Mistakes in this line of reasoning are obvious. Shakespeare's plot, in the first place, does not parallel earlier English plays or poems about shrews; it closely follows a complex of tales found mostly in oral tradition and known earlier in dramatic form only in *A Shrew*. These folktales do not show the Shrew as triumphant, but in them she is tamed just about as Katherina is in Shakespeare's play. The works which Bradbrook compares with Shakespeare's plot do not, in general, belong to the same narrative tradition at all. Shakespeare's play is not "highly original in treatment,"[39] but it is almost exactly like the analogous tale in oral circulation. Therefore, it is incorrect to make much of the dramatist's "skill in adaptation [of] the traditional image of the Shrew" as Bradbrook does.[40] Shakespeare's play may have meanings not in a simple folktale version, and there is originality in using the folktale as the subject for a comedy, but these are other matters. In short, two "traditions" about shrews exist; both are partly oral and partly popular or literary. In one tradition the Shrew triumphs; in the other she is tamed. Shakespeare wrote in the latter tradition, though he most certainly did not invent it.

The most recent discussion of sources for *The Shrew* combines judicious estimates about the extent of oral traditions (though still on the basis of the Danish tale alone) with the most elementary misunderstandings about the nature of folktales. In John W. Shroeder's note, "A new Analogue and Possible Source for the *The Taming of the Shrew*," the writer reexamines the question of sources briefly and tries to promote a claim for an early printed work as a partial source for the plays.[41] Shroeder realizes, for he has read Köhler, that the main shrew-taming plot "must surely come from some original much like the Jutland folk tale."[42] He is bothered, however, by two differences between the plots of the tale and of *A Shrew*: "Close as the Jutland tales is, in broad outlines and in particulars, to the main plot of *A Shrew*, the two narratives here and there differ considerably."[43] In the folktales, Shroeder points out, the wife is tamed on the trip home, while in *A Shrew* it is at home: by confining and starving her; and in the play a wager takes place after supper, while in the folktale there is no wager after a meal, but a prize from the father-in-law. It is true that *A Shrew* has no mention of taming the shrewish bride on the trip home by horseback, but apparently Shroeder has forgotten that this element does occur in Shakespeare's comedy, in the dialogue of act 4, scene 1. Furthermore, starving the wife as part of the taming is a common trait which is frequently combined with Type 901 in Irish versions. Three French-Canadian texts contain taming by locking-up as well as starving, just as does *A Shrew*.

Shroeder's objections to the wager episode are easy to dismiss with a little more knowledge of analogues from oral tradition. The after-dinner wager, as we have already seen, is the most common form known for this wife-testing episode; Danish tradition, as it happens, has evolved the father-in-law's prize of money in a cup as a standard variation; however, anyone acquainted with folklore would recognize this as a variant, especially when it occurs in versions of the same tale type. Furthermore, no one working with oral tradition should be surprised to find different versions of a story alike in "broad outlines" as well as "particulars" (to use Shroeder's terms) but which still differ "here and there." Such variation is simply in the nature of oral tradition. Not even two people who had just read Shakespeare's play could be expected to retell the plot exactly identically, and if their versions were to be retold a few times, more changes would surely creep in. There is nothing unusual in this Danish folktale differing slightly from the hypothesized oral version which might once have existed in England; indeed, it would be most extraordinary if *any* two folklore versions agreed in every respect. When one is considering whether Shakespeare's plot might have been derived from an original like a given folktale, this is not the same as considering whether Shakespeare used *that particular tale*. Close textual comparison is useful in studying literary influence, but it must be replaced when studying folklore by the comparison of tale traits and understanding of the effects of oral refashioning.

Shroeder did guess that there was a broader folktale tradition, but he found no examples of other oral versions. "It may be," he wrote, "to be sure that the author of *A Shrew* had as, his source a version of the tale of the Three Shrewish Sisters which differed from the Jutland version in precisely these details; perhaps we deal with nothing more than variants of an European story on that favorite theme, the Taming of the Curst [sic] Wife. . . in any case, Ferando's taming methods remain unique, and unmatched in the known analogues."[44]

Shroeder, like his predecessors, still treats oral materials as if they are literary records. He compares the two texts and since they are not exactly parallel in every detail, he rejects one as a possible prototypic form of the other; he knows that the same tale is found in different countries and even guesses that it might have been told widely, but he does not examine other oral versions and he dares not accept the clear inference that other texts might contain the elements he holds in question. Having on the basis of one folktale text set aside the oral tradition from consideration because of the supposed lack of evidence, what does Shroeder propose as his "new analogue"? His discovery is Caxton's translation of "The Tale of Queen Vastis" from *The Book of the Knight of La Tour-Landry*—the same book which provided us, from a different chapter, with a remote analogue of the wager episode (see RF Lit 5 and the discussion of the wager in Chapter III). In this tale Queen Vastis is called by her husband, king of Assyria, to come to him when he talks after dinner with some acquaintances. She does not come, so the king orders her to be locked up for a year with little to eat or drink. Shroeder finds "remarkable" similarities to *A Shrew* here, and this is in itself the most remarkable idea of his note. The full implication of this alleged source is that Shakespeare (and the unknown author of the lost original for *A Shrew*) independently selected exactly those traits from the printed text of another tale which are found in many oral versions of the tale of the Taming of the Shrew. To Shroeder, the fact that there is a reference to falconry in the Queen Vastis tale as in the English plays clinches his argument. He concludes that Caxton's book must have been one source of the lost original for *A Shrew*. The alternative hypothesis which Shroeder states, however, most assuredly is more fitting to the evidence: "Caxton's tale has material also in the lost source of *A Shrew*."[45] The plot of the Queen Vastis story is so fragmentary and the similarities to the Taming of the Shrew Complex are so incidental that there seems to be very poor evidence that the former has any genetic relationship to the latter at all.

In summary, the following techniques for analyzing oral narratives were lacking in the literary studies of sources for The Taming of the Shrew: (1) Gathering many versions of the story; (2) Distinguishing different tale types and comparing only versions of the same type; (3) Distinguishing subtypes and realizing that versions in one subtype are more closely related to each other than they are to versions of other subtypes; (4) Recognizing variations that have resulted from oral transmission; and (5) Evaluating the influence of folktales by their own principles and not by those demanded in studies of *literary* influence. These major principles have governed our new investigation of the problem.

The Shrew-Plots of "A Shrew" and "The Shrew"

Leaving aside the names of characters and the sub-plot action, for the sake of clarity and because they do not affect our subject, and including all action given in dialogue, the following summary contains the essential elements of the shrew-plot of *A Shrew*:

> The oldest of three daughters of a wealthy man is a Shrew. Her father insists that the Shrew be married before her sisters. The father offers a large dowry, and a young man—her equal in status—takes her, saying he will be able to tame her. The groom arrives late for the wedding and dressed poorly. He refuses to stay for a celebration, but takes his new wife home riding horseback. At the couple's home the husband tames his wife by confining her, depriving her of food and by pretending to get angry at minor things (throws food from the table, mistreats servants, and refuses to accept his wife's new clothing). On a trip back to visit her father, the husband says the sun

is the moon, the time of day is different than it is and that an elderly man is a young girl. He turns back when his wife disagrees; she finally agrees with him for the sake of making the trip. At the father-in-law's home, after dinner, the husbands of the three sisters lay a cash wager on who has the most obedient wife. The wives are absent, and the former Shrew must come in when called, throw her cap to the floor and step on it, place her hand under her husband's foot, and fetch the other wives in and lecture them. The husband is declared the winner and is also rewarded with extra money by his father-in-law.

The main plot of *The Shrew* differs basically from that of *A Shrew* in containing the flowing additional traits:

(1) The Shrew is the older of two daughters and the third wife is a character in the sub-plot. (2) The suitor's friends, as well as the Shrew's own father, personally warn him about the girl. (3) The groom arrives at the wedding riding an old sick horse; he behaves badly at the wedding. (4) Part of the taming takes place on the trip home from the wedding when the horses throw the riders into a muddy bog and the husband turns to beating his servant for this. (5) At home the husband says that he will also throw bedding to the floor. (6) After the wager the reformed Shrew must also kiss her husband.

One additional trait is only *mentioned* in *The Shrew*—one servant asks if the couple was riding double on the same horse on their wedding trip. *A Shrew* contains only three traits not specifically in *The Shrew*—there is no confining of the wife in the latter, and the reformed wife does not *literally* step on her cap or place her hand under her husband's foot.

In general the plot outline of *A Shrew*, which with six additions and three deletions serves for *The Shrew*, contains very little that is not found somewhere in the folktale tradition. The basic elements of the plot as well as many specific details are quite common in other versions. The exact absurd statements made by the husband in the play are not found in folklore, but similar statements are. The reformed Shrew's placing her hand under her husband's foot and lecturing the other wives are elements found in these plays only; the husband's refusing to accept the wife's new clothes is another unique trait. Even such specific traits as throwing food from the table and confining the wife are found in a few oral versions.

Only the two sisters in *A Shrew*, as opposed to one sister in *The Shrew*, puts the former text any closer to folk tradition than the latter is. In five traits, however—the second, third, fourth, fifth, and sixth listed above—*The Shrew* has material not in *A Shrew* but which is found in oral tradition. Even the mere mention in *The Shrew* of both characters riding home from the wedding on one horse points to the folktales. Only the addition of the bridegroom's bad behavior at the wedding in *The Shrew* is unparalleled in other versions. The warnings to the suitor, the old sick horse he rides, and the muddy bog they fall into in Shakespeare's plot especially link it to folk tradition; the remaining new traits in *The Taming of the Shrew* are relatively uncommon, sometimes being found only in a single other version.

The close relation of the joint plot of these plays to the oral tradition is already self-evident and consideration of the following subtype places the ultimate connection beyond question. Shakespeare's more-detailed plot is closer to folk tradition than *A Shrew* is; since this is a matter of several traits, and the forms of these traits are distinctive enough so that they could not have been invented independently by Shakespeare and by the folktale tellers, the author of *The Shrew* must have had closer contact with the tradition than did the author of *A Shrew*. If we return to the four basic theories that have been proposed about these two plays then, we see that our findings so far indicate the following corollaries for each hypothesis:

(1) If Shakespeare revised another author's play, he must have done so with reference back to the original tradition. (2) If Shakespeare revised his own early play, he must have gone back to the original tradition for a little more material. (3) If *A Shrew* is a "bad quarto" of *The Shrew*, the pirate missed some traits, changed some slightly himself, and once either returned to the tradition for a trait, or by chance hit on a traditional variation. (4) If there was an original form of *The Shrew*, now lost, of which *A Shrew* is a "bad quarto, then Shakespeare revised it with reference back to the original tradition.

Whichever origin for *A Shrew* is finally accepted, and there is still no consensus, it is clear that the plot ultimately was derived from a widespread folk tradition and that Shakespeare drew more elements from this tradition—either directly or indirectly—than did the writer of *A Shrew*.

The Northern-European Elaborated Subtype

GD 7, Grundtvig's noted text of the Taming of the Shrew, published in 1854 and translated by Köhler in 1868, is as close to Shakespeare's plot as any folktale so far recovered; it is not, however, the only such version. Most of the other texts from Denmark and a few from around Denmark contain the same elements. The distinctive elaborations that identify this group with Shakespeare's play are the details about the groom's arrival at the wedding, the absurd statements to which the wife must agree, and the wager episode. A further elaboration not in Shakespeare is found in the folktales. The husband at some time gives his wife a green branch; later when he has tamed her, he calls for it and shows other husbands how it cannot be bent. From this he draws the moral, "One must bend the branch when it is green."

The six folktales which contain all four elaborations at some length, we may designate the A Group: GD 4, 6, 7, 16, GS 7, GG 6.

Four versions make up a B-1 Group, in which three elaborations are present, but the details about the wedding are skimpy or are merely implied: GD 3, GS 1, 3, GG 9.

Another four versions we may call the *B-2 Group*; these contain three elaborations, lacking only the absurd statements: GD 2, 5, 14, 20.

A *C-1 Group* is made up of versions with only two of the elaborations, the wedding details and the wager; these include four Danish versions, one Swedish, and thirteen Irish and French-Canadian versions: GD 9, 10, 11, 15, 18, GS 8, CI 14, 16, 28, 33, 59, 69, 70, 117, 118, RFAm 1, 2, 3.

A *C-2 Group* contains four additional versions with two elaborations—the green branch motif and the wager: GD 17, CI 11, 20, 78.

Type 901: The Northern-Elaborated Subtype

Altogether there are thirty-seven versions in the Northern European Elaborated Subtype—fifteen Danish, four Swedish, two German, thirteen Irish, and three French-Canadian—which all more or less closely parallel *A Shrew* and *The Shrew*. All of the four elaborations are known over a somewhat wider area in scattered versions, but the heart of the tradition area is northern Europe, especially Denmark.

Historic-Geographic Study of the Subtype

There is never a special introduction of any kind in the oral versions of the Northern-European Subtype. Every text, save one from Ireland, opens with the description of *three* daughters (CI 14 has seven), one of whom is a shrew. The statements about the position of the Shrew in the family, however, are divided almost equally as youngest (thirteen texts), oldest (ten), and unspecified position (thirteen). All but one of the unspecified versions are Irish or Canadian (hence, Celtic-derived). In determining the position of the shrewish daughter, Danish tradition is of no help—the distribution here is an inconclusive seven for youngest daughter and eight for oldest. The remaining texts from Sweden, Germany, and Ireland divide six to two in favor of the youngest. Adding the references to oldest or youngest daughters in *all* versions which specify the point, we reach the equivocating figure of sixty-two for the oldest, sixty-six for the youngest, and sixty-six unspecified. Clearly there is no hope of establishing more than that the Shrew in this subtype is one of three sisters. The folk prefer no particular position over others, and the authors of *A Shrew* and *The Shrew* must have made the heroine the oldest daughter for artistic reasons.

The three sisters are named Karen, Maren, and Mette in Grundtvig's text and have names in some other versions in the subtype. GD 15 has the names Maren, Karen, and Sidsel and GG 6 has Katrin, Marie, and Magret. In GD 16 the name Mette only is preserved. In GD 4 the names are prefixed with terms suggesting bad temper, and have become Grøt-Grete, Morp-Maren, and Surpotte-Sidsel. In two texts where the Shrew only is named there is a similar prefix meaning "bad" or "evil"—GD 2 has Onde-Else, and GD 9 has Onde-Kristen. GD 10 and 11 both have the names Grete, Marie, and Trine, though in different order. The naming of the sisters in the tale is almost exclusively restricted to Denmark and is not found outside of this subtype. Except for one Zealand text and the Schleswig-Holstein version. GG 6, these names are not found outside of northern Jutland. It is extremely difficult to determine whether names are original in a tale since they are in the first rank of element to be lost in oral tradition.[46] They also may easily be locally attached or borrowed from other tales. About all that can be said is that certain names are traditional in Denmark and in one version analogous names have spread to northern Germany. There is no strong evidence that the names are original to the subtype.

In about one-half of the versions of the subtype the suitor's status is specified, but his different roles vary widely and no clear pattern is apparent. No particular specifications would seem to have been original. Twelve versions, representing all of the countries having the subtype, specify a position of wealth for the Shrew's father. His large dowry, gift, or prize supports this characterization, and the general idea of a wealthy father would seem to belong as an original element.

Warnings to the suitor about the Shrew, usually from his prospective father-in-law, are found in about two-thirds of the versions of the subtype and in all countries involved. Such a warning was also commonly found in other subtypes and in older literary sources. To all appearances this is a trait of long-standing in the tradition which was retained in the original form of the Northern-European Subtype. Shakespeare's use of the trait seems to derive from tradition ultimately.

Some kinds of details about the wedding of the Shrewish girl are found in about one-third of all versions of Type 901. The distribution is roughly the same as that of the wager episode—that is, the wedding details are not found in many old literary sources; the traits are most common in Scandinavia, less common in Celtic countries, thin out sharply in eastern and southern Europe and are not found in the East at all. The details about the weddings, however, are found earlier in literature than the wager was, somewhat less frequently in Slavic countries, but more frequently in Romance countries and also in the United States where the wager was unknown.

Both the medieval texts of Germany and France had elements of the wedding scene in them. GG Lit 1 had the

Type 901: The Northern-Elaborated Subtype

groom's arrival on an old horse, his dog, a falcon, and the departure riding double on the horse. RF Lit 1 had only the groom's refusal to stay for a celebration and the departure on the single horse. The other traits that are found concern the wedding—late arrival of the groom, his poor dress, arrival in a horsedrawn vehicle, a gun, and the departure on separate horses or in the vehicle—are all preserved in several folktales from different countries. Clearly, neither Shakespeare nor the author of *A Shrew* invented anything in their corresponding scenes covering this element except possibly the bridegroom's bad behavior during the ceremony which is found in *The Shrew* alone.

All but four of the Danish texts contain four to seven details pertaining to the wedding; no Danish version of the subtype is without some element of this trait. The number of details in texts drops off sharply in other countries. Ireland, for its 130 texts of Type 901, has less than ten versions with more than three details about the wedding in them. Grundtvig's 1854 text contained late arrival, poor dress (here only some large gloves), the old horse, a dog, a gun, refusing to stay for the celebration, and departure on a single horse. Only GG 6 has these same details (even to the mention of the gloves), so the influence of a printed text of GD 8 may be suspected. A comparison of the further traits of GD 7 with GG6 shows so many correspondence that print seems the most likely explanation for them. No important details about the wedding not in GD 7 are found elsewhere; other versions differ only in generalizing some traits or dropping them altogether. It may be that Grundtvig turned up an exceptionally complete text of the subtype in 1854 and everything found since then has deteriorated to some degree. The printing of GD 7 may be discounted as a possible source of the whole tradition of this episode since most of these traits occur quite widely and several were found in early literature. The possibility that Grundtvig made up a composite text for publication cannot be totally disregarded.

The bridegroom arrives late for the wedding in ten Danish versions from all parts of the country, one southern Swedish version, and one northern German text. In all of these instances he has given or sent word that he will meet the party at the church. He finally comes when all of the guests have assembled and they see his poor condition. *The Shrew* is closer to the folktales in this element than is *A Shrew*, for Shakespeare specifies that the wedding party is waiting; Kate has apparently gone off to church and meets Petruchio there. Although the trait seems to be unknown in Ireland, Shakespeare's use of it indicates that it was known further then the present oral tales extend.

The groom's dress is described in *A Shrew* as "basely attired, and a red cap on his head;" in *The Shrew* a detailed list of his poor clothing is given. The trait is known, though slightly, in folktales. In GD 7 and GG 6 only the gloves are mentioned, and in GD 3 the groom wears "traveling dress." CI 32 is the sole Irish text with a vestige of this trait. Here the groom does not take his bride home at once after the wedding, but returns after a few days to fetch her. He has put on his oldest clothes and he comes riding a horse and followed by his dog. In both RFAm 1 and 2 the suitor shows up in old clothes; in the former version the wedding in on the same day, and in the latter the man returns in the old clothing for his wedding. Examples of the groom's poor dress are not numerous, but they occur over such a wide area in oral tradition that they would appear at least to be a genuine folk trait. The author of *A Shrew* and to a greater extent Shakespeare filled out the basic idea of the trait with more specific details.

The groom's arrival riding horseback is implied in nearly every version in which a horse is later killed, but the element is *specified* early in the tale in only fifty versions. It is found in early literary sources only in GG Lit 1 and in Shakespeare's play, in both versions the horse being an old and wretched nag. The largest number of versions of the subtype (thirteen texts) simply have the groom come on horseback without specifying the condition of his horse. When the horse is described in the versions of this subtype it is more frequently a nag (eight versions) rather than a fine horse (four versions). In three versions from Ireland and Canada the groom arrives in a carriage pulled by a nag—a trait paralleled in eastern Europe with a sleigh. Beyond the versions clearly belonging to this more elaborated subtype, all possible descriptions of the groom's also occur elsewhere. The arrival on an old nag has only a slight edge over horse-unspecified versions (twenty-three to twenty-two), but its wider distribution and the older appearances tend to indicate that it is an original trait. The other forms must represent generalizations or local variations on the model. Shakespeare here is in line with the strongest traditional element.

A dog accompanies the groom in nine of the Danish versions and examples of the subtype in every other country except Canada. This element was in GG Lit 1 but is not found in the English plays. It is quite well known in other versions from northern Europe, especially the Irish. Probably it was original to the subtype.

It is specified that the groom carries a gun in twenty-two oral versions from northern Europe, only nine of which are members of the present subtype. Some kind of a weapon must have been original to the whole tradition in which an an animal is killed, but there is not sufficient evidence to believe that a gun was necessarily the original weapon in this particular subtype. At any rate, it is a natural later development in the tale and, like other traits in this section of this story, it is everywhere much more frequently implied that it is specified.

We earlier observed the groom's insistence on leaving the wedding early in RF Lit 1. It is a trait also in both of the English plays and in fourteen versions from folk tradition, most of which are clear examples of this subtype. Like the earlier traits of the warning of father and friends, this is one known in medieval literature, but retained now almost exclusively in this particular subtype, where it must have been original.

The departure of the married couple from the wedding on horseback is specified much more frequently than was the groom's arrival with a horse, since this element leads directly to the taming itself and cannot easily be dispensed with. In the oldest literary versions and most of the total number of texts, they ride together on the husband's horse; this is also the most common form of the trait in Danish versions of the subtype and others from Sweden, Germany, and Ireland. It is known outside northern Europe in one Spanish and a Spanish-American version—the only element of the wedding description known so widely. It must be the original form, with riding separate horses or riding in a vehicle being later derivations. Shakespeare may have been alluding to the trait when he has a servant in *The Shrew* ask if both rode on one horse.

The taming invariably takes place on the trip home, occasionally continuing somewhat at home. Always a horse is killed and in many texts also a dog; the dog is not included in Shakespeare or in the French-Canadian versions. Both animals are found in the older literary sources and we have already attempted to establish that the horse is a later, though now a more popular element.

The original form of the reason for which the horse is killed in this subtype would seem to be one connected with the horse doing something on its own accord—stumbling, getting stuck, splashing or throwing a rider, falling, and so forth. All of these kinds of details occur most frequently in this subtype, especially in Danish versions, but also are found elsewhere, in Ireland and French-Canada the typical local forms predominate—that is, refusing to jump an obstacle or ford a stream. Shakespeare seems simply to have enlarged on this folktale trait. The scene naturally is given in dialogue in The Shrew, as all such actions must be in drama. The horse falls in a muddy bog in The Shrew, and the bride, instead of merely being splashed, must wade through the dirt to pull her husband away from beating the hapless servant. Possibly Shakespeare declined to have Petruchio kill the horse in order to preserve his character somewhat, but there can be little doubt that he was borrowing the general scene from folklore and not simply making it up. The husband's beating the servant in The Shrew, though perhaps paralleled in a Russian versions in which the husband pushes the driver off the carriage when the horse stumbles, is probably an original touch put in to substitute for the killing.

Carrying the saddle is a trait widely known since medieval times. It does occur in this subtype, but not regularly enough to be considered an original element. A curious trait which occurs in three versions of this subtype only is that of the husband himself carrying the saddle and sometimes his wife as well. Probably this is just an extension of his general tendency in the story to put people and animals under his strict control. Except in GD 7 and GG 6 and two Swedish versions in which the dog does not retrieve an object that is dropped, this animal is most frequently killed in the subtype for the same reason as in GG Lit 1—refusing to follow closely on the trip. Probably the latter trait was the original form in the subtype and the dropped-object or other miscellaneous forms were later specializations. There is possibly the slightest hint of a dog-killed trait in *The Shrew*, at the couple's homecoming, when Petruchio calls out for water to wash before eating and then immediately afterward says, "Where's my spaniel Troilus?" This reminds one of the washing-water request from animals, in *El Conde Lucanor* and the faint echoes of the same trait, as observed in Chapter III, in a French and a Swedish-Finnish folktale.

The various taming devices applied at home in *A Shrew* and *The Shrew* are not part of the Elaborated Subtype, but are found in other versions. Depriving the wife of food specifically because she does not work (Motif W111.3.6.) is well known as a separate story and has frequently combined with Type 901 in Ireland. More simply, just keeping food from her, as in the English plays, is found in few versions. GG Lit 2, a sixteenth-century jestbook version, has the wife herself stubbornly keeping to her room and refusing to eat for three days. It is possible that this text actually was influenced by Shakespeare, since there is a servant in it who plays a part somewhat similar to Grumio's. At any rate, this version shows that such a form of Type 901 was not unknown around Shakespeare's time. GE Lit 7, from the seventeenth century, is a popular piece obviously indebted to *A Shrew*; the wife here is "mewed up like a hawk" and starved. GG 12 has starving the wife, but the taming is carried out by cutting her and not by the Type 901 device of killing an animal. In three Irish versions of Type 901 serving inferior food to the wife is part of the taming, but these may just be simpler forms of the more common no work—no food motif. In FF 35 the device is exaggerated, but in essence is quite close to the plays—the wife is locked up for four months and fed only enough to keep her alive. In one Indic text the wife is brought to a miserable little cabin and fed only bread and water for fifteen days. Three French-Canadian versions, because they are analogous to *The Shrew* in various other respects already mentioned, provide probably the best evidence that the trait got into Shakespeare via folklore. Here the wife is locked in her room with no food all day because she is not up at the first call in the morning. On the whole, there does not seem to be enough evidence to state categorically that Shakespeare or the writer of *A Shrew* must have taken the trait from folklore. Precedents, at any rate, were there and the borrowing was possible. The fact that Petruchio does not specifically mention confinement while in *A Shrew* the husband promises to mew her up like a hawk would not seem to be so important a difference as Shroeder thought. Since Petruchio intended to tame Kate by the means used to tame a falcon, he could hardly have failed to intend to keep a close check on her movements.

Petruchio's refusing to accept the new clothes ordered for Kate seems to be a unique trait in Shakespeare. Two other traits might have seemed equally so, but for two striking parallels from southeastern Europe—these elements are the casting away of food from the table and (in *The Shrew* only) the threatened casting down of bedding. One version from Yugoslavia—SY 11—has both of these traits, plus one more found in Shakespeare, and a unique element; the following is quoted from SY 11 as I have it in summary: "His behavior was impossible. He threw their dinner to the ground because, according to him, it was not pleasing. He beat the servant, threw the bedding out of the bed, and skinned a goat alive." (The throwing down of food is also found in Gre 1.) It would seem quite unlikely for these food and bedding traits from southeastern Europe to have been known in the oral tradition of northern Europe without there now being any examples from the area between. Polygenesis is the best explanation for the present evidence. The mistreating of servants could more likely have come to the English plays from tradition, being also found in RF Lit 1 and in a Danish tale. This element too, however, might have been derived independently.

The husband's forcing the wife to agree with absurd statements which he makes occurs in the ten versions of this subtype in the *A* and *B-1 Groups*—five Danish, three Swedish, and two German texts. The element also occurs separately in Norway, Estonia, and in *El Conde Lucanor* and two Spanish folktales. Linking Shakespeare's use of the same device to either the Spanish or Danish versions is a difficult step in the analysis of the tradition upon which many a previous scholar has stumbled. There is now, to our advantage, the benefit of more texts than any earlier writer had available to compare.

The first problem we must deal with is whether the absurd-statements tale in Chapter XXVII of *El Conde Lucanor* really does belong to the Taming of the Shrew at all; previous scholars have never quite been ready to accept this without some question. In the twenty-seventh chapter there is no taming like that in the tale of the Moor's wedding in Chapter XXXV. The husband only tells his future wife that he has certain shortcomings, among them that she must always agree with everything he says; she does. The husband demonstrates her obedience by calling some cows mares, some mares cows, and saying a river is running the wrong way; the wife agrees with all of his statements. Compared to Grundtvig's Danish tale and the English plays alone, there would seem to be only a general similarity in the Spanish tale. In the northern versions of Grundtvig and Shakespeare, the man and wife are on a trip and he threatens to turn back until she agrees with his absurdities. The Danish tale has statements about birds and sheep rather than larger livestock, as in Spain; the statements in the plays are unique. Further folktale versions help to clarify the situation. The trait has been collected now in two texts of Type 901 from Spain—RS 3 and 5—thereby removing doubt that the combination was known in the south of Europe. In both of these tales there is a standard Type 901 taming; the husband then sells some fat bulls and buys skinny ones. In RS 3 the wife agrees that her husband made a good deal. In RS 5 she first agrees with him that the cattle are fat, then reverses herself when he says they are lean. One Danish tale—GD 16—has also been collected which includes an absurdity about larger livestock, in this instance oxen. It is clear, then, that Spanish and northern European (most likely Danish) traditions of Type 901 must have been somehow in contact at one time. (Our previous examinations of Spanish-French-Danish similarities indicated the same conclusion.) Because in the English shrew plays continuation of a trip is involved with the absurd statements—as is *always* true in northern Europe but *never* in Spain—the route to England of this trait must have been by way of the Northern-European Elaborated Subtype.

Certain groupings of the absurd statements in folktales can be made. GD 7 closely matches GG 6, as it did in several other traits; here white birds are called black and vice versa and sheep are called dogs or wolves. GD 4 and 6 are similar in that specifically doves and ravens are confused in them. In GD 3 swans are referred to as black birds and ravens are called white birds. The latter trait also occurs separately in the text from Norway. (The Norwegian text has certain other similarities with GD 3, but it is combined with Type 1370, suggesting likely Swedish influence.) GS 3 and 7 both also involve some form of the confused bird colors. Outside of Scandinavia the bird color confusion gives way to species not necessarily of contrasting colors being miscalled. In part of GG 6 chicks and goslings are confused, and in GG 9 the birds are ravens and swallows. The only folktale version of Type 901 in which no animal is involved in the absurd statement is GS 1 where the husband calls a sunny day a rainy one.

FE 28 appears to preserve the most easterly European example of the absurd statement trait, though in a unique narrative. Here the husband of a shrew refers to some wild geese that fly overhead as swans. The wife becomes so enraged at this that she pretends to be dead; she does not agree that the birds were swans until she has been put in her grave and the first shovel of dirt is thrown in. Two separate tales from India if taken together seem to parallel this Estonian tale. In the first of these tales a raja and a rani argue whether certain birds are eagles or geese. Messengers sent to settle the question find the birds to be geese, as the rani had said, but the messengers are bribed to give the opposite answer and the rani must perform humiliating penance.[47] In the second of these tales a man and his wife quarrel and make a silence wager. When people who think they are dead begin to bury them, they speak again.[48] It seems possible that the bird dispute belongs to a separate folktale about a stubborn married person who does not give in until death is threatened. Should an independent complex of such a tale be found, it would seem likely that the bird dispute from it was later attached to Type 901. Without further evidence for this, however, no such judgment may yet be made.

In *A Shrew* and *The Shrew* no animals are involved in the absurd statements. The husband states the time of day

Type 901: The Northern-Elaborated Subtype 199

incorrectly, calls the sun the moon, and refers to an old man as a young girl. His wife disagrees with the first statement, so he turns back on a trip. She gives in and agrees with the second, so the trip is continued; and she agrees at once with the third statement. Although these absurd statements differ widely from those in the folktales, the same pattern of disagreement-agreement and trip or no-trip prevails. The use of the element in the plays could not have been a chance invention; yet one would struggle long to show how the bird and animal statements in folklore could have changed in oral tradition to the unique absurdities found in the plays. The answer lies not in any strange quirk of transmission by word of mouth, but simply in what can and cannot be acted on stage. Obviously Shakespeare could not call for a pair of doves or ravens to fly overhead; he could not write a flock of sheep or even a single ox into his comedy. He was forced to make allowance here, as in the groom's arrival and the horse-killing scenes, for limitations of his medium; in this instance he could not very well fall back on putting action into dialogue. However, in an open-air theater, the sun, or at least the sky, could readily be indicated with a gesture—this trait he may or may not have found suggested by a traditional source such as GS 1. Time in drama being strictly a convention, Petruchio could be allowed to twist it to his will for the second absurdity. For the third statement Shakespeare made use of a minor character who had to be along in following scenes anyway; he exploited comedy of contrast between age and youth, and comedy of misunderstanding. Thus the idea for this scene in the play came straight from tradition, but the themes were made to fit the medium.[49]

The green-branch-bending element with a corresponding motto ending the tale—"Bend the branch when it is green"—occurs almost exclusively in this subtype, but not in *A Shrew* or *The Shrew*. Three occurrences of it in Irish versions show that is probably passed through England and might have been known in Shakespeare's time. Most of the versions of it come from Denmark, but several times the significance of the cut branch to the story is unclear or is entirely left out. Both GD 4 and CI 20 have references to the green branch in their titles. Every occurrence of the trait in these versions comes after the wager, when the father-in-law or the other husbands ask how a wife can be tamed. Then the shrew-tamer calls for the wife to produce the bent branch, and he shows that just as it is too late to unbend this dry branch, so a wife must be trained while she is supple and young. A similar element appears in FF 43 except that the husband heats two branches in an oven before showing how only the young one will bend. In FE 4, a version of Type 1370, the hero uses two birch twigs wrapped around his finger to show his father-in-law when things must be accomplished.

The distribution of the green-branch element around Denmark and the apparent deterioration of it as one moves outwards from there clearly suggests a Danish original of somewhat limited distribution. An apparent analogue in a version published in India in 1895, however, offers startling evidence that this may be a very old element of the tale which was originally Eastern. There is no reason to suspect that the Indic version is falsified—an informant from Mirzapur is named, and the form of the taming scene conforms exactly to what would be expected there. Although it is certainly curious that such similar traits appear in the same tale type in Europe and India, the lack of versions further south and west in Europe than Estonia prevents our concluding that the element was surely disseminated. Also, the exact themes of the Indic and European tales differ. Unless some definite transitional forms come to light, polygenesis will probably best explain the coincidence of elements here. For the sake of comparison, first the ending of Ind 1 and secondly my translation of the ending scene of GD 14 are quoted below:

> Ind 1—Then Banke Chhail went out and brought the old man in. When he saw how changed his daughter was, he said to his son-in-law: "You know what a life my wife leads me. I wish you would tell me how you have succeeded in reducing your wife to order. Perhaps I may be able to deal with my wife in the same way." Said Banke Chhail: "Good, Sir, bring a brick and some moist clay and make me a lamp saucer out of each." "It is easy," quoth the old many, "to mould the soft clay but when the clay gets hard no power on earth would mould it."

"In short," said Banke Chhail, "your wife's character is fixed and cannot be mended. I dealt with my wife in season and you can see the result." The old man went home sorrowful.

GD 14—. . . she was the most obedient. They discussed this for a while and the father began to wonder about it, for she had always been the most ill-natured one when she was home. But now there was no doubt; she had won the silver cup. So her husband told them, almost like a parable, that they should bend the branch while it was young for if it got too old, then it would not bend at all. Then he asked her if she had the branch which he had once given her, and she tore it from he skirt where she kept it. It was bent, but he couldn't bend it back again, for it fell apart when he tried. They drove home again, and had the silver cup with them and they lived in the future just as well as they had in the past.

The wager has already been examined in terms of the whole tradition. It was observed that Scandinavian tradition in general and Danish versions in particular have separate and apparently later developments than are known on the periphery in Ireland, Scotland, England, Iceland, eastern Europe, and French-Canada. The versions of the present subtype follow this pattern essentially. The wager frequently takes place at the father-in-law's house, but is not specifically after dinner except in Irish versions of the subtype. A cash wager is the rule in Irish and Canadian texts (and is found in one Danish version), but the prize of coins in a cup or the like prevails elsewhere in the subtype. The wives are playing cards in most Irish and Canadian versions (and in one each from Sweden and Denmark), but more commonly in Scandinavia they are working in the kitchen or looking over clothing. The call to come is the universally known command of the husbands to their wives. Additional commands are not common in this subtype. On the whole it would appear that the wager, though regularly found with the other elaborations, is a broader and older tradition that has not been disseminated so strongly from the Scandinavian center for the subtype as have the rest. It has developed along its own lines in different areas. Shakespeare's version of the wager episode, except for some personal touches, matches the older and more widespread form which is current in England, eastern Europe and on the periphery in general, but which is not commonly found in Scandinavia. The question earlier left unanswered—whether Shakespeare's play might have given rise to the wager episode in folktales—would now, in view of the whole pattern that is developing, seem to be settled. Since all the rest of the plot, save a few rather minor details, must have derived from oral tradition, it would be unreasonable to think that one basic element of the plot has moved in the opposite direction. The wager too must be originally a folktale element.

The extra reward to the husband after the wager in the English plays is found in eastern European folktales and in one Swedish version, but it could have easily occurred to Shakespeare independently. It sounds like a contrived literary touch anyway when Baptista offers "another dowry to another daughter." There are, however, two Irish versions in which the husbands gets no dowry at all until his wife is tamed.

The Archetype for the Northern-European Elaborated Subtype

The limited distribution and the pattern of the distribution of this subtype both indicate that it is a relatively recent development, probably Danish in origin, which has drawn on and often expanded or altered elements known more widely and from an earlier period. The most striking individual trait in the subtype is the green-branch element, which, however, may have had an Indic prototype. The most significant general feature of the subtype is the bringing together in northern Europe of all of the important elaborations known in Type 901 itself. In the following archetype for the subtype which the data suggests, the particularly full or original elements are italicized; the rest of the traits are widely known and usually older:

> One of the three daughters of a wealthy man is a shrew. She is courted by a young man of unspecified status (but probably lower than her own) who, despite warnings about her, weds her. (*Full details about the wedding*): The groom *arrives later for the wedding*,

probably wearing poor clothing, riding a nag and accompanied by a dog, and bearing a weapon. He refuses to stay for a wedding celebration and departs with his bride riding on the same horse with him. On the trip home he kills his horse for committing some kind of act like *stumbling, falling, splashing the riders, or the like.* he kills his dog when it fails to obey. His wife is tamed. On a trip back to visit his in-laws, the man makes *absurd statements about birds or other animals which his wife first disagrees with and finally agrees with when her husband threatens to return home. He has given her a bent green branch to keep.* At the father-in-law's home *the wives are working in the kitchen or looking over new clothing* and the men talk separately. *The father offers a prize of coins in a cup* for the husband of the best-behaved wife. Each husband calls his wife, and only the reformed shrew comes. *The husband shows that "One must bend the branch when it's green."*

Summary of the Relationship of the English Shrew Plays to Tradition

A Shrew and *The Shrew* can be discussed simultaneously, since they share the basic traits of the tale and the differences between them consist mainly of a number of elements present only in the latter. (Details in one play only are marked with "*AS*" or "*TS*" in the following discussion.) The plays can easily be broken down with respect to the traditional bases of the elements included in them. We can begin with the oldest, most widely known and best attested traditional traits and proceed toward the least common traits which are most likely original to the English plays.

In its basic outline and in many particular details the *A Shrew-The Shrew* plot goes back to old and widespread elements of the story. In this category are the three daughters (*AS*), wealthy father, warning the suitor, the groom's arrival on an old horse, his refusing to stay for a wedding celebration, the departure on horseback, (mentioned: riding double—*TS*), taming on the trip home by punishing the horse (*TS*), depriving the wife of food, a wager at the father-in-law's home—after dinner the wives are called in and the Shrew partially disrobes.

The details about the wedding which are found in the plays are particularly typical of Ireland and the older wager tradition rather than the Scandinavian developments. French-Canadian versions, ultimately Celtic-derived, preserve two other traits known in the plays and untypical of broader tradition—the father's rule on the marriage of the Shrew first, and the groom's wearing of old clothes to the wedding. Possibly the confining and starving of the wife in Canadian versions also represents material which came to the plays from tradition.

A second category of elements in the plays belongs specifically to the Northern-European Elaborated Subtype and must have come to Great Britain by way of Scandinavia. This is not to say that many or all of the traits in the first category might not have been disseminated from Scandinavia too; as a matter of fact, the evidence from this second category tends to suggest a similar route for the first. The categories are separated here because the second group of elements is not widely known or well developed outside of the subtype, at least judging from present evidence. The elements from the subtype, then, are the groom's later arrival; the horse stumbling, falling, or splashing the riders (*TS*), and the absurd statements, made on a trip to the father's home, with which the wife must agree in order for the trip to be continued.

A third category of relatively minor elements in the plays includes elements which have parallels in folktales, but which are scattered in tradition and are so simple and general that they might easily have been invented separately. These details are two daughters (*TS*), the oldest daughter being the Shrew, beating the servant when the horse misbehaves (*TS*), confining the wife (perhaps implied: calling for water from the dog—*TS*), throwing food from the table, throwing bedding to the floor (*TS*), mistreating servants at home, making the wife kiss the husband, and an extra reward for the husband after the wager.

A few traits in the plays seem to be unique to these literary versions; these are the groom's bad behavior at the wedding, his refusal to accept his wife's new clothing, the wife putting her hand under her husband's foot, and her having to lecture the other wives.

Two basic types of literary adaptation were carried out in dramatizing the folktale—relegating unstageable action to dialogue, or otherwise altering action to fit the stage, and expanding certain elements which have particular comic appeal. The scenes which were of necessity put into the wings and rendered in dialogue were the groom's arrival on an old sick horse and the trip home on horseback during which the bride is partly tamed. The absurd statements were also altered so they could be staged. Elements which were enlarged upon for comic effect were such things as the groom's poor clothing, mistreating of servants, throwing food from the table, and making the wife do special tasks after the wager.

Similar problems in adapting the same tale to the stage were faced by the contemporary Spanish playwright Alejandro Casona, when he dramatized the version of the Taming of the Shrew from *El Conde Lucanor*; Casona's comedy, RS Lit 3 in this study, reveals in the handling of the taming device solutions different from Shakespeare's. In the old Spanish tale the hero kills the dog, a cat, and a horse which fail to bring him water with which to wash his hands before eating. In Casona's play the dog is dragged offstage and howls of fear and pain are heard; the hero returns and wipes his knife on the tablecloth. The cat is then chased offstage, and this time the hero comes back with a stuffed cat impaled on his sword—the wife pulls the cat from the sword and holds it up by the tail. Finally a horse (i.e., a prop horse-head) appears at the window. The hero pulls out a gun and shoots at the head, which is then dropped out of sight from backstage.

A Source for "The Shrew" Reconsidered

Comparative study of the available analogues of *The Taming of the Shrew* has shown that the main plot of the play must ultimately have derived from oral tradition. None of the known earlier literary versions, *A Shrew* included, could have been the sole source since none contains distinctive traits of the play which are found paralleled only in folktales. It is highly improbable that the play and the folktales could have been independently invented. *The Shrew* could not be the source of all of the traditional versions because the basic elements of the plot are found in earlier texts. *The Shrew* could not be the source even for the answering Northern-European Elaborated

Subtype because dramatically necessary alterations in it are never found in oral versions. Therefore, either directly or indirectly Shakespeare *must* have had access to the story as it was developed in oral tradition.

The Taming of the Shrew is a well-known folktale on the continent of Europe, especially in the northern countries. The popularity of the tale in Ireland and its appearance in Scotland lend support to the idea that at one time (perhaps also at present) it was known in England. Versions from French-Canada, which are borrowings from Celtic tradition in the New World, contain certain traits which closely match Shakespeare's plot and which probably belonged to the English folk prototype for the play. Irish tradition on the whole preserves the general European form of the tale which is reflected in *The Shrew* and which is also known orally in eastern Europe. A few Irish versions contain distinctive elements of an elaborated subtype which is still strongly preserved in Denmark, where it seems to have originated; this subtype has also affected Shakespeare's plot.

We cannot tell, of course, whether an actual English oral version of the tale was the immediate prototype of *The Taming of the Shrew* or whether Shakespeare used a printed version, now lost, which was closely related to the folktale. That Shakespeare knew the tale orally is at least a good possibility, for accurate recordings of tales from oral tradition are almost unknown anywhere before the late nineteenth century and are not the general rule even today. Further study of elements in Shakespeare's works which indicate the extent of his awareness of oral tradition could help to settle the question of a possible oral source here. That the model for *The Shrew* was English seems likely. There is no difficulty from the present evidence in postulating English versions of the tale; furthermore, there is definite evidence, discussed below, that the folktale was known in England in the eighteenth century. At any rate, it is far more difficult to imagine how a foreign version—which would have to have been Scandinavian or Irish—could have been known to Shakespeare in so pure a form as he must have known the tale. For the present, then, we may say that the prototype of *The Shrew* was probably an English folktale containing all of the elements of the story listed in categories one and two above

Type 901: The Northern-Elaborated Subtype

and possibly some of the traits in category three. Further collection of folktales and further analysis of the data may yield more insights.

It is unfortunate that there have been few English collections of folktales with which we might seek to corroborate this hypothesis about Type 901 in England. However, beyond *A Shrew* and *The Shrew* and a few taming stories that are either literary or which belong to another tale type, no English analogues of this folktale have heretofore been discussed. There is, nevertheless, one further version which has been long regarded as a mere copy of Shakespeare, but which in the light of present knowledge must be admitted as a separate analogue. This is the version from *The Tatler* of September 30, 1710, listed as GE Lit 3 in Table I and briefly discussed there in a footnote. Dr. Johnson's comment on this version has been quoted above; he considered it to be based on Shakespeare and either foisted off on the writer (Steele) or intended by him to fool *The Tatler's* readers. The tale was given by Steele as the report of an actual occurrence in Lincolnshire; it was written up in quite a literary style, but does not deviate in any important trait from the standard oral versions from northern Europe. *The Tatler* version may be summarized as follows:

> The youngest of four daughters of a gentleman in Lincolnshire is a shrew. A gentleman, despite the girl's well known character, decides to marry her. After living some time at her father's house, the husband goes off to prepare for her homecoming and then returns to fetch his wife. He arrives riding a nag, accompanied by a dog and with a case of pistols before him; he makes his wife mount behind him and they ride off. The dog does not obey his command to open a gate and is shot; the horse stumbles once, then again and is killed with a sword. The wife is forced to carry the saddle home. Later all of the daughters and their husbands visit the father-in-law. The husbands plan a test of their wives while the wives are apart playing cards. Each is called in turn and the first three will not come until the games is finished. The reformed shrew throws down her cards and comes at once. Her husband takes her in his arms and assures her that he will be kind henceforth.

It hardly seems necessary to point out, in view of the many similar versions already analyzed here, that this tale follows oral tradition closely. It would appear that Steele either did not recognize the similarity to *The Shrew* (which is not great, considering the play as a whole) or did not think it close enough to be worth commenting on—especially if he regarded it as a true happening. Had Johnson's note not deterred scholars from reexamining *The Tatler* story itself, it might have been noticed sooner that it matches the Grundtvig folktale in several elements lacking in Shakespeare. (Douce, in 1807, did suggest in passing that *The Tatler* version might have been based on Straparola; otherwise I have found no other references to it.)[50] On the whole the correspondence in this eighteenth-century version is to the Irish tradition. Specifically, the traits in it which are not in Shakespeare but which are matched in folktales are as follows: the Shrew is the youngest daughter of the four; the groom comes back to fetch his bride; the groom carries a gun and is accompanied by a dog; they ride double as they leave; the dog is killed for disobeying and the horse for stumbling; the wife must carry the saddle; and the wives are playing cards during the wager scene.

The Tatler version is not the missing link between the foreign tradition and Shakespeare's play; it does not contain crucial traits, especially the absurd statements, that are unknown in Irish tales and required for our English prototype of *The Shrew*. Steele's anecdote only informs us that the folktale very likely was known in England and may yet be. Any further examples of Type 901 from England could be of the greatest importance in determining more exactly the nature of Shakespeare's source. A clearer picture of his source would help in understanding Shakespeare's creative reshaping of raw folk material into dramatic literature. Moreover, should the popularity of the tale in England be discovered to be anything like it is in Ireland, we may gain new insights into the acquaintance Shakespeare's audience had with the folk tradition of his plot in *The Shrew*; hence, we may learn more about the contemporary reception of the play. For such purposes modern folktales could be of as much value as old literary sources and it is greatly to be desired that more collections will soon be made.

NOTES TO CHAPTER IV

1. Many articles and monographs have been written on the *A Shrew* question; good summaries of this scholarship can be found in Raymond A. Houk, "The Evolution of *The Taming of the Shrew*," PMLA, LVII (1942), 1009–1038 and in John W. Shroeder, "*The Taming of a Shrew* and *The Taming of the Shrew*: a Case Reopened," JEGP, LVII (1958), 424–443.
2. Francis Douce, *Illustrations of Shakespeare, and of Ancient Manners* (London, 1807), I: 345.
3. George Ticknor, *History of Spanish Literature*, 6th American ed., corrected and enlarged (Boston, 1888), I:80, n. 43.
4. Herman Knust, ed., *El libro de los enxiemplos del Conde Lucanor et de Petronio* (Leipzig, 1900).
5. *Count Lucanor; or the Fifty Pleasant Stories of Petronio*, tr. James York (London, 1888).
6. *The Remarks of M. Karl Simrock on the Plots of Shakespeare's Plays*, ed. J.O. Halliwell, printed for the Shakespeare Society (London, 1850), p. 87. This is a translation of Simrock's first edition of 1831.
7. Friedrich Heinrich von der Hagen, *Gesammtabenteuer*, I (Stuttgart and Tübingen, 1850), notes, lxxxii-lxc.
8. *Die Quellen des Shakespeare in Novellen, Märchen und Sagen* (Bonn, 1870), I: 343.
9. Ticknor. *op. cit.*, pp. 75–76, n. 31.
10. Reinhold Köhler, "Zu Shakespeare's *The Taming of the Shrew*," *Jahrbuch der deutschen Shakespeare-Gesellschaft*, III (1868), 397–401; reprinted in *Kleinere Schriften zur Märchenforschung*, J. Bolte, ed. III (Berlin, 1900), 40–44. Other notes by Köhler in the *Kleinere Schriften* were in "Anmerkungen zu Blade, *Contes populaires de la Gascogne*," I (Weimar, 1898), 137.
11. Richard Urbach, *Das Verhältniss des Shakespeareschen Lustspiels 'The Taming of the Shrew' zu seinen Quellen*, Diss. Landesuniversität Rostock (Schwerin, 1887), pp. 43–44. My translation of the quotation.
12. Albert H. Tolman, "Shakespeare's Part in 'The Taming of the Shrew'," *PMLA*, V (1890), 201–278.
13. See *The Views about Hamlet and Other Essays* (Boston, 1906), pp. 203–242.
14. Hanna Lindberg, *"The Shrew"; Argbiggans Typ i den Engelska Literaturen intill Shakespere* (Tavastehus, 1901).
15. Ralph S. Boggs, "La Mujer Mandona de Shakespeare y de Juan Manuel," *Hispania*, X (1927), 419–422.

16. In *Filosofía y letras*, Facultad de filosofía y letras, Universidad nacional de Mexico, X:19 (1945), 55–67.
17. *SFQ*, X (1946), 57.
18. Alcalá, *op. cit.*, pp. 55–57.
19. Martin Hume, *Spanish Influence on English Literature* (London, 1905), pp. 47–48. Hume reiterated these views in "Some Spanish Influence in Elizabethan Literature," *Transactions of the Royal Society of Literature of the United Kingdom.* Second Series, XXIX (London, 1909), 1–34. Here he concluded, "There is no doubt that the original European source of 'The Taming of the Shrew' was Spanish" (page 23).
20. H. Coote Lake, "Some Folklore Incidents in Shakespeare," *Folk-Lore*, XXXIX (1928), 307–328.
21. H. Thomas, "Shakespeare and Spain," The Taylorian Lecture, 1922, in *Studies in European Literature, Being the Taylorian Lectures Second Series, 1920-1930* (Oxford, 1930), p. 15.
22. Felix E. Schelling, *Foreign Influences in Elizabethan Plays* (New York and London, 1923), p. 58–59. James Fitzmaurice-Kelly, who was one of Schelling's sources, commented in a similar vein in *The Relations between Spanish and English Literature* (Liverpool, 1910); he concluded, "*The Taming of the Shrew*, is a recast of a previous play which dramatized a story that was common property everywhere" (page 20).
23. E.K. Chambers, *William Shakespeare. A Study of Facts and Problems* (Oxford, 1930), I: 328.
24. Wilhelm Creizenach, *Geschichte des neueren Dramas*, IV (Halle 1909), 687. My translation of the quotation.
25. G.I. Duthie, "*The Taming of A Shrew* and *The Taming of the Shrew*," RES, XIX (1943), 352. (For folktale analogues, Duthie referred only to Köhler's, Simrock's, and Tolman's articles.)
26. R. Warwick Bond, ed., *The Works of Shakespeare* (Indianapolis, [n.d.]), p. li.
27. George Lyman Kittredge, ed., *The Complete Works of Shakespeare* (New York and elsewhere, 1936), p. 325.
28. Charles Jasper Sisson, ed., *William Shakespeare. The Complete Works* (London, 1953), p. 291.
29. John Munroe, ed., *The London Shakespeare*, I (New York, 1957), p. 67.
30. Sir Arthur Quiller-Couch and John Dover Wilson, eds., *The Taming of the Shrew* (Cambridge, Eng., 1928).
31. *Ibid.*, p. xv.
32. Geoffrey Bullough, ed., *Narrative and Dramatic Sources of Shakespeare*, I (London and New York, 1957), 61–64.
33. Werner P. Friederich, *Outline of Comparative Literature* (Chapel Hill, N.C., 1954), p. 39

34. Kenneth Muir, *Shakespeare's Sources*, I (London, 1957), p. 259.
35. Selma Guttman, *The Foreign Sources of Shakespeare's Works (An Annotated Bibliography, 1904–1940)*. (Morningside Heights, N.Y., 1947), Chapter 5, pp. 124–134.
36. *Shakespeare Jahrbuch*, XCIV (1958), 132–150.
37. *Ibid.*, p. 133.
38. *Ibid.*, p. 134.
39. *Ibid.*
40. *Ibid.*, p. 135.
41. *Shakespeare Quarterly*, X (1959), 251–255.
42. *Ibid.*, p. 251.
43. *Ibid.*, p. 252.
44. *Ibid.*, p. 253.
45. *Ibid.*, p. 254.
46. This is one of the principles established by the experiments of F.C. Bartlett described in *Remembering* (Cambridge, England, 1932).
47. Verrier Elwin, *Myths of Middle India* (Madras, 1949), pp. 184–185.
48. *Ibid.*, p. 432.
49. In other newer media for presenting drama—motion pictures and television—such dialogue is often translated back into action. Thus in a television production of *The Taming of the Shrew* on the "Hallmark Hall of Fame," March 18, 1956, according to a review, the trip home was staged as a ride out to a ranch in a covered wagon. On the way Petruchio kills a bear. The reviewer comments, "Nichols [the director, William Nichols] never forewent the chance to dramatize episodes that Shakespeare had chosen merely to narrate." See Paul A. Jorgensen, "The Taming of the Shrew: Entertainment for Television," *The Quarterly of Film, Radio and Television*, X (1956), 395. (Compare also the techniques used by Casona, discussed below.)
50. Douce, *loc. cit.*

CHAPTER V

Type 901: "That's Once," The American Subtype

Survival of the European Tradition in the New World

European versions of Type 901 in North America, transplanted but unaltered, have already been discussed from Canada and New Mexico. Three French-Canadian versions are particularly well preserved specimens, probably of Irish origin. (No Irish-American texts, however, have yet been reported.) The Southwestern version, RSAm 1, is told in Spanish and contains older elements not current in Spain; like the Canadian versions it otherwise is not far removed from European tradition. All four of these North American texts of Type 901 are anachronistic remainders from a tradition that has generally changed in the homelands and does not appear to be very well known here.

Only some traces of the Taming of the Shrew Complex among other immigrant groups in America have come to light. A prize find was a version of Type 1370 known by the daughter of a Polish immigrant family; this text, SP 1, has been considered as a Polish source and is discussed with the rest of the 1370 tradition. A clear instance of Scottish influence in Kentucky was identified in a text of the "Who will not work, shall not eat" tale, GEAm 18. As for Type 901 itself, no direct

European borrowings could be traced. Reverend Thomas R. Brendle, collector of Pennsylvania-German folklore, sent a negative report on the tale from his area.[1] Dr. Jones Balys, Lithuanian-American folklorist, has collected one or two versions of Type 901 from Lithuanians in the United States, but as yet, he informs me, these particular tape recordings have not been transcribed.[2] Searches in various private or university archives have turned up no further pure European versions in America.[3]

Type 901 is by no means moribund in the United States, however. On the contrary, the tale is quite popular in a new form that has penetrated into several areas of modern life. Aside from four longer texts collected by folklorists from relatively isolated areas, twenty-four short versions were collected, mostly from college students, and three texts were found in popular periodicals. These contemporary urban versions of the Taming of the Shrew show drastic simplification of the old European theme. They are too brief and standardized to reveal their exact origins, but further details in the longer versions help to pin down the most likely possibilities. The best and most revealing of these versions was collected by a music professor in Illinois, but unfortunately, no information is available on the informant's family background. The story, called "You Haven't Packed the Saddle," was told by Miss Una Keeling on January 16, 1947, at a meeting of an extension course sponsored by Southern Illinois University at Pinckneyville, Illinois. Professor David S. McIntosh, who taught the course, asked Miss Keeling to write out the story and send it to him, and the text was subsequently printed in the first number of *Illinois Folklore*; it is listed in the present study as GEAm 10.

Una Keeling's version was learned from her mother, who had heard it from her own mother; no further background information was recorded, except that the final line, "You haven't packed the saddle," had been applied in the Keeling family, "to calm the younger folk when we got to expressing ourselves too forcefully as to what we would or wouldn't do."[4] This scrap of information, however, is a valuable clue to the tale's possible origin. Carrying the saddle is a widely known trait in European versions, especially in northern countries, but only seven other tales conclude with *a motto* about carrying the saddle; these are GI 1, 2, GS 2, GSF 2, GD 6, FF 10 and 13. In all of these versions the situation is comparable—the reformed Shrew obeys her husband's command, and when her sisters reproach her for this, she recalls how she had to carry the saddle. In GI 1 the phase refers specifically to a broken saddle which the bride must carry; an allusion to it is the title—*Borinn brotni söðullinn*—"The Broken Saddle Carried." When the wife misbehaves in this tale, "the husband needed only to remind her of the broken saddle girth to calm her."[5] GI 2 was summarized in German; the corresponding phrase is *Ihr habt nicht, wie ich, den Sattel getragen.* In the Swedish tale the wife tells her sister, *Ni har inte burit sadeln*—"You haven't borne the saddle." the Swedish-Finnish statement is almost identical to the Swedish, and the Danish statement is *De havde ikke baaret paa Saddel.* Both Finnish texts end with the saying *että oo satulata kantanna*; in FF 13 there is the interesting conclusion, ". . . and that's where the saying, 'You haven't carried a saddle' comes from." Evidently the Keeling family tradition of applying the statement separately from the tale was also known in Finland. So much at least is now clear: Una Keeling's version shows the marked influence of Scandinavian tradition; quite likely it originated there. (I sent this guess to Professor Jesse W. Harris at Southern Illinois University, who edited *Illinois Folklore* when the tale was printed. He was unsuccessful in a search for more information on Una Keeling, but wrote, "There *is* one old Danish settlement in her home county.")[6]

Other traits in GEAm 10 mark it as a particularly full and interesting text, closer to European tradition than are most of the American versions. The Shrew is designated the youngest daughter of a family, while in other American texts no specific position is named. The father warns the suitor about his daughter, a trait commonly found in Europe, but one that occurs in only two other American versions. In GEAm 10 the groom arrives for the wedding on a horse and with a dog and a gun; the couple depart riding double. No other American versions are so specific as this about the wedding. This is the only American version in which both a horse and a dog are killed. There is also a trace of the wager element in GEAm 10— the husbands and wives are visiting the father-in-law and the husband of the reformed Shrew demonstrates her obedience by making her leave the party at his call. No other version from the United States has even the visit to the in-laws.

In the longer texts from backwoods America and in some shorter texts we do find a few of these traits occasionally preserved, but Una Keeling's version alone has so many of the elements combined.

Sources of the American Versions

The thirty-one American versions of Type 901 gathered for this study are perhaps not representative of the whole tradition in the United States, since a majority of them resulted from personal collecting efforts by the writer while the research was in progress. With the cooperation of several correspondents, however, a fair geographical sampling was achieved and much interesting material came to light. The texts may be divided into two small groups of "folk" versions and printed texts and a third larger group of short urban versions.

The longer versions of Type 901 from the United States, besides Una Keeling's text, were collected by Vance Randolph in the Ozarks (GEAm 23), by Richard Chase in Virginia (GEAm 20), and by myself in Kentucky (GEAm 16).[7]

Versions of Type 901 from popular printed sources are GEAm 1 (from the joke page of *Boy's Life*), GEAm 24 (in *The Emancipator* of San Antonio, Texas),[8] and GEAm 26 (from a recent book of "sick" jokes).

The largest group of short urban texts is in the Indiana University Folklore Archives. One text, GEAm 2, was collected in 1954 while this archive was located in Michigan. The rest were submitted by students on the Bloomington campus in 1959 and 1960; these are GEAm 5, 8, 13–15, and 27–32. Most of these texts were elicited from folklore classes by asking for "any stories you know about a bad wife who is cured by her husband."

Another seven versions were collected by me either from local acquaintances (GEAm 6, 9, 21, 22, and 25) or through correspondence with friends elsewhere (GEAm 4 and 19). A number of passive reports of the tale also were given directly to me.

Three teachers at other colleges secured texts from their classes. Professor Jesse W. Harris at Southern Illinois University collected GEAm 7, 11 and 12; Mrs. Marie Walter at Brooklyn College, New York, sent GEAm 3; and Professor Leonard Roberts at Morehead [Kentucky] State College sent GEAm 17.

The considerable variety of details within a standard framework in the American versions seemed to indicate that there had been no serious influence on informants by specifically requesting a particular kind of tale. In all attempts to collect the story from college students response was positive and often remarkably good. It is noteworthy that none of the teachers who asked for the tale failed to turn up at least one version or a report of a version. There is every indication from all of these texts that the folktale is known widely in the United States at various levels of society and that it is reasonably popular.

The American Subtype

In Una Keeling's version of Type 901 when the dog misbehaves, the bridegroom says, "That's the first time," then "That's the second time"; after a third warning the dog is shot. The horse is warned three times in the same words before being killed; when the wife complains, she is warned for the first and second times too. In all the rest of the American versions a simplified warning, "That's once" or "That's one," is found. The tale is often entitled "That's once." In almost every instance the American story ends when the bride has been given one such warning, and generally there has been little, if any, prefatory material. Thus the basic development of the tale here is that it is greatly simplified and the husband's warnings are formularized and made the point of the jest. Only by implication is the bride threatened, but she is made to think that her death would swiftly follow any disobedience. The most extreme stage in the reduction of the old folktale to a joke fitted to the pace of modern times is perhaps represented by the *Boy's Life* text which is quoted in its entirety below:

> A newly married couple were leaving the church they were married in, in a horse-drawn carriage. The horse stumbled on a rock. "That's one," said the groom. Later on the horse stumbled again. "That's two," he said. A

while later the horse tripped on a rock, "That's three," the man said as he pulled out a gun and shot the horse. His wife said he was too cruel. "That's one," said the man, and they lived happily ever after.

Repeated warnings, often three in number, are not uncommon in European versions, but nowhere is the element so effectively condensed as in the "That's once" of the United States. In European versions the wife is specifically told that if she does not behave herself, quiet down, carry the saddle, or the like, she will be killed just as the animals were. In American versions there is only the fearsome implication of the groom's "That's once." This new verbal tag is the "punch line" which is essential to a modern funny story; it makes a joke out of a more diffuse narrative. Thus, a line like "That's once" is the defining characteristic for the American Subtype of Type 901.

Historic-Geographic techniques are useless with respect to a story that has probably been transmitted largely by mass communications media. The "That's once" joke has essentially the same form everywhere in the United States that it has been collected. This is the result of its rapid passage in standardized form through radio, television, print, and oratory rather than by gradual oral dissemination going outward from an original center. Despite the pressures for standardization, however, certain typical tendencies in the texts can be observed in a general comparative survey of their elements.

The three longer American versions from the Ozarks, Virginia, and Kentucky contain details reminiscent of the Old World sources and not commonly found in the shorter joke versions. All three of these texts introduce the Shrew before her marriage, while other American versions begin on the wedding trip. The Ozark text is localized and the character's names are given. In this version the husband (who is part Indian) first warns, then slaps, and finally kills his wife's pet dog for biting him. When his wife curses and slaps him, he says, "That's one." Richard Chase's text from Virginia begins with a brief description of the Shrew, "a woman . . . couldn't nobody get along with. Good worker, good cook and housekeeper and all, but she was so vigorous nobody 'uld marry her." The wedding in this version is briefly described, including the groom's arrival on a nag. The wife must carry the saddle home, and the tale ends there. The longer Kentucky text (GEAm 16) introduces the Shrew as, "the ill-tempered young lady that lived in pioneer days." As in the Virginia tale, the couple rides double on the horse, the wife must carry the saddle home, and the story ends at that point.

The major difficulty in adapting the Taming of the Shrew tale into a modern urban joke has been to find a way to keep the horse (or other draft animal) *logically* in this plot. Most of the changes we find in the shorter examples of the American Subtype resulted from efforts to create a situation in which the essentials of the tale—bride, groom, and horse or other animal—could be brought together in a context that is meaningful to a modern audience. (In GEAm 11 the difficulty is avoided by having a mild-mannered husband suddenly perk up and kill *a fly* at mealtime to frighten his wife. This change, however, definitely weakens the tale; it is not resorted to by other storytellers.) Two rather common solutions to the problem have been to put the story in the mouth of an old-timer from the horse and buggy days, and sometimes also to give the plot a remote setting.

Eight American versions are told as legends; that is, a man is asked for the secret of his happy marriage, and he describes the way he tamed his wife on their wedding day. In GEAm 2, 4, 15, and 24 a husband is asked for his secret on the occasion of the fiftieth wedding anniversary. In GEAm 5, 19 and 29 the taming method is requested at no specific time. In GEAm 25 the husband's father-in-law requests information on shrew taming and he is told the narrative. A typical opening sentence is, "A man was being congratulated on fifty years of wedded bliss and he was asked to give the secrets of why he and his wife had never had any arguments. This was his answer . . . (GEAm 2)." Probably an important factor bringing on the development of such an introduction is the American newspaper reporter's tendency always to ask this question whenever a couple is interviewed on the occasion of the anniversary of a long marriage. (It should also be noted, however, that the Persian texts had the same kind of beginning.)

The most elaborated introductions in urban American versions are those which have the husband divulging his taming secret in a rural or backwoods setting. Thus, GEAm 5 begins, "A fella in the Ozarks had the best wife. Why she did everything he asked and never talked back or complained. All the other men around had troubles with their wives, so one day they asked him how he got her to behave so well." GEAm 12 is set in "the hills of Arkansas"; GEAm 29 is supposed to have been told by an old farmer in Vermont; and GEAm 7, though no location is specified, was said to have taken place "two hundred years ago." The informant for GEAm 13 was of Italian background and believed that his version was a family story from the Old Country. This would be most interesting, if true, since no Italian folktale analogues are known. Except for the mention of Italy in the introduction, however, there is nothing in the text to distinguish it from other American tales.

All of the settings so far mentioned were remote from the storytellers themselves, but in two instances the setting is only in another part of the informant's own state. The printed version from Texas begins, "An old West Texas ranch couple, married for 50 years, were noted for their serene, happy home life. Many wondered why they had gotten along so well." Version GEAm 15, from Louisville, Kentucky, begins, "This Quaker couple over in Eastern Kentucky were being interviewed on the occasion of their fiftieth wedding anniversary. When asked why his marriage had been so long and happy, Friend Jones told of an incident which happened on his wedding day as he and his bride drove home from the meeting with a mule and a wagon." (The Quaker characters in this tale raise the interesting question whether sects, like the Amish, who still normally use horse-drawn vehicles, also have the tale told on them. No other versions mentioning such religious groups have been reported so far.)

The husband is often identified as a farmer, hillbilly, pioneer, or the like in the American versions; if nothing is specified, it is usually *implied* that he is a farmer. No other character except the Shrew appears in most versions, though GEAm 7 contains the Shrew's father warning the suitor about his daughter's bad nature. No details about the wedding are ever given except to mention that the taming occurs on the trip home from being married. In fourteen versions the couple ride in a horse-drawn vehicle, and in four versions (besides three longer texts already discussed) they ride double on one horse.

Type 901: "That's Once," The American Subtype

Only in GEAm 24 do they ride separate horses. A few texts vary the occasion of the taming slightly. In GEAm 3 the characters are country people in town with their rig to do some shopping. GEAm 14, from an undergraduate coed, is about "a guy and his girl out on a date riding in a buggy." The "slick" joke text describes a couple going horseback riding while on their honeymoon. (Probably the informant for GEAm 32 picked up the same detail from the printed text.) All of these variations on the wedding trip, it seems obvious, are merely further devices to keep the horse or other animal logically in the joke.

With very few exceptions the horse is killed for stumbling, or, some versions add, for throwing the riders, falling, or the like. Sometimes it stops, drinks water, or shies at something. Often the horse commits a different mistake each one of the three times. In GEAm 22 the horse breaks wind three times—a slightly off-color modern touch. In versions GEAm 3, 5, 7, 15, and 27 the animal killed is a mule, and in GEAm 13 it is a donkey. Of the shorter versions in only GEAm 25 does the wife carry the saddle, but in two other American texts, GEAm 3 and 7, the wife must carry some baggage home.

A few other unique elements in this subtype may be noted. There is a general tendency to enlarge on the wife's verbal reaction to the killing of the horse. Often, even in short texts, there is a digression just before the conclusion to tell what the wife said and how vehemently she protested the animal's death. This may be interpreted mainly as delay of the punch line for comic effect. In Richard Chase's version this speech of the wife's is especially extended;[9] in the Ozark text the wife even slaps her husband. The whole idea of the wife resisting her husband after the animal is shot is a departure from European versions, where she is usually subdued by observing the slaying itself rather than by a direct threat to her own safety. Some protest on the part of the wife is necessary to lead up to the American punch line, and this detail has been expanded for the sake of comedy. GEAm 8 strangely weakens the point of the joke by having the husband tame his wife merely by describing to her how he shot the horse. In GEAm 12 there is a unique element—the husband clubs the horse to death, instead of shooting it. In GEAm 6 the husband beats the horse, then shoots it.

Taking from shorter American versions the traits that are known to be originally found in Europe, we can see at least approximately that the Old World prototype must have contained the following elements: the father's warning to the suitor, the trip home by horseback or in a horse-drawn vehicle, riding double, killing the horse for disobeying or misbehaving, and making the wife carry the saddle or other baggage. Such an "archetype" is sufficiently general so that we can only say that these jokes could have evolved from any of the general European versions which we surveyed earlier. There are simply not sufficient details in the texts to link them with specific Old World prototypes. Judging from the relative popularity of the folktale in European countries, and taking into account where such a possible prototype exists, as well as immigration to the United States, Irish tradition would seem a likely source for the tale. Perhaps even English versions have been preserved here, though they are unknown in present-day England. It is possible that further tracing of the backgrounds of the informants for the longer texts would lead to some direct Old World sources.[10] The Una Keeling text suggests that Scandinavians were influential in transmitting the tale to the United states, but if this were the only source we would expect to find more of the typical elaborations of Scandinavia here. Probably a combination of several European forms was transmitted originally to the United States. It is quite possible that other American printed versions of the tale or its early use by radio comedians could have given rise to the tradition here. The homogeneity of the texts certainly supports this possibility.

Although nothing further can be determined at this point on exact sources of the Taming of the Shrew joke in the United States, there are other aspects of the tradition that can be investigated—the place of the folktale in our contemporary culture, and the media of its dissemination.

Dissemination and Functions in the United States

The dominant mode of transmission of the Taming of the Shrew in the United States is decidedly oral, judging from informants' comments about sources of the versions gathered for this study; still, print and broadcasting as well as public oratory have played a part in shaping the tradition. Information presently available is fragmentary, but it serves at least to produce the general outlines of a picture which can be filled in with the results of continued collecting. Data on the media of transmission of the American versions are recorded in Table I, in note 10—giving quotations from passive reports of the tale—and in notes 11 through 20—quoting from major informants.

Fifteen informants, or about one-half of those who told the American versions of Type 901, could recall their direct sources. In all instances the tale was learned orally, usually when delivered as a joke. Randolph's Ozark informant and my storyteller from Kentucky both claimed to recall an oral source from near the turn of the century. All the rest of the versions date from the 1940's or later. Four informants (see GEAm 11, 13, 14 and 15), besides Una Keeling, knew the tale as a family story. The informant for GEAm 11 was told the story by his or her father just before marrying; unfortunately, this informant's sex was not reported to me. Version GEAm 14 too was told as marriage advice, but in this instance by a husband to his wife. In the family of the informant for GEAm 13, as was already pointed out, the tale apparently was being passed down as an Old Country tale. Another instance of family transmission is GEAm 22, a text learned by the informant's mother from a laborer on the family farm and then told to her son. A version of the tale was reported to me *directly* from a natural joke-telling situation only one time: GEAm 9 had been told during a bridge game by an acquaintance who a few days later heard of my research and repeated his version for me. The informants for GEAm 7 and 8 also knew the tale from such a casual joke session. Versions GEAm 3 and 21 were learned orally while the informants were serving in the army. The former text came from an officer encouraging his men (and probably also humorously threatening them) on a hot day's march; the latter was told by one American soldier in Formosa to another.

More formal oral delivery was the origin of three versions. GEAm 19 was learned from an economics professor in a college in West Virginia who told it to a class. (Another classroom use of the story was reported to me by David Reibel of Bloomington, Indiana, who used it in a course in English for foreign students he taught in Illinois. Mr. Reibel said he found the story somewhere in print and that his foreign students, whatever their nationalities, always seemed to like it.) GEAm 5 was learned from a speech delivered by a public school official to a group of teachers in South Bend, Indiana. Three informants from two different states reported that they had heard the tale from the pulpit. My source for GEAm 21 knew the story from other sources, but had learned it originally from a Baptist sermon in Topeka, Kansas. A young married couple, who could give only passive reports of the tale, both had heard it separately in their church, The Church of the Brethern, in different cities of Indiana. A point suggested by ministerial uses of the table, and one well worth examining, is the possible printing of the Taming of the Shrew in modern *exempla* collections or other works used in preparing sermons. Whether by way of print or otherwise, the folktale in the United States evidently has found its way back to its medieval Spanish function as an instructional example.

One version, GEAm 32, apparently was picked up from a recent paperback "jestbook"—a collection of "sick" jokes. Though there have been varied kinds of printings of the Taming of the Shrew, no informant claimed to tell a version learned from print. The person who told GEAm 15 did recall seeing the joke in a newspaper Sunday supplement, but she had known the tale earlier from her father's telling. The level of publications of printed versions found of the tale was ephemeral and popular, but ranged, in terms of audience, all the way from the Boy Scout readers of *Boys' Life* to the young bachelors who buy *Playboy*. The attempt to make the story fit a fad for "sick" humor was weak, the only alterations being a setting on a honeymoon jaunt and having the bride call the tamer a "sadist." This printing can be put down as an obvious attempt to capitalize on a joke fad by slightly refurbishing an old jest for new publication. Nothing was reported on the nature of *The Emancipator* or the source from which its version was clipped, *The Scandal Sheet* of Graham, Texas.

Radio and television, like print, have transmitted the American subtype of the tale, but no present oral versions are attributed directly to them. Baughman, however, did hear a version (but did not collect it) that had been learned from a TV show the night previously. Four others of my informants had heard the tale told on radio or television, but these people had never retold it. Broadcasting personalities named were Groucho Marx, Tennessee Ernie Ford, Jack Paar (on whose show it was told in a New England dialect), and an eastern radio "raconteur" (unknown to me), William B. Williams. Evidently the tale has been adaptable to a range of commercial comic styles from Marx's biting wit and Paar's sophisticated humor to Ford's somewhat contrived homespun comedy. An effort has been made to find out if the Taming of the Shrew is contained in the voluminous joke files of the radio and television comedian Milton Berle, who in 1961 willed a microfilm copy of his twenty-eight indexed cabinets of accumulated jokelore to the Library of Congress.[11]

Scant as data are on the American Subtype of Type 901, it is clear that the tale not only has sturdy roots in rural and European-derived folk tradition in this country, but also that it has gained popularity as a current joke, entered the repertoires of public speakers, teachers, and even ministers, and has become grist for the mills of the jokesmiths of print and the airwaves. The tale evidently appeals to Americans from backwoodsmen to college students, from boy scouts to playboys, and from GIs to preachers. So far the Taming of the Shrew has been reported from only sixteen states, but it is safe to anticipate that it could be found in the other thirty-four as well, thanks mainly to mass communications. (It is almost frightening to think how many more listeners are reached by one television comedian telling the story on one show than are heard by the oral efforts of all the Irish informants of our tale put together.)

Folklorists have not yet studied in any depth a phenomenon such as this—the full-scale acceptance of a European folktale in America by rural and city storytellers in different age, educational, and occupational levels and through modern communications media. Type 901 is not the only folktale that illustrates these characteristics, though it seems to be an outstanding example. Modern joke analogues of the following other tale types are all to be found in the Indiana University Folklore Archives: Type 750A, *The Wishes*; 1365A and B, *The Obstinate Wife (Falls into a Stream* and *Cutting With the Scissors)*; 1675, *The Ox as Mayor*; 1825C, *The Peasant as Parson (The Sawed Pulpit)*; and 2300, *Endless Tales*. Other tales, such as

Type 440, *The Frog King*, circulate in modern parodies, and some popular "shaggy-dog" stories are based on narrative motifs from European traditions. Even the literary nursery tale *The Three Bears* is current among adult American jokesters in at least four comic variations. Whether any of these or other European tales could be found in as great a variety of sources as Type 901 has been remains to be studied. At any rate, the Taming of the Shrew shows a sufficiently interesting development in the United States to justify continued collecting of oral and published texts and further analysis. Because the tale was dramatized by Shakespeare and used in other literary works, and since it deals with such a fundamental theme as the relations of husbands and wives, it offers a particularly fine opportunity to compare the history of an idea in folk and popular tradition in relation to its employment by the creative writer.

The American Subtype in Ireland and Mexico

Two versions of Type 901 have come to light which show a quite unexpected development—transmission of the American Subtype of the folktale back to Europe and, in Spanish translation, to Mexico. American jokes, in company with other aspects of our popular culture—movies, chewing gum, popular music, and the like—seem to have won widespread acceptance abroad. Both of these texts are relatively inaccessible, and they are short enough in the summaries I have to be quoted. The versions both show the same characteristic American traits—a husband's secret for his happy marriage, lack of plot elaborations, and the phrase "That's once" as a punch line.

The Irish version, CI 140, was published in the popular English-language magazine *Ireland's Own* in 1953. It was summarized for me as follows:

> An American farmer, who had just celebrated his golden wedding anniversary, was asked for some advice on how to achieve a happy married life. He said he had 50 years of such and told the following story to illustrate his methods.
> When he got married he and his bride rode out to his farm. After about a mile of the journey his horse faltered

and fell. The farmer forced the animal up again and wagging his finger at it said menacingly—"That's once." Further along the way the animal fell again. Once more the farmer forced it on saying—"That's twice." Near the end of the journey the poor animal fell a third time. The farmer became very angry and said—"That's three times," and promptly shot the horse.

His wife was furious. She vehemently reproached him for shooting a good horse, and told him he was a brute and a bully. The farmer listened patiently to her, and when she had finished her tirade, he said, "That's once." She never gave him any further trouble.

The Mexican version, originally told in Spanish to a school principal from Texas and retold in Spanish to another Texan—both times in Mexico—was summarized for me by the last auditor, as follows:

Two Mexicans were talking about their wives. One of them asked the other, "How is it that your wife is so "*consecuente*," so compliant? You never have trouble with her." The other told him the following.

When we got married we got on my burro and rode along until the burro stepped on a stone and stumbled. "That's one," (*Esa es una*) I said. After a little while the burro stumbled again. "That's two," (*Esas son dos*) I said. Then the burro stumbled once more. "That's three times," (*Esas son tres*) I said. "*La tercera es la vencida.*" (The third time is the charm.) I got off the burro, took out my revolver and shot him dead.

My wife screamed at me, "*Imbecile!* What have you done?"

I threw a look at her and said, "That's one." She's been a good wife since.

One final ironical twist of the American tradition which relates to Mexico has been pointed out to me. It is reported that "That's One" is sometimes told in a Spanish dialect along with a cycle of tales about a comic Mexican character. The details are the same—the horse is warned *uno* and *duo* (sic) and then dispatched with a *pistolo*, and the wife is warned when she objects to the killing.[12]

NOTES TO CHAPTER V

1. Letter dated December 16, 1959.
2. A letter including information from Dr. Balys was sent to me on January 14, 1960, by Sergius Yakobson, Chief of the Slavic and Central European Division of the Library of Congress. I spoke to Dr. Balys about his collection on November 18, 1960, on the Indiana University campus.
3. I personally examined the folktale material in the Indiana University Folklore Archives. The other archives searched are referred to in the preface.
4. *Illinois Folklore*, I: 1 (1947), 17. (Quoted there from a letter that accompanied the text.)
5. Quoted from the English translation of GI 1 made for me by Bo Almqvist of Reykjavik, Iceland, and sent in a letter of May 1960.
6. From a letter dated December 1, 1959.
7. Randolph wrote me in December 1959 that he had no further versions. Chase in his book asked readers to send in their own versions of stories printed there; I mailed him a query about new texts of Type 901, but got no reply. My text from Kentucky was sent to me as a result of a query I printed in the *Courier-Journal*.
8. Baughman lists this version in his note to Randolph's text.
9. In his telling of the tale on an LP recording, Chase strives for the maximum comic effect from the wife's protestations by imitating her voice and her excitement at some length.
10. Leonard W. Roberts exemplified the process of this kind of source-hunting in his *Up Cutshin and Down Greasy* (Lexington, Ky., 1959).
11. According to a United States Press release from Hollywood, January 7, 1961, Berle had by then kept track of all the jokes he had used for the past thirty-two years. His sources included print, oral tradition, and material from other comedians. At one period, the release states, Berle employed ten people to cross-index everything.
12. Heard by Miss Judith Binkele of Bloomington, Indiana, at a student gathering at Indiana University in January 1961.

CHAPTER VI

Type 1370 and the Combination of 1370 and 901

The present number of collected texts of Type 1370 and their variety and extent of distribution is surprising since only Estonian, Finnish, and Finnish-Swedish versions were known when the Aarne-Thompson *Type-Index* was published. Stith Thompson commented in *The Folktale*, on the basis of these few indexed versions, that the stories about lazy wives "show neither the originality nor the interest to be found in stories of shrews or overbearing women. Of this group," he continued, "perhaps the best known, at least in eastern Europe, is the tale of the cat which is beaten for not working."[1] Although Thompson here alluded to the Taming of the Shrew, he was discussing Type 1370 separately along with other stories about laziness; in conclusion he suggested that a comparative study of all the various tales about lazy people might be worthwhile.

Examining many versions of Type 1370 has resulted in the need to discard generalizations about the tale which information in the Aarne-Thompson *Type-Index* had suggested. Fully seventy-two texts of the tale are now known from seventeen countries; the area of distribution extends from England to Russia and from Scandinavia to Spain and Greece; one version has been found in French-Canada and another (from a Polish-American informant) in the United States. I previously noted that Type 1370 exists in two subtypes besides that dealing with the lazy cat; each involves beating an inanimate object—an animal hide or something else—on the wife's back. Versions of these subtypes were in European literature as early as the thirteenth century. In structure as well as in connections with other tale types, Type 1370 belongs in the Taming of the Shrew Complex and not with other stories about laziness. The form of the narrative in Type 1370 (marriage-taming-peace) and the taming device (punishing an animal or something else that disobeys) are essentially the same as in Type 901. The only tale types with which Type 1370 regularly has combined are those which are also connected with the Taming of the Shrew or other tales about bad wives. In short, the proper context for study of Type 1370 consists of all the other facets of this complex.

Versions of Type 1370 are considerably simpler and more homogeneous than are versions of Type 901. The tale contains basically only the account of improving the bad wife. Whatever the subtype, the story is always about a lazy girl, without sisters, who gets married to a man who knows her nature but thinks he can improve her. Her husband cures her of laziness at home by beating the cat or other object while she holds it or has it on her back. The beating is usually "punishment" for the cat or object not doing housework. The wife, thus, gets beaten more or less by proxy, but she realizes that to escape future pain she must do work herself.

Almost no internal elaboration has developed in this basic plot of Type 1370. Sometimes there are a few humorous examples of how lazy the wife is, and in some versions the suitor claims from the start that he has a cat or something else at home to do housework; otherwise the individual texts differ very little in anything except the animal or object that is the recipient of the beatings. When versions of Type 1370 are longer than usual it is because of the addition of other narrative elements from the Taming of the Shrew Complex, such as the "Who will not work, shall not eat" tale or Type 901B. Combinations of Type 1370 with Type 901 employ either the wager episode alone or the whole taming device and occasionally other details.

The total number of texts of Type 1370 now assembled still is insufficient to prepare a well-documented life history of the tale. The subtypes separate the collection of versions into such small groups spread over so wide an area that it is difficult to determine accurately the original forms of the traits, the subtype to which the archetype corresponded, or where the tale originated. Now that the story is to be rescued from the oblivion of "Types Not Included" in the revised *Type-Index*, it can be hoped that more texts will eventually be collected so a thorough biography of the type can be worked out. Our present purposes will be primarily to delineate the subtype structure of the tale and to describe its relationship to the rest of the Taming of the Shrew Complex; secondarily, as far as possible, a hypothesis will be suggested about the tale's origin and history. Since the versions of each subtype are already listed in Chapter II, these lists are not repeated here; individual tales are simply identified as they are discussed.

The Object-Beaten Subtype

Perhaps one of the most logical applications of the system in Type 1370 for curing a wife's laziness is found in RS Lit 4 from a sixteenth-century Spanish story collection. This text effectively demonstrates the underlying principle involved in the cure and, thus, is a good starting place for a survey of the versions of Type 1370. In RS Lit 4 the lazy wife complains that she needs a servant to do the cooking. Her husband hangs up a picture of servant instead and when still no cooking is done, he places the picture on his wife's back and beats it. This is the only version in which a representation of a servant is brought in to do the work. In all other variations of this laziness cure some different object or a cat is ordered to do the wife's work for her. In all versions no housework is done until the disobedient "servant" is punished and the wife takes over herself. The Spanish story, being unique and relatively late, cannot easily be defended as an archaic form, yet it may represent a general step in the development of our tale from beating a servant, to beating a picture of a servant, to beating on or with something else which is treated like a servant.

Other versions of the Object-Beaten Subtype fall into two groups—those in which a stick or other such object is ordered to work, and those in which some kind of a bag is ordered to work. The former group consists of five versions from Yugoslavia and one from Greece, all of which continue as Type

901B. The latter group contains nine versions, mostly combined with other types and found further north and west in Europe.

The Yugoslavian versions are all short and direct. A lazy girl gets married and her husband tells her that a stick (SY 6, 10), a poker (SY 9), or an ax (SY 13, 14), will do all the housework for her. When the object does not bring him his meals or do other work, he "punishes" it by beating it on his wife's back. The Greek version, Gre 5, has the reluctant stick handled in a manner more like that of Type 901. The stick is ordered to work; it does not obey, so the husband angrily breaks it over his knee and burns it. The wife is frightened by this demonstration of how idlers fare, and she becomes industrious.

Between the "stick" and the "bag" forms of this subtype stands a version in which a stick-like object *inside* a bag is beaten on the wife. In RF Lit 3A, from a thirteenth-century sermon book (the oldest literary version we have of the type) the wife is beaten with a plowshare placed in a bag. When the neighbors take the couple before a judge, the husband swears he touched his wife only with the bag; the witnesses must agree, and he is acquitted. Although neither the plowshare nor the bag were ordered to work in this version, it must surely have some connection with the other tales we are studying. Perhaps it is even close to a prototypic form to which later the trick about the object supposedly doing work was attached to make the tale apply specifically to *lazy* wives. (It should be noted that the labeling here of RF Lit 3A as a French version refers only to the *nationality* of the author, Jacques de Vitry. As bishop of Acre, Palestine, de Vitry traveled to Rome and lived long in the Near East. The sermon book in which this version appeared was undated, but probably it was written late in his life, after much time abroad when he could have learned stories from diverse sources. It is impossible, thus, to attribute this particular narrative to any specific location.)[2]

Three of the other "bag" versions of the subtype also have something inside the bag when it is beaten on the wife. SRUk 2 might have been classed as a version of the Cat-Beaten Subtype, for a cat upon refusing to work is put in a bag, hung on the wife's back, and beaten. (This tale concludes with Type 901B.) In BLi 4, the only version of the Object-Beaten Subtype which is combined with Type 901 (a horse, cat, cock, and pig are killed), a bag full of wooden shoes is commanded to do the housework and then is hung on the wife's back and beaten for not obeying. In FE 26 a motif occurs which was probably adapted from *The Table, the Ass and the Stick* (Type 563)—magic sandals in a bag jump out and beat the wife until she works. The sandals also serve food to the father-in-law when he visits and beat the mother-in-law when she gives bad counsels (i.e., Type 901B). In all of the "bag" and "hide" tales the object is hung on a nail in the wall when it is commanded to work and it is taken down later for the punishment.

Two versions from Polish tradition have only an empty bag which is supposed to do the work. SP 1, known by a second-generation Polish-American informant, has a linen bag. SP 2, taken directly from a Polish collection, has a knapsack (more logically, perhaps) which the wife must hold on her back when it is beaten for not working. BLi 6, apparently an offshoot of this kind of version, has a basket substituted for the bag. All three of the versions just mentioned are without elements of other tale types.

Three final versions of the subtype may be transitional between the "bag" and "hide" forms; in these a *leather* bag is involved. All three—RR1, RS 1 and, apparently, RS 2 (Which is only briefly described in a footnote)—are nearly the same. A leather bag is beaten for not working; in RS 1 the bag is violently beaten; but not on the wife's back; the woman only fears what may happen when it is beaten next, so she begins to work. The other two versions are standard, and all three are without other narrative elements.

The Hide-Beaten Subtype

The versions in which the hide of some animal is beaten on the wife's back can be divided into two groups which seem to represent on the one hand mainly oral material, and on the other hand literary or literary-derived material. The former group is more true to the rest of the tradition in that the hide has always been ordered to do some work; in the latter group the beating is just a direct punishment of the wife for her own laziness. Another partial distinction can be made between the groups because of the species of animals that are involved; in the oral versions usually a small animal's skin is employed, while in the literary versions there is a larger animal's skin.

Four versions of the folktale from southeastern Europe have a sheepskin beaten on the wife's back for failing to do the housework on command. Gre 3 is unique in that the wife instead of the husband commands the skin to work. The other versions—SY 12, RR2, and 3—are short and standard. Only the Yugoslavian version ends with Type 901B. FF2 has a few more details about the characters' backgrounds, but is essentially the same tale except that a goatskin is here beaten for not working. In GSF 3 the hide is from a calf, but the tale otherwise is similar. Neither of these latter two northern European versions contains other narrative elements. The other version in this group of folktales with a larger animal's skin in it is SY 17, in which an ox hide is beaten.

The second group of versions of the Hide-Beaten Subtype is mostly from old printed sources, and the analogues from folklore seem to be quite closely related to the printed texts. The oldest version of this group is GNe Lit 1, a play written in Latin by a Dutchman and published in 1538. In the section of this play which is analogous to our tale the husband beats his wife until she is bloody and wraps her afterward in a horsehide. GNe Lit 2, a play from around 1550, has the same device except that the hide is well salted. Here the horse is named "Moorken" and the name is included in the title, "Moorkensvel." The oldest known German printed versions of this episode is GG Lit 5, from about 1540 to 1550; here the wife is beaten, rubbed in ashes, and wrapped in the horsehide. GG Lit 6 is the first of the German analogues to have the distinctive name for the horse, here "Morgen." The action in this play is close to that in GNe Lit 2, to which it undoubtedly is closely related. GG Lit 7, from a seventeenth-century jestbook, has the wife beaten and wrapped in a salted cowhide; this version ends with an echo of the wager episode, for the wife is called away from a bath to demonstrate her obedience. Two eighteenth-century German plays also have the animal-hide taming. GG Lit 8, written in 1710 by an exiled German in France, has the beaten wife wrapped in a salted and peppered ox hide, then rocked in a cradle. In GG Lit 9, from 1716, the cowhide again appears, probably borrowed from the jestbook tale.

Bolte and Seelmann, who edited the literary hide-beaten versions, felt that the story must have been well known in Germany and in the Netherlands before it appeared in England in the poem *A Merry Jest of a Shrewde and Curste Wyfe Lapped in Morrelles Skin*, GE Lit 4. In their last study of the subject, these editors remained in doubt as to whether *Morrelles Skin* might be either an analogue of a lost Dutch tale which lay behind the earliest play, or a free translation of one of the continental literary versions.[3] The English poem being apparently so little known there and the Dutch play being early, the editors tended to favor the theory of a lost Dutch tale.

Morrelles Skin is a curious piece. It has certain features paralleled in other folktales but not found in the other literary hide-beaten versions. The lazy wife in it has a good sister at home. The suitor is poor, but the father-in-law is wealthy, and he gives a large dowry, but warns the suitor about his daughter. After the wedding (and following some incidental description of the wedding night) the husband finds that he cannot live with his bad-natured wife. He beats her and then kills his old horse "Morrell," and wraps the woman in the salted hide. Later he tames the mother-in-law by threatening her. Some scholars have seen parallels to Type 901 here in the second sister and the killing of the horse; we may add to their list the taming of the mother-in-law and the father's warning. The possibility that has been suggested that *Morrelles Skin* might have given a few details to Shakespeare's play seems remote. By a dated reference in a letter we know only that *Morrelles Skin* was popular in England by 1575, but this indicates that it must have been known there somewhat earlier.[4] Shakespeare, thus, could easily have known the poem, but his details are all closer to the forms found in the regular folktale tradition of Type 901 than to *Morrelles Skin*.

The basic core of the plot in *Morrelles Skin*—the method of curing the wife—is more closely related to Type 1370 than to Type 901. The plot is closer to folk tradition than are the plots of the continental printed texts; thus, Bolte and Seelmann's hypothesis that *Morrelles Skin* is derived from a tale and not from the plays is supported by more recent field data.

Francis James Child thought that GE Lit 5, the ballad "The Wife Wrapt in Wether's Skin" (Child 277), was derived from

Morrelles Skin; hence the title he used. (It is discussed with the present group because of this theory.) In the ballad, however, the wife is wrapped in a sheepskin, then beaten—a curious echo of the oral prose versions of Type 1370 from southeastern Europe. The point is especially made in the ballad that the wife's higher social status makes her too proud to do any housework. The husband cannot beat her directly, and so he pretends to tan his sheepskin by beating her on her back. Thus, unlike all of the other literary "hide" versions of the tale, we have here a more direct parallel to the folktales. Child's theory of the origin of the ballad, therefore, must be discarded.

The wife's unwillingness to work because of her natural prerogative to rule her husband has been pointed out already in some versions of Type 901 where it seemed to be one of the oldest elements of the tale. It occurs less frequently, though over a fairly wide area, in Type 1370. Only GG Lit 7 and 9 of the "hide" versions have a lower status husband, but this point is not much stressed in them. The same can be said of GD 13, FF 2, FH 2, and SRW 2, and other versions of Type 1370 with this element. RR 3 does have the request of the lazy wife before the wedding that she will not have to work, and in FH 1 the father of the bride contracts with the husband that his daughter will not have to do work; nowhere, however is there found a close parallel to the characteristic ballad lines about the wife's refusal to work and the husband's trick in punishing her. Thus, though it appears obvious that Child 277 must have derived from prose versions of Type 1370 somewhat like the sheepskin folktales found in southern Europe, the path from this tale plot to English balladry cannot yet be mapped. In a study of six English and Scottish texts and forty American texts of Child 277, William Hugh Jansen, although he did not refer to Tale Type 1370, drew the following conclusion concerning the ballad's prototype:

> It seems evident that the ballad originally presented the situation of a husband confronted by a wife whose high birth made the chores of a housewife distasteful to her, yet whose high birth also prevented him from chastising her. So he wrapped her in a wether's skin, which he proceeded to beat. Upon her threat to tell her parents or family of the indignity, the husband assured her that he

was only tanning his wether's skin—that she happened to.
be inside was unfortunate.⁵

This plot outline applies equally well to the Hide-Beaten Subtype of Type 1370. A larger collection of texts of the ballad would help to determine its source, especially if parallels in continental balladry were found.

One folktale text, FF 14, does closely match the German-Dutch literary tradition of the Hide-Beaten Subtype. Here Type 901 (a horse and dog are killed) is combined with the episode of the husband skinning the dead horse, salting the hide, and *threatening* to wrap his wife in it. Other Finnish versions of Type 901 mention skinning the dead horse, and one Finnish and one Canadian version also have the wife carrying the dead horse's skin home. In these versions we seem to find further evidence that *Morrelles Skin* has a relationship to Type 901.

The Cat-Beaten Subtype

There are somewhat more than twice as many versions of Type 1370 in which a cat is beaten on the wife's back as there are versions of the other subtypes combined. Although found in more individual countries than the other variations, the Cat-Beaten Subtype is more restricted in distribution, being known mainly in northeastern Europe. It has not been found in literature earlier than the fifteenth century. Like the versions of the preceding subtype, the "cat" stories can be divided into one group in which the cat is applied to the wife's back simply as punishment of her laziness, and a second group in which the cat was first commanded to do housework and *it* is supposedly being punished for laziness. A third group of "cat" stories contains combinations of Type 1370 with Type 901.

The only version of the Cat-Beaten Subtype found in southern Europe is SY 7; here, since a wife always defies her husband, he puts a cat inside her blouse and beats it to punish her. Four other version similarly have direct punishment of the wife's laziness by application of the cat to her. In all of these—FF 36, GS 5, GD 13, and RFAm 5—the cat is dragged along the wife's bare back until she submits. In the Finnish tale the wife is tied face down on a table for her punishment. In the Swedish and Danish versions the wife is in bed when the cat is dragged along her back, but in the French-Canadian version she is tied naked to a post and scratched front and back. GD 13 and RFAm 5 both conclude with the wager episode, but the other versions in this group are without further elaborations. The two Wellerisms from Sweden must refer to this form of the subtype; they attest to its further popularity in that country. In none of these tales is there any mention of the cat doing housework.

GD 13, containing one of the two traces of Type 1370 from Denmark, belongs to a small subgroup with three northern German versions, GG 3, 4, and 5. The taming method in the German tales is simply beating the wife, but otherwise all of these versions are very similar and are distinct from the rest of the tradition. The Shrew here is always a widow and a tenant on the estate of a landholder. A servant on the same estate is married to the widow, and he bets his master that he can tame her. Later, when both men are at a smithy, the husband demonstrates his wife's cure by sending home for money with which to gamble, and she brings more money than was required. GD 13 lacks a few details that are in the German versions, probably an indication of faulty borrowing from Germany to Denmark.

The oldest literary texts of the Cat-Beaten Subtype are in two German manuscripts from the fifteenth century, GG Lit 3 and 4. In the former version the wife must have the cat on her back when it is beaten for not working, and in the latter version the wife is naked in bed and has to hold the cat by the tail during its beating. In both versions the wife promises to work if the cat will not be beaten any more. GG Lit 4 concludes with the advice for husbands, "If your wife is stubborn, then beat the cat with a club." Both of these literary versions mention the husband's skill in taming wild horses as well as shrewish women, and GG Lit 4 ends with the horse-taming test and leading the stubborn animal with food.

Three versions of the subtype are found in eighteenth-century Russian printed sources—SR Lit 1, 2, and 3. All three plots are basically the same. The cat is commanded to cook, and it is beaten for disobedience while the wife holds it. In SR Lit 2 and 3 the cat is held over the wife's back. The latter version was rendered in verse and illustrated with a print.

The present oral versions of the Cat-Beaten Subtype in Germany and Russia are apparently neither direct copies of the literary versions nor prototypes of direct sources for the literary versions. There are three texts of the tale from German tradition, GG 8, 10, and 14. The first of these versions is quite simple—the cat is beaten while the wife holds it, and she reforms. GG 10 is elaborated with an opening borrowed from Type 1461*, *The Unwilling Suitor Advised from the Tree* and with Motif W111.3.6. Both the cat and the wife get progressively more food as more and more housework is performed during the days while the husband is out working. GG 14, like the "Wife Wrapt in Wether's Skin," has the wife of higher status beaten by proxy. The comment is made that "the wife was ashamed to admit to her father that she was being beaten." In Russia proper two oral versions have been collected. SR 11, in combination with Type 901, is discussed below with other such combination. In the other Russian version, SR 6, the husband claims that before the wife came home with him, the cat always did his housework; now it has stopped working. The husband pretends to get drunk on water (a trait known in two other Russian tales), beats the cat on his wife's back, and plows with his mother-in-law. Two Ukrainian versions, SRUk 1 and 4, are made up of the same combination of Types 1370 and 901B. In the first of these versions the wife holds the cat for beating, but in the second she is beaten *with* the cat.

The greatest concentration of versions of cat story is found in Estonia, where eight texts have been collected—FE 4, 8, 15, 16, 18, 19, 24, and 27. Only FE 4 has any other narrative elements in it, in this instance the green-branch incident, which we saw earlier in the elaborated subtype of Type 901. In all of these Estonian texts except FE 15 the cat is bound to her leg. All of the Estonian versions are filled out with details about the wife's laziness and the husband's patience with her at first. In FE 19 there are whimsical passages about the cat actually doing some housework—licking the plates clean—and then resting from its labors. When the wife promises to work, it is "to help out the cat with its chores." Possibly such touches are the result of rewriting, but this is impossible to determine.

There are four Finnish versions combining Types 901 and 1370 and only one text, FF 23, exists which has no elements of

Type 901; this story concludes, however, as Type 1383, *The Woman Does Not Know Herself.* In Hungary, in FH 1, 2, and 3, as was true in Estonia, Type 1370 is found separately; all of these versions have the cat put on the wife's back.

One version of the Cat-Beaten Subtype is known from Swedish-Finland and one from Lithuania. The former version, GSF 4, is quite standard, but the latter, BLi 7, is combined with Motif W111.3.6. and this element becomes so much emphasized in the tale that, although the cat is ordered to do work, it is never beaten; the wife is cured by starving instead.

Type 901 Combined With Type 1370

We have encountered two versions of the previous subtypes of Type 1370 which are combined with the basic shrew taming tale, Type 901. BLi 4 included the killing of animals and also beating a bag of shoes on the wife's back for not obeying orders to work; FF 14, a story of killing a horse to tame the wife, concluded with skinning the horse and wrapping her in the hide. Both of these tales had a wager on the wives' obedience. Eight further versions consist of Type 901 combined with Type 1370 in the Cat-Beaten Subtype. Four of these combinations are Finnish, and there is one text each from Russia, White Russia, Norway, and Denmark. Different methods of integrating the two plots (and sometimes parts of other tale types) can be observed, so the eight versions must be taken up individually.

FF 1 is the only tale in this group in which the cat is simply dragged along the wife's back to punish her; in this instance the punishment comes after returning home from a trip which was interrupted by the husband killing the horse and dog when his wife did not open a gate. After the cat treatment, however, the trip is completed with no further delay. In FF 6, 20, and 24 the beating of the cat has been lost, but the command to it, as well as to a dog and a rooster, remains. When the animals do not obey, they are killed. FF 6 contains only these elements plus part of Type 1453, *The Slovenly Fiancée*. In FF 20 and 24, more of Type 901 is preserved; after the smaller animals are killed at home for not doing the housework, a horse is killed on a trip. Both versions end with the wager episode.

SR 11 combines Types 901 and 1370 in the same manner as did FF 6, that is the cat is commanded to do housework and then is killed for not working. The next time the husband in this version comes home and finds no work done, he drinks water, pretends to be drunk and beats his wife. The tale concludes with Type 901B. SRW 2 is the only one of these combined versions in which the disobedient cat is actually put on the wife's back to be beaten; this version continues with the killing of a horse on a trip to the in-laws and a wager on the wives.

Two Scandinavian versions contain rather garbled combinations of these types. GN 1, the only example of the Taming of the Shrew Complex from Norway (and probably a direct borrowing from Sweden or Denmark) has the cat beaten while the wife holds it. Then on a trip the husband makes absurd statements about birds, and when his wife disagrees, he shoots her horse; later they arrive at the in-laws and the tale ends with a wager. GD 19 has the couple riding home from the wedding in a horse-drawn vehicle. The husband gives commands to drive through obstructions, and the wife must intervene with the driver to save them; the horse, however, is not killed here. At home the husband beats the cat while his wife holds it. The tale ends with a reward from the father-in-law of gold coins in a cup for the husband—a carry-over from the usual Danish form of the wager.

Towards the Life History of Type 1370

The only previous attempt to deduce the possible origin of Type 1370 and to explain its relationship to Type 901 was that made by Dragomanov in his article on the Taming of the Shrew in Ukrainian folklore, already discussed in Chapter I. Dragomanov's conclusions seem sound, considering the versions available to him in 1893. He recognized the basic similarity between the tales we now label as Types 901 and 1370; knowing only the former tale in the East, he attempted to explain the development of the latter from an Asiatic original. Taking the Persian texts, in which the husband slays a cat in front of his wife, as a sample of the prototype, Dragomanov reasoned that this Oriental tale had been "suggested by the life of the harems" and, thus, it was only with great difficulty made suitable for the simpler, less restrained, and more coarse folk culture of Western Europe.[6] He summarized his case as follows:

> In reading the Ukrainian variants of the tales upon the taming of the shrew, it is seen that we have to deal with a foreign theme upon which the people have seized because it lends itself to pleasantry—doubtless rather coarse—but whose details even are not familiar to them, from which comes often the confusion in the tales which cannot be explained except by the aid of comparative study. The imagination of the people of Ukraine ended by the creation of a new tale which had arranged quite freely the details of the strange story, and at the same time had changed its dominant idea. This new recital commences by transforming the episode of the refractory animal.[7]

The Ukrainian variants which he said showed the people's confused rendering of the Eastern tale were all texts of Type 1370 belonging to the subtype in which the lazy cat is beaten on the wife's back, a story which, Dragomanov felt, "disfigures the Persian variant which is to frighten the lady without touching her body."[8] The new invention of the people to which Dragomanov referred was a version of the no-work—no-food tale (Motif W111.3.6.) which began with a demonstration of the suitor's skill in driving oxen.[9]

Although our advance from Dragomanov's position is considerable, due to our larger collection of texts of Type 1370, our problems are also correspondingly greater, because of new knowledge of the variety of the forms of the tale and of the broad areas in which they are known. Still, more versions of the tale must throw new light on its history; unfortunately, the present texts of Type 1370 do little else for us than to reveal unsuspected complications in reconstructing the history of the tale.

Dragomanov's ideas about the origin of Type 1370 are too narrow to fit the present information on the tale. The further subtypes in which animal hides and other objects are beaten cannot readily be explained either in his terms as confused retellings of Eastern versions of Type 901 or as further developments of the Cat-Beaten Subtype. The suitor test concerned with inducing the stubborn draft animal to work we have already found to be well known outside of the Ukraine and to be frequently combined with various plots in the Taming of the Shrew Complex, especially the older northern European Subtype of Type 901 which is now well preserved only in Canada and Ireland. This new evidence does not support the theory that such a suitor test was a secondary adaptation of the animal-killed tale from the East. Rather than further belaboring Dragomanov's early theories, however, which seem quite reasonably drawn from his evidence, we can make some fresh inferences on the basis of the present texts.

Having identified the three distinct subtypes of Type 1370—the cat, hide, and other-object variations—the most basic problem that arises is to establish which subtype is the oldest and to explain how other subtypes could have been derived from the prototype. In other words, the archetype for the tale appears to be simply that a lazy wife is cured when something else is beaten (usually while she holds it), ostensibly for not working, but she suffers. The question, then, is "What was the original *something* which was being 'punished'?" The possibility may be discarded at once that there were not three distinct and separate *traditions* of one tale, but that individual though similar variations on the basic archetype were invented independently in different places. Such might be a reasonable supposition if we had discovered only two or three isolated examples of the non-cat subtypes. But each of our subtypes has its own fairly restricted geographical limits and its own distinctive details; a connective oral tradition for each subtype and some kind of sequence of development of them is clearly implied.

The possibility that a tale consisting of Type 901 plus Type 1370 was the original for the whole complex must also be discarded after initial consideration; such well-integrated examples of this combination of types as FF 20 and 24 or SRW 2 would exemplify the parent form for such a hypothesis. In these versions the husband commands the cat and other animals to work and kills them for disobeying, or he first beats the cat on his wife's back or scratches her with it and then kills her horse on a trip. The examples of such versions, however, are too irregular in form and too restricted in distribution for a plausible prototype of this tradition. Were a 901-plus-1370 tale older than the individual types, we would expect the examples of this combination to be consistent with each other; instead they differ from country to country quite erratically in the manner of linking the two elements of the taming; probably, therefore, they represent individual combined versions inspired locally by the popularity of both types. (The fact that combinations appear in all three subtypes of Type 1370 further corroborates this line of reasoning.) The distribution of the combined texts is a further clue to their origin. Type 901, as we have seen, is generally well known all over Europe except in France and Italy, while Type 1370, especially the Cat-Beaten Subtype, has been collected mainly from eastern Europe. The Cat Killed Subtype of Type 901 was also found well preserved in Europe in the northeastern countries, especially in Finland. The combined texts are only found in Finland, parts of Russia, and in a single text each from Lithuania, Denmark, and Norway. Therefore, only where the two types overlap rather strongly has this particular combination of types occurred; in the area around Finland a tradition of this combination may be detected. We may conclude that the combined form is more recent than the individual types and that it gained a foothold in those few countries where both tales were well established earlier.

  The distribution of the three subtypes gives some indications of their development. We have seen that versions of the Object-Beaten Subtype in which a stick or other such object is beaten are found in Yugoslavia and Greece; a picture of a servant is known in a Spanish literary text, and various kinds of bags are found in versions from Spain, Romania, the Ukraine, Poland, Lithuania, and Estonia. The distribution of the Hide-Beaten Subtype is thin through southeastern Europe, scattered in northern Europe and is found rather strongly represented in German, Dutch, and English popular literature of the sixteenth century and later. The Cat-Beaten Subtype centers on Estonia and extends to Scandinavia, then westward as far as Germany and southward through the Ukraine, and Hungary and in one Yugoslavian text. Taken together, then, the two first subtypes with inanimate objects beaten have a broader distribution than the tale about the cat. The Object- and Hide-Beaten Subtypes, unlike the Cat-Beaten Subtype, are known in Romance countries (Spain and Romania), in Poland, quite well in Yugoslavia and Greece, in England, and in the Netherlands. Furthermore, these subtypes are encountered more frequently than the cat story is in older literary sources. These facts about the distribution of the known versions make it appear that the subtypes concerning an inanimate object beaten on the wife's back were invented first and then reworked, perhaps under the influence of Type 901, into the story about the beating of the lazy cat. If such were true, then Type 1370 would seem to have originated somewhere generally in southern Europe by the early Middle Ages and to have been disseminated northward, being changed in the process of oral transmission.

It seems likely that versions of the tale in which the animal or object is *not* commanded to work are closer to the original form of Type 1370 than are the versions which include the command. The former texts are simpler in conception, containing only the basic idea of a ruse by which the husband may punish his wife and then declare himself innocent. Our oldest literary version, RF Lit 3A, is such a tale; here the husband beats his wife with a plowshare placed inside a bag, then swears he touched her only with the bag. In the English ballad "Wife Wrapt in Wether's Skin" we see what may be early advances in the development of the tale, for here the necessity for a ruse in punishing the wife is supplied ("her noble kin") and rationalization for beating the hide is given ("only tanning my old sheepskin"). A second basic strain in the tale is represented by the rest of the versions without the command to work; this strain involves the cruel punishing of a wife, either by wrapping her bleeding body in an animal skin or by scratching her with a cat. This application of straightforward wanton cruelty for which no particular reason is given stands in contrast to the other versions of the tale in which the animal or object is first commanded to work and then is beaten while it is in the wife's hands or on her back. The latter form of the story is more fully motivated, and the cruelty somewhat less central in the tale, while the husband's cleverness is emphasized more. If the two basic strains—punishment by a ruse and cruelty—are behind all later forms of the tale, then the development of Type 1370 has consisted of improving the plot by making it more logical and by supplementing the characterization of the husband to bring him more in line with the cleverness of a hero such as there is in Type 901.

We may, for the present, regard the thirteenth-century text of undetermined geographical origin (RF Lit 3A) as representative of the earliest versions of our tale of punishment by a ruse. Possibly under the influence of such a tale as RS Lit 4, in which the picture of a servant is commanded to work, the object with which the wife was beaten in the prototype was eventually also required to work. If the plowshare type of object (stick, ax, poker) represents one development of the old tale, the various bag versions are other offshoots. The latter element, the bag, had the more far-reaching influence; not only is it now more widely known and has received other elaborations (i.e., something else inside the bag) and taken on new forms (i.e., a knapsack), but it also has joined with the Hide-Beaten Subtype in those versions where a leather bag is beaten. The Cat-Beaten Subtype, then, seems to be a more recent development in Type 1370, though it was known by the fifteenth-century; it must have felt some influence from Type 901, where animals are also mishandled in order to tame a wife. Those versions in which the cat is scratched on the wife to punish her may show the oldest form of the Cat-Beaten Subtype; these versions, it will be recalled, occur on the furthest extremities of the area of distribution—Yugoslavia and Canada. Estonia and Hungary appear to have been centers for the dissemination of the Cat-Beaten Subtype; but, although the tale remains best known in eastern Europe, it is still told in Germany and Scandinavia. In the area around Finland combinations of Type 1370 and Type 901 have developed recently, but the two types must have been well known there first.

Such is as much of the life history of Type 1370 as the present data suggests. The conclusions should be regarded as provisional—subject to revision by the discovery either of new oral texts or of further old literary versions of the tale.

NOTES TO CHAPTER VI

1. Stith Thompson, *The Folktale* (New York, 1946), p. 211.
2. Information on Jacques de Vitry from Thomas Frederick Crane, ed., *The Exempla of Jacques de Vitry* (The Folk-Lore Society: London, 1890), Introduction.
3. W. Seelmann, ed., *Mittelniederdeutsche Fastnachtspiele* (Norden and Leipzig, 1885), pp. xii–xxvi; J.Bolte and W. Seelmann, eds., *Niederdeutsche Schauspiele älterer Zeit* (Norden and Leipzig, 1895), pp. *16–*18.
4. See Frederick J. Furnivall, ed., *Captain Cox, His Ballads and Books; or Robert Laneham's Letter*. . . (London, 1871), p. 29.
5. "Changes Suffered by 'The Wife Wrapped in Wether's Skin'," *Hoosier Folklore Bulletin*, IV (1945), 45. Jansen found that "All the American versions omit the motif of gentle birth," and that this democratization of the story was the most important single point in the study of these texts (pp. 45–46).
6. M. Dragomanov, "Taming of the Shrew, in the Folk-Lore of the Ukraine," *The International Folk-Lore Congress of the World's Columbia Exposition. Chicago, July, 1893* (Chicago, 1898), pp. 368–369.
7. *Ibid.*, p. 372.
8. *Ibid.*, p. 370.
9. Version SRUk 5.

CHAPTER VII

Other Tales in the Complex

Four miscellaneous groups of tales about ways to improve a bad wife belong to the Taming of the Shrew Complex. Although none of these stories has been connected with Types 901 or 1370 in folktale indexes, they have frequently been confused with these tale types by folklore archivists; hence, some of the miscellaneous tales came into the net which was cast for versions to use in this study. The four groups all relate to the rest of the complex not only because the tales deal with a husband's clever method of curing his bad wife, but also because some versions in every group are combined with elements of Types 901 or 1370. For example, as the chart and Chapter II show, in every group there are some versions which end with a wager on the wives' obedience. Because of the casual way in which the versions from these four groups were gathered, and since no regular index numbers exist for three of the tales, the present collection cannot be assumed to be representative; therefore, it is fruitless now to search for the archetypes and origins of the tales. There is value, however, in characterizing the groups as to their known forms, their distribution, and their relationship to the rest of the complex. This will not only fill out our conception of the whole Taming of the Shrew Complex; it will also lay the groundwork for future indexing and study of these miscellaneous groups.

Motif W111..3.6. "Who will not work, shall not eat"

Although the cure for a lazy wife listed in the *Motif-Index* as W111.3.6. is attributed there to Lithuanian folklore alone, we have found it to occur quite widely elsewhere in Europe, and to have a significant place in the Taming of the Shrew Complex. The essence of this taming device is summarized in its title; until the lazy wife does some work, the husband either gives her no food at all, or serves meals to her which are inferior to those the servants eat. Often she receives progressively more food (or better food) as she gradually begins to do more work. We have already encountered this motif in combination with some fifty-one versions of Types 901, 901B, and 1370 from several countries. It is useful to recapitulate these sources before going on to examine the separate occurrences of the motif.

The only country from which Motif W111.3.6. combined with Type 901 has been collected is Ireland. The forty-four Irish examples of this form of the tale constitute the majority of the sixty-one assembled texts of the motif, both in combined form and as a separate tale. Thirty-nine of the Irish versions end with a wager. One Scottish version, CS 2, contains the motif as an introduction to Type 956B, *The Clever Maiden Alone at Home Kills the Robbers*. GEAm 18, from Kentucky, is made up of the same combination of types as CS 2 and has a striking verbal parallel ("the girl wouldn't do a hand's turn of work"); probably it goes back to Scottish tradition. Balys listed four versions of Type *1370A, the Lithuanian form of the tale containing Motif W111.3.6., and this was the *Motif-Index* reference to the story.[1] Only one of these texts, BLi 7, was available for this study; it contains Type 1370 (Cat-Beaten Subtype) plus Motif W111.3.6. Another combination of the same subtype and motif occurs in GG 10 with the added element of an introduction based on Type 1461*, *The Unwilling Suitor Advised from a Tree*. The combination of 1370+W111.3.6.+901B occurs in FE 26 (the sandals-in-the-bag tale) and SY 6 (Object-Beaten [stick] Subtype). Finally, SY 4 consists of Motif W111.3.6. plus Type 901B.

Motif W111.3.6. occurs as a separate tale in ten versions collected in Ireland, Sweden, the Ukraine, Yugoslavia, Spain, Portugal, and Romania; four of these texts are from Ireland and one each come from the other countries. These texts increase by five the number of countries where the motif is known, bringing the present total to twelve. The single-motif tales are C1 1, 4, 5, 9, GS 6, SRUk 5, SY 1, RS Lit 5, RP 1, and RR 4.

Motif W111.3.6. is not reported as a *separate* tale from three of the countries—Estonia, Lithuania, and Germany—where it occurs in combinations with Type 1370; quite possibly such versions were known but were not cross-indexed with the shrew taming tales in the archives. Since the motif occurs in more countries as a complete tale rather than in combinations with other types, it seems to have been a distinct and separate story originally which later became attached to other folktales. We can make out at least the general features of the separate tale type by comparing the versions now available.

Except in Irish versions, where three daughters have become the rule in all of these shrew stories, the lazy girl in the no-work—no-food tale is the only child. The suitor, usually a farmer, either is warned by the father about the girl or sees some demonstration of her laziness. After the wedding he informs her that in his house, "Who will not work, shall not eat"; this line, sometimes given as a moral for the tale, is a fixed feature in all of these versions. Another element found almost exclusively in connection with this particular taming device, though not in the majority of the texts, is that of the suitor's mother assisting in the taming by helping to deprive her daughter-in-law of food until she learns to work. The husband's mother's role is found in five Irish versions, two from Yugoslavia, and one each from Lithuania and the Ukraine. FE 15 also has the husband's mother help in the taming but contains only a trace of Motif W111.3.6. when the bride complains that she is hungry. After the lazy wife is made industrious, the standard ending for the tale is a visit from one of her relatives, usually her father. The visitor is amazed to find the girl working. The reformed wife warns the visitor that he too must work for that is his rule. Only Irish versions conclude with a wager on the obedience of wives.

Motif W111.3.6., the evidence shows, should be regarded as a distinct tale type generally known all over Europe and especially popular in Ireland as a supplement to Type 901. Less frequently in eastern Europe it has been combined with Type

1370. There is no direct evidence that the tale is known outside of Europe except in one Scottish-American version, but an element of the normal form of the tale, the father's visit to his reformed daughter, is known in one Indic version of Type 901. Certainly the taming device in Motif W111.3.6. is simple and obvious enough to have appeal anywhere, even to have been invented independently in different countries. The relatively fixed form of available versions, however, and the standardization of the line "Who will not work, shall not eat" indicates that we are dealing with a genuine traditional series of retellings of a single original tale. Version RS Lit 5 shows that a prototype for the tale was known in Europe by the sixteenth century, but this version is so skeletonized that we cannot deduce anything further from it. It seems likely, judging from the fairly wide distribution of the tale, that at one time it must have been rather popular in Europe.

The Broken Arm

In 1779 an editor of the fabliau text of Type 901 (RF Lit 1) included in a note a French story about a husband who, on the first day of his marriage, beat his wife until he broke one of her arms (RF Lit 4). When the doctor asked 100 pounds for setting the arm, the husband replied, "Take 200! That's for the next arm that I will break." His wife overheard this and decided she should reform. The editor remarked, "One finds this story in a thousand places."

This tale has not yet been recognized by type or motif indexes, and, consequently, even if it be widely known, as the eighteenth-century editor claimed, it has not been much noticed by modern folklorists. It showed up in six further texts from three other countries for the present study; all of these texts were identified by folktale editors or archivists with Type 901, an apparently justifiable idea, since two of the versions include the wager on the wives' obedience. Because of the husband's clever method of taming his wife, the tale deserves mention in a study of the Taming of the Shrew.

Two German versions, though both from Schleswig-Holstein, differ from one another. GG 1 begins with a coachman marrying the shrewish daughter of his master, a nobleman; he is promised a farm as her dowry. After a few days, when she begins to slack off on her work, the man beats her with a club until her arm is broken. When a doctor asks five *daler* for a fee, the man pays him ten, saying, "It won't be long until I break the other one." In GG 7 a farmer's widow marries one of her servants but insists on keeping the keys to their money chest and paying all of the bills herself. In an argument over this the husband breaks one of her arms clean off; later he pays the doctor twenty marks instead of the required ten and says, "It won't be long until the other one is off too."

In a Spanish version of the broken arm tale the husband endures his wife's refusing to bring him his lunch in the fields for three days. Then he beats her, breaking her arm. He pays the doctor a whole *duro* when he only asked for one-half. The tale ends with the moral, "Twist an arm to break a bad habit."

Three Irish versions of the tale have been collected: CI 53, 79, and 124. The first two of these texts have two sisters of the lazy wife and a wager. In all three texts the husband is a farmer and the arm is broken when the woman is beaten with a stick. In CI 53 the doctor's fee is one pound, and in CI 124 the fee is thirty shillings; no exact account is specified in CI 79. The texts come from three different counties in Ireland—Galway, Kerry, and Donegal.

One must conclude from the extent of distribution and the variety of forms in these versions that the broken arm tale was quite widely known in Europe. As to its age, we know only that it is at least as old as the late eighteenth century, and that the most recent text is CI 79 from 1936.[2]

The Cradle

We previously observed in GG Lit 8—an eighteenth-century text of the Hide-Beaten Subtype of Type 1370—the rocking of the bad wife in a cradle as part of the taming process. The element has also been found in four Finnish folktales and one Russian tale.

FF 33 has only the rocking of the wife in a cradle as the taming device; other oral versions are more detailed. SR 9 is about the student son of one landowner who marries the spoiled daughter of a second landowner. The girl's nursemaid confides in the husband that since her charge's upbringing was French and German, she had never been swaddled and rocked in a cradle. When the husband performs these acts, his wife improves. The three remaining Finnish versions all end with a wager on the obedience of the wives. FF 35 describes a petty officer who marries a higher officer's daughter who is spoiled. He subdues her by first starving her, then rocking her alternately in a dozen cradles which have been painted different colors. In FF 40 the girl is one of three sisters and the suitor is a soldier. In FF 42 the bad wife is the youngest of the czar's three daughters and the suitor, again, is a soldier. In this version the cradle is made of copper. The czar is so pleased with his daughter's reform that he promotes his son-in-law to general.

The only hypothesis we can make on the basis of these six examples of the cradle tale is that since it is found in eighteenth-century literature in Germany as well as in later Finnish and Russian oral tradition, it may at one time have had a wider oral circulation. Possibly it is still told. (The most recent is FF 42 from 1897.) Until more texts come to light, however, we cannot tell more about the tale.

Miscellaneous Cruel Taming Devices

A final miscellaneous group of fifteen versions which describe various cruel devices to tame a wife are related to the Taming of the Shrew either because similar devices sometimes appear attached to the regular tale types or because some versions of these odd tales have taken on the wager episode. Four of these versions—GG 3–5 and CS 1—were previously discussed in connection with other subtypes.

GG 12 may be a version derived ultimately from the old anger mole tales; here the wife is tamed when she is forced to get up on a table and have wounds cut in her body and salt and pepper put into them. Possibly there is an echo here of the salted animal-hide tales too. Three literary versions from England, GE Lit 6–8, also seem to have a relation to the anger moles. The wife is told that her "hot blood" causes bad temper. After some blood is let, the woman promises that she is cured; henceforth she obeys her husband. (Both GE Lit 7 and 8 contain other references which show that they derived partly at least from Shakespeare's play, which they postdate.)

The simple beating of a wife to cure her we have occasionally observed as part of a longer taming method. This very obvious taming device also occurs as a separate tale. In FE 25 the wife is hitched up with a horse (probably an element carried over from Type 901B) and both are beaten as they work, until the wife promises to reform. CS 4 has the taming of the bad wife by beating and ends with a standard form of the wager episode—the wives called away from their card game.

SRW 1 apparently contains a unique taming device. The wife is put on an anthill and left to be bitten until she promises to reform. The tale, however, has other elements from the standard types—the horse taming test of the suitor and the final wager scene.

Two Finnish and two Irish versions have the wife tamed by some kind of threat made by her husband. In CI 12 the man drops his stick over a cliff and offers to push his wife after it if she does not climb down and retrieve it of her own accord. In CI 23 the husband keeps a gun handy and threatens to shoot his stubborn wife as soon as she disobeys him. Both Irish versions end with a wager on the wives' obedience. In FF 37 and 38 the wife is threatened with a gun, then actually shot at, until she saddles (#37) or unsaddles (#38) her husband's horse. The former of these versions ends with a wager. It might be significant that in both of these tales the wife is actually being forced to carry a saddle, as in Type 901, although the horse has not been killed.

The four miscellaneous groups of tales just surveyed represent individual traditions about shrew taming which have sometimes joined with the major folktale types dealing with the same theme. Possibly other miscellaneous taming devices also exist as separate tales; if so, they have not been sufficiently similar to Types 901 and 1370 to come to view for this study. Just how minor these miscellaneous tale traditions are cannot now be determined, but it is quite possible that they are better known than current evidence indicates. The most significant result of the present chapter may be to call the attention of archivists, indexers, and collectors of folktales to these groups. From their work only can the material come for a better history of these tales.

NOTES TO CHAPTER VII

1. Jonas Balys, "Motif-Index of Lithuanian Narrative Folk-Lore," *Folk-Lore Studies*, II (Publication of the Lithuanian Folk-Lore Archives: Kaunas, 1936).

2. A modern comic strip episode built on a similar basic idea shows that the germ of the broken arm tale at least may still be known in the United States. In the series "Nancy" drawn by Ernie Bushmiller the following sequence occurred in April, 1959 (I saw it in the Louisville [Kentucky] *Courier-Journal*): Nancy's aunt learns that her niece has squirted one of her little companions with a water pistol. As a punishment Nancy must write "I'm sorry" 100 times. In the last picture the aunt is shown looking at two stacks of paper and exclaiming "I wonder why she wrote it *200* times": through a window we see little Nancy outside giving her playmate another squirt with the water pistol. Here punishment for the next time is performed in advance of the deed, while in the folktale advance payment is made for correcting the effect of a punishment which never has to be administered.

CHAPTER VIII
Summary of Conclusions

In our analysis of the oral and literary versions of the Taming of the Shrew tales, various conclusions have been drawn about the relationships of different aspects of this tradition, the origins of the subtypes, and the interplay of printed and oral transmission. It remains now to consolidate and summarize these conclusions and to weld them into a coherent statement about the apparent life history of the whole complex. For this purpose we may dispense with detailed references to data that support each theory and concentrate on the findings themselves. We may divide this summary into three parts: (1) the nature of the Taming of the Shrew Complex, (2) the life histories of the tales in the complex, and (3) Shakespeare's relationship to the tradition.

THE TAMING OF THE SHREW COMPLEX

Aarne-Thompson Type 901, the tale in which a husband kills a disobedient animal in order to tame his shrewish bride, is at the heart of a large group of related folktales and literary stories which I have called the Taming of the Shrew Complex. A typical ending of Type 901, a wager on the obedience of wives, has become free-floating in tradition and occurs with other tales more or less closely connected to the rest of the complex. Another supplemental episode of Type 901, the story of taming the mother of the shrew (Andrejev's Type 901B) is also free-floating; it occasionally appears as a separate tale. Type 901 may end with an episode in which a second husband unsuccessfully tries to use the taming method on his wife.

Aarne-Thompson Type 1370, *The Lazy Cat*, is structurally similar to Type 901; here a cat is punished for not obeying a command to work by being beaten while the lazy wife holds it. Two other subtypes of Type 1370 involve the beating of an animal hide or some other inanimate object while it is on the wife's back. All three subtypes may end with a wager or may be combined with the taming device in Type 901.

Another cure for a lazy wife is represented by Motif W111.3.6. "Who will not work, shall not eat." This motif occurs as a separate tale, usually without the wager; in Ireland it is found in combination with Type 901. Types 1370 and 901B and Motif W111.3.6. also combine with each other independently of Type 901.

Three further miscellaneous groups of tales about taming shrews are loosely connected to the complex. The "broken arm tale" is about a husband who breaks his wife's arm and pays the doctor twice his fee in order to cover the charge for setting the next arm he will break. The "cradle tale" is about a husband who rocks his bad wife in a cradle until she reforms. A third group contains tales about miscellaneous cruelty used to tame wives—blood-letting, beating, and so forth. Tales from all three of these groups sometimes conclude with the wager episode and occasionally are combined with the taming portion of Type 901.

The Taming of the Shrew Complex as a whole is made up mostly of versions from Indo-European oral tradition, but there are literary and subliterary analogues such as a Middle High German poem, an Old French fabliau, a fourteenth-century Spanish story, an Italian *novella*, Shakespeare's comedy, jestbook texts, and recent printings of a modern joke subtype in the United States.

THE LIFE HISTORIES OF THE TALES

Type 901 has been analyzed in seven groups of versions. There is considerable overlapping among these groups, but at least a few relatively pure versions of each subtype have been found. The distribution of the subtypes, the presence of some

Summary of Conclusions

dated literary versions and the recognition of normal changes that oral transmission brings about have been aids in plotting the probable age of the subtypes and their order of development.

In general it appears that a fairly simple original Eastern tale, perhaps from India, told of a husband who killed a cat (probably also a bird; possibly a dog) in front of his bride in order to frighten and subdue her. Although the original cat subtype left traces on the periphery of Europe, a new form in which a horse is killed has largely supplanted it there. This tale was developed in various ways in European tradition. A distinct subtype found in medieval French and German texts is still reflected in some modern folktales. A number of unusual elements in Spanish, French, and Danish versions indicate direct influence northward along that axis. Versions of an older English-Irish Subtype are still known in French-Canada through Celtic influence there. The tale reached its most elaborated stage in Scandinavia (probably Denmark) and is known in this form throughout northern Europe; the elaborated subtype was known in England by the late sixteenth century, as Shakespeare's play shows. The majority of present European versions are short and generalized, probably being simply degenerated remains of the more complex earlier subtypes. Traces of pure Old World tales can be found in the United States, but a short modernized American subtype with a punch line ending has surpassed them in popularity.

Particulars of each subtype of Type 901 and the suggested pattern of development of the tale may be summarized as follows:

(1) In the *Cat Killed Subtype*, a man marries a girl of higher social position. On the wedding day, when a cat begs for food or mews, he kills it with his bare hands. He also kills a bird and possibly a dog which annoy him. A friend tries the same trick, but he fails because he waited too long. Originally from the East, and best preserved in versions from India and Persia and in proverbial sayings from Burma and Turkey, the subtype had reached Spain by the fourteenth century; it can be traced in oral tradition in Greece, Yugoslavia, Russian, Estonia, Finland, Lithuania, Swedish-Finland, and Ireland.

The sequence of animals that are killed developed further in European tradition; in the early Spanish versions the horse had already appeared as the last, the largest, and the most valuable member of the series. The horse received a function in the plot when description of the wedding trip was added; then the horse was killed on this journey home. Eventually in most countries the smaller animals which were killed at home dropped out of the narrative. In northeastern Europe, mainly in Finland, however, the whole sequence of smaller to larger animals has remained and the horse is generally killed last on a trip back to visit the wife's parents.

(2) In the *Medieval Subtype*, exemplified by a French and a German version which may be as old as the thirteenth century, the Shrew's father is a knight who is henpecked by his wife; the suitor also is a knight. The girl is counseled by her mother to treat her new husband badly and to keep him under her control. The bridegroom's bizarre arrival for the wedding—riding on a nag, followed by a dog, and carrying a falcon—is described. Directly after the wedding he insists that they leave; both then ride on his one horse. The falcon is killed for disobeying a command. The dog is killed when it does not follow closely or chases after a hare. The horse is shot for disobedience during the trip. The bride then must carry the saddle and perhaps even her husband on her back. She decides to improve. The mother-in-law is tamed by bogus surgery which is claimed to cool her temper.

Elements of this subtype are preserved in oral versions from Germany, the Netherlands, Scotland, and Ireland. Some details, such as the knightly characters and the falcon, have been lost or changed, but other elements, such as carrying the saddle, the hare-chasing trait and the wedding elaborations have survived in later subtypes.

The henpecked father opening of the subtype in which the suitor comes upon the father of the Shrew working outside in the fields on a bad day, derives from the southeastern European form of the Slavic tale about taming the mother-in-law—Type 901B. This tale seems to have originated in Russia as a supplement to Type 901 and then to have spread throughout eastern Europe. In the original form of Type 901B the mother gave her married daughter bad counsels and was forced to pull the plow by her son-in-law; the father gave good counsels and was rewarded with drink and presents. Seeing him come back home, the mother thought that he too had been forced to pull a plow. The description of the henpecked father developed differently in Yugoslavia, and it is this form which is reflected in western Europe. Probably under the influence of printed versions in which bogus surgery is used on the shrewish wife, the anger mole taming of the mother-in-law replaced the plowing in western Europe, but this episode never seems to have had great popularity in oral tradition. Other isolated traits in western Europe and in Yugoslavia further indicate that the area of southeastern Europe must have been important in the transmission of the whole tale from east to west in Europe.

(3) Seven versions of a *Spanish-French-Danish Subtype* and a number of distinctive traits shared between other texts from Spain and Portugal on the one hand and Scandinavia on the other hand show that there must have been a direct line of transmission between these two areas. In this subtype the Shrew is a widow. Friends of the suitor warn him about her bad temper. They marry early in the morning at her home. When the horse is killed on the wedding trip, she must carry the saddle the rest of the way, but at home husband and wife pull off each other's boots and the husband promises to continue to reward her with whatever treatment she uses on him.

Two Scandinavian texts mention France, and one has a Spanish character in it; there is one French example of the subtype; the washing-water request known in the earliest Spanish literary version may also have survived in northern Europe; all oral Spanish tales are in this subtype; the Spanish folktales preserve elements of Old Spanish literary versions. All of these facts indicate that probably the typical Spanish development of the tale was transmitted to Denmark by way of France; at least partly this happened through print. The subtype has only weakly penetrated outside of Denmark in the north.

(4) An early *English-Irish Subtype* of the tale has left traces in three French-Canadian versions which must have been learned in the New World from Celtic sources. The same subtype is still reflected in many Irish versions; ten of them in particular retain a distinctive sequence of traits. Elements of the subtype occur also in Scandinavia, Estonia, Finland, and parts of

Russia. In this subtype there are three sisters; the father requires that the Shrew be married before the others. The suitor demonstrates his skill in taming a stubborn horse. He wears old clothes to the wedding and kills his horse on the way home for refusing to jump a fence. There is a wager ending, and the wives are playing cards when called.

The father's rule on the marriage and the bridegroom's old clothes are closely paralleled only in Shakespeare, showing that elements of the subtype were known in England by this time; the wager is widely known in oral tradition, but does not appear in the same form in literature earlier than in *A Shrew* and *The Shrew*. The horse training test is even more widely known, being found in a Greek and a Ukrainian text; the fence-jumping incident is mainly Irish.

The wager as it appears in the Taming of the Shrew seems to have originated in northern Europe in connection with Type 901; it is probably not much earlier than Shakespeare's time. The wager has combined with other tales in the complex. Originally the form of the wager incident was as follows: At the father-in-law's house, probably after a dinner party, the women retire and the men lay a cash wager on which wife is most obedient. When the wives are called for, they are in, or are commanded to assume, some state of undress. Only the reformed Shrew obeys. The wager episode in *this* form spread throughout Scandinavia, Ireland, and northeastern Europe; new elements later appeared in Denmark in a more elaborated subtype of the whole tale.

(5) The *Northern-European Elaborated Subtype* centers on Denmark, where it is apparently originated, and has influenced European tradition mostly in the area immediately surrounding Denmark. *A Shrew* and *The Shrew* belong to this subtype, and elements of it are current as far afield as Ireland and Canada. In the archetype there were two sisters of the Shrew. A horse and dog were killed on the wedding trip, and later, on a visit to his in-laws, the husband won a wager on his wife's obedience. The subtype is defined by the following elaborations on the basic core of the plot: full details about the groom's arrival at the wedding, absurd statements about birds or other animals to which the wife must agree, the bent branch element, and the wager. In Denmark the typical form of the

wager episode is for the wives to be working in the kitchen or looking at clothes when they are called for; the Shrew's husband receives a prize of coins in a cup. In most other countries older traits of the wager episode remain. In this subtype we can see that a number of older elements in the tradition have been expanded or altered. This development would appear to be one of the latest changes in the tale's history.

(6) A group of *General European versions* including about sixty percent of the texts of Type 901 consists of fairly standardized and shorter texts which probably developed as the more complex earlier subtypes gradually were modernized and simplified in oral tradition. Such versions are scattered throughout Scandinavia and are especially numerous in Ireland; they are found throughout the Finno-Ugric and Slavic countries in eastern Europe. A normal form for western Europe has three sisters, a farmer as suitor, riding double on the horse, killing the horse for failing to obey a command, carrying the saddle, killing a disobedient dog, Motif W111.3.6. (in Ireland only), and a wager. A normal form for eastern Europe differs in that the wedding trip is in a buggy or sleigh; sometimes the taming is on a trip back to visit the in-laws; the wife must pull the vehicle when the horse is killed; a dog is also killed; there may be taming of the mother-in-law.

(7) The *American Subtype*. Only French-Canadian and Spanish-American versions of Type 901 have been collected so far to represent survival of the pure European tradition of the tale in the New World. There are twenty-eight versions in this study, however, of a new joke form that appears to be quite popular in the United States. Four texts, somewhat longer than the rest, were collected by folklorists in relatively isolated areas; the remainder of the versions are mainly from college students or from popular periodicals. The defining characteristic of the American Subtype is the husband saying "That's once; that's twice," and "that's three times" to warn his horse before killing it; then he says the same things to his wife to frighten her. The story has sometimes been altered in order to make the horse appear logically in the plot either by relating the taming as the experience of an old-timer or by giving the plot a remote setting. The longest version of the American Subtype has a recognizable Scandinavian trait—the motto ending "You

haven't carried the saddle." This indicates that the American Subtype may have been derived, in part at least, from Scandinavia. Ireland, and England are other good possibilities for the sources of borrowings.

The subtype is well known orally in the United States, but popular printings, radio, television, and public oratory have all had a part in the dissemination of the tale. It has been reported told as simple entertainment, as advice to the newly married, as encouragement to tired soldiers, as classroom or lecture anecdotage, and as a pulpit exemplum. Although informants report the story from radio and television, no one so far interviewed tells a version he learned this way. The American Subtype has spread abroad recently in at least two instances to Mexico and Ireland.

In summary we say that Tale Type 901, an old Indo-European story, has survived well in contemporary culture because it deals with a theme of enduring interest, because it has been effectively modernized, and because it was then picked up by media of mass communications.

Type 1370 has a more complex history than the *Type-Index* references might suggest. It seems probable that the cat, hide, and other-object subtypes do have distinct traditions which are ultimately related to each other in origin. It seems likely too that Type 1370 as a separate tale predated the combination of Type 901 plus 1370, which is found mainly in the area around Finland. I have suggested that the original tale developed by the early Middle Ages in southern Europe and had an inanimate object beaten on the wife's back; later the Cat-Beaten Subtype developed, perhaps under the influence of the animal punishment in Type 901. The versions in which the animal or object is *not* first commanded to work may represent the oldest form. If these hypotheses are correct, then the tale must have become more logical and the characterization of the husband more fully developed as the tale evolved.

Four miscellaneous groups of tales which occasionally combine with Types 901 or 1370 can only approximately be placed in the history of the complex. A tale based on Motif W111.3.6. "Who will not work, shall not eat" has a separate tradition distributed generally throughout Europe; in Ireland only it combines regularly with Type 901. This tale was recorded in the sixteenth-century in Spain, but appears from its distribution to have been popular earlier. The tale about the husband paying in advance for the next arm of this wife's that he will break was recorded in France in 1779 and is still known in oral tradition in Germany, Spain and Ireland. The only actual connection of the story with Type 901 is in two Irish versions ending with a wager. This tale may have been more widely popular, but presently we lack further evidence of this. A recent American comic strip seems to indicate that the germ of the tale is still alive here. The story about the husband rocking his wife in a cradle is known only in Finland, in Russia, and in one German literary version from the eighteenth century. The Finnish versions end with a wager, and the German text is a version of Type 1370. The cradle tale does not appear to have had more than restricted regional distribution. There are a few taming tales in oral tradition based on miscellaneous cruelty to the wife. These are variously related to the Taming of the Shrew Complex, but they are neither numerous nor very widely known. Generally they appear to be either literary plots, unique inventions, or garbled versions of more standard tales.

SHAKESPEARE'S RELATIONSHIP TO THE TRADITION

Previous studies of sources of Shakespeare's *The Taming of the Shrew* were deficient because they failed to include the full oral tradition of Type 901, because different tales in the complex were often confused, and because a few known oral versions were analyzed as if they were literary texts; as a result, the folktales were always misinterpreted. Undue emphasis has been put on earlier literary versions, and too little weight has been given to oral tradition in these studies. Until recently some scholars still felt that there was a direct connection between *El Conde Lucanor* and the English plays. Other students of the problem have been content to say that *The Shrew* is only a revision of *A Shrew* in which form the much-traveled folktale had reached England. Some scholars, however, have ventured to postulate that further versions of Type 901, now lost, were once known in England.

Even a superficial comparison of the plots of the thirty-fifth chapter of *El Conde Lucanor*, the two English plays, and the one well-known Danish folktale reveals that Shakespeare could not have derived his plot solely from either the Spanish story, *A Shrew*, or even from both, but that he must have known a version from oral tradition in a form resembling the Danish oral text. Implicit in these data, then, is the broad tradition of this tale type which is discoverable with the aid of folktale research tools; however, the resources for locating folklore analogues have never been employed in these studies of Shakespeare's comedy.

Both *A Shrew* and *The Shrew* belong to the Northern-European Elaborated Subtype of Type 901; Shakespeare's version of the plot is closer to oral tradition than is the plot of *A Shrew*. In its basic outline and in a number of specific points, the plot goes back to old and widespread elements of the story which may have been popular in England, as they were on the continent, since the Middle Ages. Some elements of the plot, notably the absurd statements, must have reached England by way of Scandinavia. Some minor elements of Shakespeare's plot are paralleled in scattered folktales, but could not have been invented separately. Only a few traits in the main plot of *The Shrew* are not found in any folktales. Certain changes which were necessary for the dramatic adaptation of the folktale plot can be identified, but the traditional pattern in the oral tales is otherwise well preserved in the comedy.

Shakespeare must have known, either directly or indirectly, the plot of the tale as it was developed in oral tradition. Most likely he used an English version. The possibility that the folktale spread orally to England is supported by the present Scottish and Irish versions, by the distribution of the Northern-European Elaborated Subtype, and by Canadian texts from oral tradition which preserve traits peculiar to Shakespeare's plot. There is evidence that Type 901 was told in England in the eighteenth century. A version of the tale printed in *The Tatler* in 1710 paralleled the oral tradition, and this text was not, as Dr. Johnson supposed, adapted from Shakespeare's plot. If Type 901 was circulating orally in England in the eighteenth century and in Shakespeare's time, it may still be current there, just as it now is in Ireland and Scotland. Folktale

Summary of Conclusions

collections from oral tradition in England could establish this point and thereby help to clarify further the nature of Shakespeare's possible source for *The Taming of the Shrew*.

Appendix

The following additional Icelandic version of Type 901, text GI 3, was sent to me by Bo Almqvist, who had earlier supplied me with version GI 1. It was received too late to be treated in the body of the study. The story was collected by Þorður Tómasson of Vallnatúni from Hallbera Halldórsdóttir of Selfoss, who heard it from her grandmother. Professor Einor Ól. Sveinsson made the copy from Tómasson's manuscript. The text had been used on a radio program in Iceland early in 1960, when Mr. Almqvist first heard it.

Harkalegt ráð
("Doing Things the Hard Way")

It is said, that once upon a time there was a girl who was unusually domineering. There were many who prophesized that she would not be easy to deal with if she were married, and that her husband was not to be envied. At last, however, a young man asked for her hand and was accepted. Their wedding took place a short time later. The bridegroom gave his bride a horse on which she rode from church. It could hardly have been worse, an old nag, not worth many pence. On their way was a quagmire and it was difficult to pass over it. The bride's horse sank down to its belly and could not stir. Then the bride jumped off the horse's back and stood there at the edge of the quagmire. Her dress was dirty and disordered and she did not know what to do. The bridegroom then pretended to be very angry and spoke sharply. He quickly drew his sharp knife, ran toward the horse and cut its throat. Then he ordered his wife to take the saddle and to carry it the rest of the way up to the farm. His behavior had had such an influence on her temper, that she took the saddle without saying a word and put it on her back.

Many years went by and the evil prophecies about her marriage were not fulfilled. On the contrary, it was proverbial how fine the marriage was and how obedient the wife was to her husband in all respects.

Once the couple went to a party in the neighborhood. After having eaten, the gentlemen and the ladies went into different rooms. Then they talked about many things. The farmers started to talk about who had the best wife and each of them boasted about his own wife. Our man was no worse than the others. At last he said, "Let us call for our wives. She who obeys first, she is the best." This was agreed upon and the farmers called for their wives. When the ladies were called for, our woman was talking to her sister. She stood up in a hurry. Her sister said: "You are in no hurry," and asked her to stay for awhile. She answered immediately, "No, you have not carried the saddle like I have" (*þú hefur ekki borið söðulinn eins og ég*). So she was the first to come to her husband and so she proved that he was right.

In common with the majority of versions collected recently in Europe, this new Icelandic text is quite generalized and cannot be assigned to one of the distinct subtypes of Type 901. However, it shares two special features with the other Icelandic texts, and one of these elements is found in Shakespeare. Since GI 1 was a *Mischvariant* and GI 2 was merely a summary, the new version also serves to validate the form of the Icelandic tale, and it thus affords a better basis than before from which to discuss the possible origin of Type 901 in Iceland.

The two most distinctive elements of the Icelandic versions are the horse's getting stuck in the mud (trait IVB1biv) and the concluding motto that refers to the bride's having to carry the saddle (trait VIIC3). The former element occurs in Shakespeare's play, in nine versions of the folktale from Ireland, and in one each from Estonia and Lithuania. The Icelandic examples conform to the English and Irish rather than to the

Appendix

Estonian and Lithuanian tales, for in the latter versions the horse is pulling the wedding pair in a carriage when it gets stuck in the mud. In Shakespeare and in all nine Irish tales, as in Iceland, the characters are mounted. Four of these Irish texts also have carrying the saddle; six end with a wager. The tamed Shrew's statement about carrying the saddle is also found in two Finnish versions and in one each from Sweden, Swedish-Finland, Denmark, and the United States. (This element was briefly discussed above on pages 214 to 215.) The wordings of the statements are about the same wherever they occur.

It is interesting to note that only in Iceland are found *both* the statement about carrying the saddle and getting stuck in the mud; however, the bride is splashed in versions from Sweden and Denmark, and one of these texts, GD 6, also has carrying the saddle and the statement about doing it. The Icelandic tradition, which has no counterpart in Norway (where only a single, garbled text has been collected; see page 241 above), seems most likely to have entered from Denmark. Getting stuck in the mud must have died out in the rest of Scandinavia, though it is still found in Ireland. It seems unlikely that Irish tradition gave rise to the tale in Iceland, since no example of the statement about carrying the saddle has shown up in the many texts collected there, but this element *is* found in all three Icelandic versions and elsewhere in Scandinavia. The new Icelandic version of the tale further corroborates the oral source of the trait in Shakespeare, while the date of this literary appearance in turn indicates how early the element could have entered the British Isles.